LLEWELLYN'S

MAGICKAL ALMANAC

Edited by
Ray Buckland

Printed in the United States of America
Typography property of Chester-Kent, Inc.

ISBN: 0-87542-455-4

Edited and Designed by Ray Buckland
Cover Painting by June Zenner

Contributing Writers: Ted Andrews, Raymond Buckland, Scott Cunningham, David F. Godwin, Gordon Hudson, deTraci Regula, Alan Richardson, Gerald and Betty Schueler, Diane Stein, Donald Tyson

Published by
LLEWELLYN PUBLICATIONS
P.O. Box 64383-455
St. Paul, MN 55164-0383

..

1989

JANUARY
S	M	T	W	T	F	S
1	2	3	4	5	6	7
8	9	10	11	12	13	14
15	16	17	18	19	20	21
22	23	24	25	26	27	28
29	30	31				

FEBRUARY
S	M	T	W	T	F	S
			1	2	3	4
5	6	7	8	9	10	11
12	13	14	15	16	17	18
19	20	21	22	23	24	25
26	27	28				

MARCH
S	M	T	W	T	F	S
			1	2	3	4
5	6	7	8	9	10	11
12	13	14	15	16	17	18
19	20	21	22	23	24	25
26	27	28	29	30	31	

APRIL
S	M	T	W	T	F	S
						1
2	3	4	5	6	7	8
9	10	11	12	13	14	15
16	17	18	19	20	21	22
23	24	25	26	27	28	29
30						

MAY
S	M	T	W	T	F	S
	1	2	3	4	5	6
7	8	9	10	11	12	13
14	15	16	17	18	19	20
21	22	23	24	25	26	27
28	29	30	31			

JUNE
S	M	T	W	T	F	S
				1	2	3
4	5	6	7	8	9	10
11	12	13	14	15	16	17
18	19	20	21	22	23	24
25	26	27	28	29	30	

JULY
S	M	T	W	T	F	S
						1
2	3	4	5	6	7	8
9	10	11	12	13	14	15
16	17	18	19	20	21	22
23	24	25	26	27	28	29
30	31					

AUGUST
S	M	T	W	T	F	S
		1	2	3	4	5
6	7	8	9	10	11	12
13	14	15	16	17	18	19
20	21	22	23	24	25	26
27	28	29	30	31		

SEPTEMBER
S	M	T	W	T	F	S
					1	2
3	4	5	6	7	8	9
10	11	12	13	14	15	16
17	18	19	20	21	22	23
24	25	26	27	28	29	30

OCTOBER
S	M	T	W	T	F	S
1	2	3	4	5	6	7
8	9	10	11	12	13	14
15	16	17	18	19	20	21
22	23	24	25	26	27	28
29	30	31				

NOVEMBER
S	M	T	W	T	F	S
			1	2	3	4
5	6	7	8	9	10	11
12	13	14	15	16	17	18
19	20	21	22	23	24	25
26	27	28	29	30		

DECEMBER
S	M	T	W	T	F	S
					1	2
3	4	5	6	7	8	9
10	11	12	13	14	15	16
17	18	19	20	21	22	23
24	25	26	27	28	29	30
31						

1990

JANUARY
S	M	T	W	T	F	S
	1	2	3	4	5	6
7	8	9	10	11	12	13
14	15	16	17	18	19	20
21	22	23	24	25	26	27
28	29	30	31			

FEBRUARY
S	M	T	W	T	F	S
				1	2	3
4	5	6	7	8	9	10
11	12	13	14	15	16	17
18	19	20	21	22	23	24
25	26	27	28			

MARCH
S	M	T	W	T	F	S
				1	2	3
4	5	6	7	8	9	10
11	12	13	14	15	16	17
18	19	20	21	22	23	24
25	26	27	28	29	30	31

APRIL
S	M	T	W	T	F	S
1	2	3	4	5	6	7
8	9	10	11	12	13	14
15	16	17	18	19	20	21
22	23	24	25	26	27	28
29	30					

MAY
S	M	T	W	T	F	S
		1	2	3	4	5
6	7	8	9	10	11	12
13	14	15	16	17	18	19
20	21	22	23	24	25	26
27	28	29	30	31		

JUNE
S	M	T	W	T	F	S
					1	2
3	4	5	6	7	8	9
10	11	12	13	14	15	16
17	18	19	20	21	22	23
24	25	26	27	28	29	30

JULY
S	M	T	W	T	F	S
1	2	3	4	5	6	7
8	9	10	11	12	13	14
15	16	17	18	19	20	21
22	23	24	25	26	27	28
29	30	31				

AUGUST
S	M	T	W	T	F	S
			1	2	3	4
5	6	7	8	9	10	11
12	13	14	15	16	17	18
19	20	21	22	23	24	25
26	27	28	29	30	31	

SEPTEMBER
S	M	T	W	T	F	S
						1
2	3	4	5	6	7	8
9	10	11	12	13	14	15
16	17	18	19	20	21	22
23	24	25	26	27	28	29
30						

OCTOBER
S	M	T	W	T	F	S
	1	2	3	4	5	6
7	8	9	10	11	12	13
14	15	16	17	18	19	20
21	22	23	24	25	26	27
28	29	30	31			

NOVEMBER
S	M	T	W	T	F	S
				1	2	3
4	5	6	7	8	9	10
11	12	13	14	15	16	17
18	19	20	21	22	23	24
25	26	27	28	29	30	

DECEMBER
S	M	T	W	T	F	S
						1
2	3	4	5	6	7	8
9	10	11	12	13	14	15
16	17	18	19	20	21	22
23	24	25	26	27	28	29
30	31					

1991

JANUARY
S	M	T	W	T	F	S
		1	2	3	4	5
6	7	8	9	10	11	12
13	14	15	16	17	18	19
20	21	22	23	24	25	26
27	28	29	30	31		

FEBRUARY
S	M	T	W	T	F	S
					1	2
3	4	5	6	7	8	9
10	11	12	13	14	15	16
17	18	19	20	21	22	23
24	25	26	27	28		

MARCH
S	M	T	W	T	F	S
					1	2
3	4	5	6	7	8	9
10	11	12	13	14	15	16
17	18	19	20	21	22	23
24	25	26	27	28	29	30
31						

APRIL
S	M	T	W	T	F	S
	1	2	3	4	5	6
7	8	9	10	11	12	13
14	15	16	17	18	19	20
21	22	23	24	25	26	27
28	29	30				

MAY
S	M	T	W	T	F	S
			1	2	3	4
5	6	7	8	9	10	11
12	13	14	15	16	17	18
19	20	21	22	23	24	25
26	27	28	29	30	31	

JUNE
S	M	T	W	T	F	S
						1
2	3	4	5	6	7	8
9	10	11	12	13	14	15
16	17	18	19	20	21	22
23	24	25	26	27	28	29
30						

JULY
S	M	T	W	T	F	S
	1	2	3	4	5	6
7	8	9	10	11	12	13
14	15	16	17	18	19	20
21	22	23	24	25	26	27
28	29	30	31			

AUGUST
S	M	T	W	T	F	S
				1	2	3
4	5	6	7	8	9	10
11	12	13	14	15	16	17
18	19	20	21	22	23	24
25	26	27	28	29	30	31

SEPTEMBER
S	M	T	W	T	F	S
1	2	3	4	5	6	7
8	9	10	11	12	13	14
15	16	17	18	19	20	21
22	23	24	25	26	27	28
29	30					

OCTOBER
S	M	T	W	T	F	S
		1	2	3	4	5
6	7	8	9	10	11	12
13	14	15	16	17	18	19
20	21	22	23	24	25	26
27	28	29	30	31		

NOVEMBER
S	M	T	W	T	F	S
					1	2
3	4	5	6	7	8	9
10	11	12	13	14	15	16
17	18	19	20	21	22	23
24	25	26	27	28	29	30

DECEMBER
S	M	T	W	T	F	S
1	2	3	4	5	6	7
8	9	10	11	12	13	14
15	16	17	18	19	20	21
22	23	24	25	26	27	28
29	30	31				

Table of Contents

Phases of the Moon

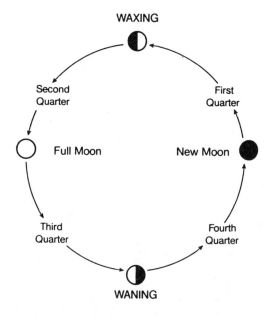

1st Quarter: begins when the Sun and Moon are conjunct, just after the New Moon.

2nd Quarter: begins halfway between the New Moon and Full Moon. The Sun and Moon are at 90° or squaring each other.

3rd Quarter: begins with the Full Moon when the Sun and Moon are in opposition.

4th Quarter: begins halfway between the Full Moon and New Moon when the Sun and Moon are again squaring each other.

TABLE OF TERMS REFERRING TO LUNAR QUARTERS (PHASES)

Sun-Moon Angle	MAGICKAL ALMANAC TERM	Common Terms	Division by:		
		2	4	8	
0-90° after Conjunction	First Quarter	Increasing Waxing Light New	New Moon	New Moon	
				Crescent	
90-180°	Second Quarter		First Quarter	First Quarter	
				Gibbous	
180-270°	Third Quarter	Decreasing Waning Dark Old	Full Moon	Full Moon	
				Disseminating	
270-360°	Fourth Quarter		Last Quarter	Last Quarter	
				Balsamic	

Magick

*"There are more things in Heaven and Earth, Horatio,
than are dreamt of in your philosophy."*
Shakespeare—*Hamlet* (Act I, Scene v)

Science has barely scratched the surface of human knowledge. It is slow and ponderous, being by nature cautious and skeptical. It demands proof one hundred (if not one thousand) times over before any theory is accepted as fact. Any event or occurrence that cannot be immediately explained by previous scientific experiment and conclusive proof, does not fit under the scientific umbrella and is usually immediately discarded out of hand as impossible, as mistaken, or as outright charlatanism. Such questions as "Does *magick* really exist? And if it does, how does it work?" are unlikely to even be addressed.

More questions that get scant attention from the main scientific community are: Is there any real significance to the numerological equivalent of your name? Do you have the power to heal the sick from a distance? Can you create your own reality? Are there "entities" that can be conjured?

Yet there are many people who feel that these, and other similar questions, have already been answered and proven, though others think they never will be. The answers actually lie in our freedom to believe or to disbelieve, as we see fit. Belief is not a sign of gullibility, but a sign of honest inquiry, a desire to expand our horizons and not be limited by what we have been told to believe.

It is generally conceded that there are many as-yet-undiscovered forces of Nature, including those of the human mind. The mind is an incredibly powerful force in and of itself. *Magick* can be looked upon simply as a term for the use of some of these forces; and *Magicians* as people who know how to use these

1

The Burgher in Winter

The Sower

Lovers in Springtide

The Sheep Shearer

A Ride in Summer

The Reaper

Miniatures from the Calendar of a "Book of Hours" manuscript of the beginning of the sixteenth century.

The table shows the cipher alphabet with correspondences:

a	b	c	d	e	f	g	h	i	k	l	m	n

o	p	q	r	s	fch	t	th	u	x	y	z	&

The Secret Cipher of Trithemius

forces but who are not yet "accepted" by the scientific community.

Magick is as old as humankind itself. Martin del Rio, in 1592, said "Magick is the art and power to produce extraordinary and marvellous effects by resort to an existing natural force." Aleister Crowley said that magick is "a question of employing hitherto unknown forces in Nature."

A further distinction between a scientist and a Magician is that the latter seldom seeks to reveal his discoveries. Magick is traditionally shrouded in secrecy, one of the reasons for scientific skepticism. Paracelsus said that magick is "a great secret wisdom." The Magician frequently works as long and as hard on his theories as does the scientist, but when he gets results he goes to great pains to hide and protect them. In past centuries Magicians have employed secret forms of writing to safeguard their notes. *Theban, Malachim, Passing the River, Angelic, Runic,* were some of the styles used.

In the pages that follow we examine some of the many forms that Magick can take. We try to draw back the veil of secrecy, if only a fraction, to give a glimpse behind it. Egyptian Magick, Enochian, Shamanic, Wiccan . . . they are as varied as any other aspect of Nature. And each is as fascinating and as complex. With this brief introduction to the subject we hope to lead you to the hidden world, the world that science tries so hard to ignore.

The word "almanac" probably comes from an Arabic word meaning "to reckon," though it first appears in popular usage in the thirteenth century as the Latin *almanach*. Almanacs have actually been around since Egyptian times; the British Museum has a fragment of one, dating from three thousand years ago, giving dates for festivals, and lucky and unlucky days. Over two hundred years ago, in France, an *Almanac of the Devil* was very popular and stayed so for most of the eighteenth century.

This present *Magickal Almanac*, as an annual, represents a brief introduction to the magickal world. But, as is the nature of an almanac, it will be back again next year, with additional insights and more tidbits for you. And the year after that. Let us know what you would like to see in the almanac, where *your* interests lie, so that we can address them.

Raymond Buckland

Almanac Pages

The almanac pages for each month give information important in the many aspects of working magick. For example, in many magickal systems the phases of the Moon are strictly adhered to, together with the times for the Moon's rising and setting. The times for sunrise and sunset are likewise frequently necessary (Where there are local variations in time, these must be taken into consideration. Most local newspapers give exact times for different geographical areas).

The *phases* of the moon are especially important. *Constructive* magick must be done in the waxing phase, and *destructive* magick in the waning phase.

The various dates for the celebration of many different Festivals are included in the almanac. Included also are the Tarot Card, Herb, Incense, Mineral, Color, and Name of Power associated with the particular day. Names of Power are especially important in many forms of magick. The god/goddess/entity whose name is particularly associated with the day of working should be given due honor on that day.

Each of the Full Moons is traditionally named to reflect the time of year at which it occurs. January's is the *Wolf* Moon, since January is a time (in Europe) when the wolves are especially prominent and dangerous (due to a scarcity of food). Wolves are frequently credited with preternatural cunning and are featured in many old tales and legends. Feburary's Moon is the *Storm* Moon, since February is frequently marked by turbulent weather. The *Chaste* Moon of March symbolizes the purity of the new spring, while April's *Seed* Moon marks the sowing season.

Tables of Spirits and Planets

Angels and Planets Ruling:

Hours NIGHT	SUNDAY	MONDAY	TUESDAY	WEDNESDAY	THURSDAY	FRIDAY	SATURDAY
1	♃ Sachiel	♀ Anael	♄ Cassiel	☉ Michael	☽ Gabriel	♂ Samael	☿ Raphael
2	♂ Samael	☿ Raphael	♃ Sachiel	♀ Anael	♄ Cassiel	☉ Michael	☽ Gabriel
3	☉ Michael	☽ Gabriel	♂ Samael	☿ Raphael	♃ Sachiel	♀ Anael	♄ Cassiel
4	♀ Anael	♄ Cassiel	☉ Michael	☽ Gabriel	♂ Samael	☿ Raphael	♃ Sachiel
5	☿ Raphael	♃ Sachiel	♀ Anael	♄ Cassiel	☉ Michael	☽ Gabriel	♂ Samael
6	☽ Gabriel	♂ Samael	☿ Raphael	♃ Sachiel	♀ Anael	♄ Cassiel	☉ Michael
7	♄ Cassiel	☉ Michael	☽ Gabriel	♂ Samael	☿ Raphael	♃ Sachiel	♀ Anael
8	♃ Sachiel	♀ Anael	♄ Cassiel	☉ Michael	☽ Gabriel	♂ Samael	☿ Raphael
9	♂ Samael	☿ Raphael	♃ Sachiel	♀ Anael	♄ Cassiel	☉ Michael	☽ Gabriel
10	☉ Michael	☽ Gabriel	♂ Samael	☿ Raphael	♃ Sachiel	♀ Anael	♄ Cassiel
11	♀ Anael	♄ Cassiel	☉ Michael	☽ Gabriel	♂ Samael	☿ Raphael	♃ Sachiel
12	☿ Raphael	♃ Sachiel	♀ Anael	♄ Cassiel	☉ Michael	☽ Gabriel	♂ Samael

Angels and Planets Ruling:

Hours DAY	SUNDAY	MONDAY	TUESDAY	WEDNESDAY	THURSDAY	FRIDAY	SATURDAY
1	☉ Michael	☽ Gabriel	♂ Samael	☿ Raphael	♃ Sachiel	♀ Anael	♄ Cassiel
2	♀ Anael	♄ Cassiel	☉ Michael	☽ Gabriel	♂ Samael	☿ Raphael	♃ Sachiel
3	☿ Raphael	♃ Sachiel	♀ Anael	♄ Cassiel	☉ Michael	☽ Gabriel	♂ Samael
4	☽ Gabriel	♂ Samael	☿ Raphael	♃ Sachiel	♀ Anael	♄ Cassiel	☉ Michael
5	♄ Cassiel	☉ Michael	☽ Gabriel	♂ Samael	☿ Raphael	♃ Sachiel	♀ Anael
6	♃ Sachiel	♀ Anael	♄ Cassiel	☉ Michael	☽ Gabriel	♂ Samael	☿ Raphael
7	♂ Samael	☿ Raphael	♃ Sachiel	♀ Anael	♄ Cassiel	☉ Michael	☽ Gabriel
8	☉ Michael	☽ Gabriel	♂ Samael	☿ Raphael	♃ Sachiel	♀ Anael	♄ Cassiel
9	♀ Anael	♄ Cassiel	☉ Michael	☽ Gabriel	♂ Samael	☿ Raphael	♃ Sachiel
10	☿ Raphael	♃ Sachiel	♀ Anael	♄ Cassiel	☉ Michael	☽ Gabriel	♂ Samael
11	☽ Gabriel	♂ Samael	☿ Raphael	♃ Sachiel	♀ Anael	♄ Cassiel	☉ Michael
12	♄ Cassiel	☉ Michael	☽ Gabriel	♂ Samael	☿ Raphael	♃ Sachiel	♀ Anael

May's moon is called the *Hare*, traditionally a sacred animal, frequently associated with the Moon. Witches were once thought to be able to turn themselves into hares, and did so when meeting at the full of the Moon. June's is the *Dyad* Moon, the Latin word for "a pair," marking the Moon of the astrological sign of Gemini. In July there is the *Mead* Moon, which some people attribute to the honey wine aptly described as "the nectar of the gods," though others ascribe it to the *mead*ows and their readiness for mowing.

August's *Wort* Moon is named from the old Anglo-Saxon word *wyrt*, meaning "plant." This was the month when the *wyrts* would be gathered and stored. In September there was the barley harvest, hence the *Barley* Moon of that month. The *Blood* Moon of October reflected a time of sacrifice; domestic animals were slaughtered to prepare for winter food storage and wild animals were thinned out for the coming season. November saw the *Snow* Moon and December brought the *Oak* Moon, the latter relating to the sacred tree of the Druids. Incidentally, it is interesting that the Moon, although frequently associated with the Goddess, is in the legends and myths of many different peoples a *male* figure (the Man in the Moon), while the sun is a female.

On pages 6 and 7 is a table of correspondences of spirits and planets for the different *Hours* of the day and night. The hours of the day run from Noon to Midnight. Those of the night run from Midnight to Noon.

In the back of the book you will find special tables for calculating the planetary hour for your magickal workings or rituals. This is done with the help of sunrise and sunset tables also provided. We have included moonrise and moonset tables for your convenience and information as well.

All lunar information provided in this almanac is set for Central Standard Time. Please adjust to your time zone if different. Llewellyn uses the four quarter system as described in earlier pages. If you are interested in more detailed astrological information, please refer to *Llewellyn's Daily Planetary Guide*.

Following the monthly almanacs there will be articles on various magickal systems. In most cases there is a major article followed by related articles. One particular form of magick is addressed each month. All of these are written by authorities in their fields. The authors are as follows:

Ted Andrews Author of *Simplified Magic*, the ultimate beginner's guide to the New Age cabala and to magic.

Raymond Buckland Author of such best-selling books as *Buckland's Complete Book of Witchcraft, Practical Candleburning Rituals, Practical Color Magick* and *Secrets of Gypsy Fortunetelling.*

Scott Cunningham His ever-popular books include *Cunningham's Encyclopedia of Crystal, Gem & Metal Magic, Magical Herbalism, The Magical Household,* and *Wicca: A Guide for the Solitary Practitioner.*

David F. Godwin Expert on the cabala and author of *Godwin's Cabalistic Encyclopedia.*

Gordon Hudson Egyptologist and author, born and raised in Cairo, Egypt. Founder and Preceptor of the University of Egyptian Arts.

deTraci Regula Priestess of Isis and author of an upcoming book on that Goddess.

Alan Richardson Author of *Ancient Magicks for a New Age.*

Gerald Schueler Recognized authority on Enochian Magick, member-at-large of the Theosophical Society, author of such books as *Enochian Magick, Advanced Enochian Magick, Enochian Physics, The Electric Tarot,* and *The Enochian Tarot.*

Diane Stein A leader in women's spirituality, author of *The Goddess Book of Days, The Women's Spirituality Book, The Kwan Yin Book of Changes, Stroking the Python,* and *The Women's Book of Healing.*

Donald Tyson A Rune Master, author of *Rune Magic* and creator of the *Rune Magic Deck.*

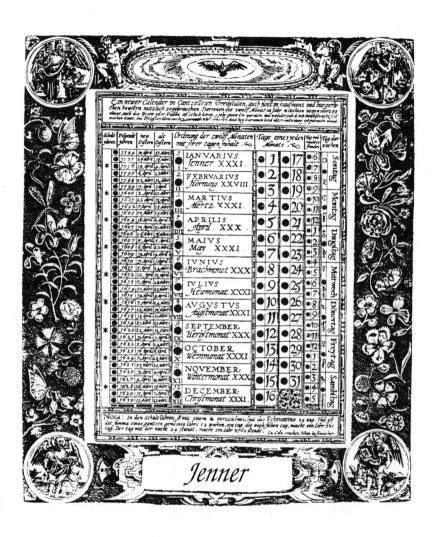

Jenner

January

1 *Monday*

Moon Sign: Pisces
Moon Phase: 1st Quarter
Festival: San-ga-nichi
    (1st Day)
    Good Luck Day

Tarot Card: The Lovers
Herb: Acacia
Incense: Jasmine
Mineral: Black Opal
Color: White
Name of Power: Fortuna

2 *Tuesday*

Moon Sign: Pisces
Moon Phase: 1st Quarter
Festival: Advent of Isis
    Nativity of
    Our Lady

Tarot Card: The Chariot
Herb: Angelica
Incense: Benzoin
Mineral: Chalcedony
Color: Red
Name of Power: Isis

3 *Wednesday*

Moon Sign: Aries
Moon Phase: 1st Quarter
Festival: San-ga-nichi
    (last day)

Tarot Card: Justice
Herb: Bedstraw
Incense: Pine
Mineral: African Jade
Color: Purple
Name of Power: Benten

4 *Thursday*

Moon Sign: Aries
Moon Phase: 2nd Quarter

Tarot Card: The Hermit
Herb: Blackberry
Incense: Cinnamon
Mineral: Green Feldspar
Color: Blue
Name of Power: Strenia

5

Friday

Moon Sign: Taurus
Moon Phase: 2nd Quarter
Festival: Pagan Feast of
      the Epiphany
      Good Luck Day

Tarot Card: Wheel of Fortune
Herb: Briar Hip
Incense: Frankincense
Mineral: Smithsonite
Color: Green
Name of Power: Kore

6

Saturday

Moon Sign: Taurus
Moon Phase: 2nd Quarter
Festival: Twelfth Night

Tarot Card: Strength
Herb: Cardamom
Incense: Sandalwood
Mineral: Green Zircon
Color: Black
Name of Power: Persephone

7

Sunday

Moon Sign: Gemini
Moon Phase: 2nd Quarter
Festival: Distaff Day
      Seven Herbs
      Festival

Tarot Card: The Hanged Man
Herb: Chive
Incense: Myrrh
Mineral: Amethyst
Color: Yellow
Name of Power: Amethyst

JANUARY

S	M	T	W	T	F	S
		1	2	3	4	5	6
7	8	9	10	11	12	13
14	15	16	17	18	19	20
21	22	23	24	25	26	27
28	29	30	31			

8　　*Monday*

Moon Sign: Gemini
Moon Phase: 2nd Quarter

Tarot Card: Death
Herb: Cotton
Incense: Jasmine
Mineral: Jet
Color: White
Name of Power: Justitia

9　　*Tuesday*

Moon Sign: Cancer
Moon Phase: 2nd Quarter

Tarot Card: Temperance
Herb: Dog's Mercury
Incense: Benzoin
Mineral: Yellow Carnelian
Color: Red
Name of Power: Nephthys

10　　*Wednesday*

Moon Sign: Cancer
Moon Phase: 2nd Quarter

Tarot Card: The Devil
Herb: Evening Primrose
Incense: Pine
Mineral: Yellow Diamond
Color: Purple
Name of Power: Securitas

11　　*Thursday*

Moon Sign: Leo
Moon Phase: Full Moon
　　　　　(Wolf)

Tarot Card: The Tower
Herb: Fragrant Valerian
Incense: Cinnamon
Mineral: Opal
Color: Blue
Name of Power: Carmentis

12
Friday

Moon Sign: Leo
Moon Phase: 3rd Quarter
Festival: Compitalia
       (Household)

Tarot Card: The Star
Herb: Goldthread
Incense: Frankincense
Mineral: Cape Ruby
Color: Green
Name of Power: Lares

13
Saturday

Moon Sign: Virgo
Moon Phase: 3rd Quarter

Tarot Card: The Moon
Herb: Hemlock Spruce
Incense: Sandalwood
Mineral: Black Amber
Color: Black
Name of Power: Mania

14
Sunday

Moon Sign: Virgo
Moon Phase: 3rd Quarter
Festival: Hindu Makar
       Sankrati

Tarot Card: The Sun
Herb: Hops
Incense: Myrrh
Mineral: Garnet
Color: Yellow
Name of Power: Makar
       Sankrati

JANUARY

S	M	T	W	T	F	S
	1	2	3	4	5	6
7	8	9	10	11	12	13
14	15	16	17	18	19	20
21	22	23	24	25	26	27
28	29	30	31			

15   *Monday*

Moon Sign: Virgo
Moon Phase: 3rd Quarter
Festival: Carmentalia

Tarot Card: Judgment
Herb: Indian Pipe
Incense: Jasmine
Mineral: Red Tourmaline
Color: White
Name of Power: Porrima

16   *Tuesday*

Moon Sign: Libra
Moon Phase: 3rd Quarter

Tarot Card: The World
Herb: Kousso
Incense: Benzoin
Mineral: Sodalite
Color: Red
Name of Power: Concordia

17   *Wednesday*

Moon Sign: Libra
Moon Phase: 3rd Quarter

Tarot Card: The Fool
Herb: Lobelia
Incense: Pine
Mineral: Pearl
Color: Purple
Name of Power: Felicitas

18   *Thursday*

Moon Sign: Scorpio
Moon Phase: 4th Quarter

Tarot Card: Ace of Swords
Herb: Matico
Incense: Cinnamon
Mineral: Chalcedony
Color: Blue
Name of Power: Surya

19
Friday

Moon Sign: Scorpio
Moon Phase: 4th Quarter

Tarot Card: Two of Swords
Herb: Peppermint
Incense: Frankincense
Mineral: Pyrite
Color: Green
Name of Power: Prisca

20
Saturday

Moon Sign: Scorpio
Moon Phase: 4th Quarter
Sun enters Aquarius

Tarot Card: Three of Swords
Herb: Monkshood
Incense: Sandalwood
Mineral: Orange Spinel
Color: Black
Name of Power: Postverta

21
Sunday

Moon Sign: Sagittarius
Moon Phase: 4th Quarter

Tarot Card: Four of Swords
Herb: Nasturtium
Incense: Myrrh
Mineral: Tourmaline
Color: Yellow
Name of Power: Agnes
Tree: Rowan

JANUARY

S	M	T	W	T	F	S
	1	2	3	4	5	6
7	8	9	10	11	12	13
14	15	16	17	18	19	20
21	22	23	24	25	26	27
28	29	30	31			

22 *Monday*

Moon Sign: Sagittarius
Moon Phase: 4th Quarter

Tarot Card: Five of Swords
Herb: Olive
Incense: Jasmine
Mineral: Black Pearl
Color: White
Name of Power: Selena

23 *Tuesday*

Moon Sign: Capricorn
Moon Phase: 4th Quarter

Tarot Card: Six of Swords
Herb: Squaw Balm
Incense: Benzoin
Mineral: Fire Opal
Color: Red
Name of Power: Venus

24 *Wednesday*

Moon Sign: Capricorn
Moon Phase: 4th Quarter
Festival: Start of Burgeoning
        Time in Celtic
        calendar

Tarot Card: Seven of Swords
Herb: Ribwort
Incense: Pine
Mineral: Moonstone
Color: Purple
Name of Power: Daena
Tree: Birch

25 *Thursday*

Moon Sign: Capricorn
Moon Phase: 4th Quarter

Tarot Card: Eight of Swords
Herb: Prickly Ash
Incense: Cinnamon
Mineral: Peridot
Color: Blue
Name of Power: Ardisvang

26 *Friday*

Moon Sign: Aquarius
Moon Phase: 4th Quarter

Tarot Card: Nine of Swords
Herb: Queen of the Meadow
Incense: Frankincense
Mineral: Jade
Color: Green
Name of Power: Arstat

27 *Saturday*

Moon Sign: Aquarius
Moon Phase: New Moon

Tarot Card: Ten of Swords
Herb: Red Eyebright
Incense: Sandalwood
Mineral: Obsidian
Color: Black
Name of Power: Diana

28 *Sunday*

Moon Sign: Pisces
Moon Phase: 1st Quarter

Tarot Card: Page of Swords
Herb: Saffron
Incense: Myrrh
Mineral: Vesuvianite
Color: Yellow
Name of Power: Zamyad

JANUARY

S	M	T	W	T	F	S
		1	2	3	4	5	6
7	8	9	10	11	12	13
14	15	16	17	18	19	20
21	22	23	24	25	26	27
28	29	30	31			

29 *Monday*

Moon Sign: Pisces
Moon Phase: 1st Quarter
Festival: Roman Peace
        Festival

Tarot Card: Knight of Swords
Herb: Senega Snakeroot
Incense: Jasmine
Mineral: Yellow Sapphire
Color: White
Name of Power: Mene

30 *Tuesday*

Moon Sign: Aries
Moon Phase: 1st Quarter

Tarot Card: Queen of Swords
Herb: Speedwell
Incense: Benzoin
Mineral: Red Zircon
Color: Red
Name of Power: Livia

31 *Wednesday*

Moon Sign: Aries
Moon Phase: 1st Quarter
Festival: Hecate's Feast

Tarot Card: King of Swords
Herb: Woodruff
Incense: Pine
Mineral: Black Tourmaline
Color: Purple
Name of Power: Hecate

JANUARY

S	M	T	W	T	F	S
	1	2	3	4	5	6
7	8	9	10	11	12	13
14	15	16	17	18	19	20
21	22	23	24	25	26	27
28	29	30	31			

Dr. John Dee

Enochian Magick

Gerald and Betty Schueler

Enochian Magick is a special branch of magick that was begun in modern times by Dr. John Dee, court astrologer to Queen Elizabeth I, and his psychic partner, Edward Kelly. Dee and Kelly discovered an ancient language which they called the "Angelic" or Enochian Language. The alphabet of this archaic language has twenty-one letters. It has its own grammar and syntax, but only a small sample of it has ever been translated into English. Dee and Kelly were directed by "Angels" to produce several tablets containing squares, with a letter in each Square. Kelly would gaze into a crystal *shewstone* where he could see Angels and communicate with them, and Dee would record the conversations. Together, they produced many curious tablets. Five of these are especially important—the four Watchtower Tablets and the Tablet of Union.

Each square on these tablets represents a region in the subtle invisible worlds that surrounded the Earth. Each tablet represents a map of one of the five Cosmic Planes of Manifestation. These planes exist in the regions between the divine plane of God, and the matter of our gross physical plane. In addition, a person's body is made of the elemental substance of each plane. The planes interpenetrate each other and are named after the five known cosmic elements: Earth, Water, Air, Fire, and Spirit. Each tablet corresponds with a color, a direction, and a cosmic plane and subtle body, as shown below.

Watchtower	Color	Direction	Plane/Body
Earth	black	North	etheric
Water	blue	West	astral
Air	yellow	East	mental
Fire	red	South	causal
Tablet of Union	white	———	spiritual

In addition to the Watchtower Tablets and the Tablet of Union, thirty special regions, called the *Aires* or *Aethyrs*, were also investigated. They ranged in serial order, from the most material to the most spiritual, and are complementary to the Watchtowers. The Watchtowers and Aethyrs of Enochian Magick have striking similarities with the Sephiroth and paths of the Tree of Life as taught in Qabalistic Magick.

Enochian Magick is a comprehensive system of magick. Besides the basic system (see *Enochian Magic: A Practical Manual* and *An Advanced Guide to Enochian Magick*) there is Enochian Physics (see *Enochian Physics*), Enochian Tarot (see *Enochian Tarot*), and Enochian Yoga (see *Enochian Yoga*).* Enochian Physics is a structural analysis of the Magical Universe as taught by Enochian Magick. Enochian Tarot is a new system of divination using the deities and locations of Enochian Magick. Like the traditional Tarot system, it can also be used for meditation. Enochian Yoga uses the system of Yogic meditation, instead of rituals, to fulfill the goals of Enochian Magick.

The basic teachings relating to Enochian Magick and the Angelic Language, as revealed by Dee and Kelly, were taken up at

---

*These books are currently available, or soon to be available, from Llewellyn Publications.

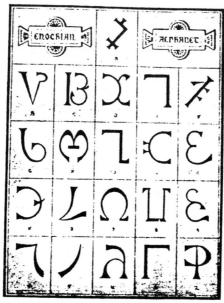

The Enochian Alphabet, the cipher of Dr. John Dee

the end of the last century by a secret occult group known as the Hermetic Order of the Golden Dawn. The Golden Dawn used the mysterious tablets and language in their rituals and magical ceremonies. They amplified Enochian Magick by creating what are known as the "signposts" of the squares. Just as a good map points out the major sites of an unknown area for a traveler to prevent him from getting lost, so the signposts predict the general atmosphere, the names of the local deities, and so on, for each of the Watchtower Squares. Two of the methods used by the Golden Dawn to visit these regions were skrying and traveling in the Spirit Vision. Skrying was the method used by Kelly to discover the Tablets. It involves gazing into a crystal, or similar material, and recording whatever visions are seen or voices heard. The Spirit Vision method is similar to what is known today as astral traveling—a consciously directed out-of-body experience.

The primary goal of Enochian Magick is the attainment of knowledge and power. This is accomplished by visiting the subtle regions of the Cosmic Planes of Manifestation, and conversing with the inhabitants and rulers of the regions. The knowledge and power gained should give the magician a better understanding of man and the universe. According to Enochian Magick, man does not have to be a slave to the forces of cosmic justice (karma) that always seem to control our lives. Man can, through Enochian Magick, consciously direct his life and therefore his destiny.

The highest Watchtower deities of Enochian Magick are the four Kings who rule over the Watchtowers. Immediately below them are the Seniors, six in each of the Watchtowers. Below the Kings and Seniors is a hierarchy of lesser deities. The lesser deities of the Watchtowers are Demons and various ranks of Angels. The Sephirothic Cross Angels rule over the sixteen subquadrants (each Watchtower can be subdivided into four subquadrants). Below them are the Kerubic Angels. Below these are the Archangels, Ruling Lesser Angels, and lastly, the Lesser Angels. There are also said to be Demons whose nature is to oppose the general angelic rulership. The Demons can be found in the Lesser Squares, the lowest, or most dense, regions of each Watchtower. Each of the Lesser Squares also contains one of 15 Egyptian deities and one of a wide variety of sphinxes who embody the natural creative and preservative forces of the atmosphere of these subtle regions. This association with ancient Egypt helps lend an air of authenticity to Enochian Magick as a special school of Western occultism.

Probably the most popular operation used in Enochian Magick is the invocation of an Angel or other Enochian deity. To call forth such deities, Dee and Kelly devised Keys (Calls). These were channeled to Kelly in the Enochian language, and later translated into English. Each Call was used to address a specific group of deities according to their location in the Watchtowers. Only one Call was made for all thirty Aethyrs, the name of the respective Aethyr being used in a blank provided for it. In general, the technique used was to speak the Call out loud while facing the direction of the desired Watchtower from within a specially consecrated magick circle. Then, the ritual words of invocation would be spoken. The invocation was usually built around the name of the desired deity, whose name was derived from the letters of the tablets.

Enochian Magick has its own alphabet, which resembles no other known alphabet. The table on page 25 lists the letters and their correspondences with the Zodiac and Tarot.

Enochian Alphabet Correspondences

Letter	Zodiac/Element	Tarot
A	Taurus	Hierophant
B	Aries	Star
C,K	Fire	Judgment
D	Spirit	Empress
E	Virgo	Hermit
F	Cauda Draconis	Juggler
G	Cancer	Chariot
H	Air	Fool
I, J, Y	Sagittarius	Temperance
L	Cancer	Chariot
M	Aquarius	Emperor
N	Scorpio	Death
O	Libra	Justice
P	Leo	Strength
Q	Water	Hanged Man
R	Pisces	Moon
S	Gemini	Lovers
T	Leo	Strength
	Caput Draconis	High Priestess
U, V, W	Capricorn	Devil
X	Earth	Universe
Z	Leo	Strength
	Caput Draconis	High Priestess

The general rules of pronunciation given by the Golden Dawn are:

> Most consonants are followed by 'eh' (B is *Beh*, D is *Deh*). Most vowels are followed by 'h' (A is *Ah*, O is *Oh*). In general, each letter forms a syllable. The letters Y and I are interchangeable, as are V and U, and S and Z. Z is pronounced *zod*. S is pronounced either *ess* or *seh*. R can be either *reh, rah, or ar*. I is pronounced *ee* (TI is *Teh-ee* or simply *Tee*).

The truth is, no one really knows the "correct" pronunciation of Enochian today. The rules established by the Golden Dawn, as given above, were slightly bent by Crowley and others. Today, they have undergone even more changes in other groups. For example, Z was pronounced *zod* (like *zoad* or *zode*) by the

Golden Dawn, but it is frequently heard as *zeh* today. It is some-times uncertain when R is to be pronounced *ar* or *rah*, or even *reh*. Similarly, S can be *ess* or *seh*. Israel Regardie, one of the foremost experts on Enochian Magick, clearly stated that as far as he knew, there was no right or wrong way to pronounce the Enochian language, though he followed the general Golden Dawn rules. Our advice is to use whatever you feel is sonorous or melodic within the general rules. The syllables should flow with a rhythm that is almost musical. Success in a magickal operation depends on more than just properly pronouncing the words or names. You must also concentrate strongly on their meanings while speaking them.

During ritual invocations, Enochian words and names must be vibrated properly. There is a special 7-step procedure devised for this as follows:

(1) Stand upright with your arms outstretched before you.

(2) Breathe in deeply. Imagine that the name is entering your body with the air.

(3) Imagine the name descending down your legs and into your feet.

(4) When the name is in your feet, advance your left foot about 12 inches. Draw back your hands to the sides of your eyes and lean forward.

(5) As you lean forward, shoot your arms forward with fingers together and pointed before you. At the same time, exhale and imagine the name rising upward through your body with the air.

(6) Imagine the name leaving your body and thundering out-ward into the world. Imagine it vibrating through the whole universe.

(7) Withdraw your left foot and stand upright again. This pro-cedure must always be used, rather than simply saying a name out loud. When you vibrate a name in this way the name becomes psychically charged with energy, which greatly increases the likelihood of success.

A potential danger is believed to exist in the use of the letters of the Enochian Alphabet. If you write out the name of a deity using the angelic letters, and speak the name aloud but once, you could be visited by that deity in one form or another. If you are a beginner, you should avoid calling down to yourself things best left in their natural place. Dee and Kelly used to spell deity names backwards to avoid this danger. This phenomenon is one of the

Osiris seated in a shrine from the roof of which hang bunches of grapes. From the Papyrus of Nebseni

reasons why Enochian Magick should only be practiced by those individuals who are sincere in their desire to learn the system and are willing to put the time into learning to use the system properly.

The fact is, by speaking a deity's name out loud, or in your mind, you can create a psycho-magnetic link between yourself and that being. When you give something a name, you invest it with life—at least to a degree. To that degree, you are subconsciously accepting its existence and establishing a connection with it. If you form a mental image of the deity, the link is strengthened. If left open, the deity could use the link to establish contact with you—even against your will. Such contact would probably occur in a dream, but it is possible for a deity to affect you in some way even in the waking state—possibly quite unconscious to yourself. For example, suppose you desire to attain the mystical state of *samadhi* (an exalted state of consciousness which is said to be the goal of yogic meditation). You invoke the Angel *SIODA*, from the subquadrant of Earth of Fire, who is known to be of help in attaining *samadhi*. By vibrating his name, you will establish a psycho-magnetic link. Let's further suppose that you have negative results with your invocation, and fail to properly sever

The cipher of the Order of the Golden Dawn

the link. Four nights later, you become extremely sleepy and drift off into dreamless sleep for a whole twenty-four hours, rather than your normal seven hours. You would probably think to yourself that you were simply extra sleepy for some reason. Maybe you will think that you are sick. The real cause, however, is that you have left open the link with SIODA, whose power to cause an exalted state of consciousness is affecting you sub-consciously. You may even find your mind drifting off during the day. Your ability to concentrate on your surroundings could have unexpected lapses. If you are driving a car, the consequences could be serious. This danger can be eliminated, or at least con-trolled, by severing the link that the invocation established. This can be done in several ways—the best is to use a suitable banish-ing ritual.

The real danger with Enochian Magick is not in having an angry fanged monster materialize before you and do you bodily harm. The danger is that the practice of Enochian Magick will, by its very nature, precipitate much of your stored karma. Past karmic debts, known collectively as your karmic burden, will naturally be worked off over many future lifetimes. When you practice Enochian Magick, one of the results is the dissipation of your karmic burden. In effect, the karma that would normally take lifetimes to work out may be worked out in this lifetime.

There are several safeguards that you can use to reduce the possible dangers involved in the practice of Enochian Magick. The most obvious is to obtain knowledge. Know what you are doing, and why you are doing it. Ignorance, even if your motives are the highest, could end in disaster. Another is to cultivate a sincere love for your fellow man—a true desire to help others. Compassion is a necessity for work in the higher Aethyrs and without it you would be in very great danger indeed. Morality aside, it turns out that strong feelings of compassion and selfless love will coat the aura with a protective shield that few demons can penetrate. Without compassion, the ego will have fear—fear for itself in some form or another. Fear attracts demons of the worst sort, and can be fatal for many magickal operations. You must conduct your magickal operations without fear. Perfect love casts out fear, and though it may sound trite in today's world, nevertheless it is true that love is the best and surest safeguard that a magician can have.

An Enochian Invocation Ritual

Gerald and Betty Schueler

For this ritual, you will need to use either actual weapons or their psychic equivalent. The four main weapons used in Enochian Magick are a red Wand, a yellow Sword or Dagger, a blue Cap, and a black Pantacle (sometimes spelled Pentacle). As an alternate to making physical weapons you can use your magickal imagination to create 'astral weapons'.

STEP 1. Consecrate a circle around you in which to perform the operation. You can either paint or draw a circle on the floor, or create a psychic circle with your magickal imagination. Hints for creating a magick circle can be found in many books, including *An Advanced Guide to Enochian Magick*, pages 60-62 (Llewellyn).*

STEP 2. Hold your Wand before you and stand facing the Watchtower of Fire in the South. Imagine that a burst of fire shoots from your Wand while you say the following:

OIP-TEAA-PDOKE
(pronounced Oh-ee-peh Teh-ah-ah Peh-doh-keh)
In the names and letters
Of the Great Southern Quadrangle,
I invoke you,
Angels of the Watchtower of the South.

Vibrate the Great Holy Name of OIPTEAA-PDOKE and feel the Angels of the Watchtower of Fire rising up from within you.

*See also page 328 of this almanac—Ed.

STEP 3. Hold your Cup before you with water in it and stand facing the Watchtower of Water in the West. Turn your Cup over so that the water spills out while you say the following:

MPH-ARSL-GAIOL
(pronounced Em-peh-heh Ar-ess-el Gah-ee-oh-leh)
In the names and letters
Of the Great Western Quadrangle,
I invoke you
Angels of the Watchtower of the West.

Vibrate the Great Holy Name of MPH-ARSL-GAIOL and feel the Angels of the Watchtower rising up from within you.

STEP 4. Hold your Pantacle before you and stand facing the Watchtower of Earth in the North. Shake the Pantacle three times while you say the following:

MOR-DIAL-PDOKE
(pronounced Moh-ar Dee-ah-leh Peh-doh-keh)
In the names and letters
Of the Great Northern Quadrangle
I invoke you,
Angels of the Watchtower of the North.

Vibrate the Great Holy Name of MOR-DIAL-PDOKE and feel the Angels of the Watchtower of Earth rising up from within you.

STEP 5. Hold your Sword or Dagger before you and stand facing the Watchtower of Air in the East. Slice the air before you three times with your Sword (or stab the air three times with your dagger) while you say the following:

ORO-IBAH-AOZPI
(pronounced Oh-roh Ee-bah Aah-oh-zod-pee)
In the names and letters
Of the Great Eastern Quadrangle
I invoke you,
Angels of the Watchtower of the East.

Vibrate the Great Holy Name of ORO-IBAH-AOZPI and feel the Angels of the Watchtower of Air rising up from within you.

STEP 6. Remain facing the East and look up toward the Tablet of Union that is above all manifestation. Say the following:

EXARP (Ehtz-ar-peh)
BITOM (Bee-toh-meh)
NANTA (Nah-en-tah)
HKOMA (Heh-koh-mah)
In the names and letters
Of the mystical Tablet of Union
I invoke you,
Angels who are the divine forces
Of the Spirit of Life.

Vibrate the names of the four elements, BITOM (Fire), HKOMA (Water), NANTA (Earth), and EXARP (Air). Feel the Angels of the Tablet of Union rising up from within you.

STEP 7. Feel all of the Angels of the Watchtowers and Tablet of Union rising up together within you. Say,

I am the Lord of the Universe.
I am He Whom Nature Has Not Formed.
I am the Vast and Mighty One,
Lord of the Light and of the Darkness,
Lord and King of the Earth.

See yourself as the embodiment of the spiritual forces of the universe.

Hold this image of yourself for as long as you can.

Note: Because you are invoking helpful forces which you want to stay with you, it is not necessary to perform a banishing ritual. The above ritual can be performed as often as desired.

Edward Kelley

The Enochian Language

John Dee was the son of Rowland and Jane Dee, and was born in London on July 13, 1527. His father was a gentleman server to King Henry VIII. At the age of ten, young John was placed in the hands of Peter Wilegh at the Chantry School at Chelmsford, in Essex. At fifteen he moved on to St. John's College, Cambridge. He graduated from there in 1546 with a B.A. degree, and within a few months was selected as one of the Founder Fellows of Trinity College.

The Enochian Language was brought to Dr. John Dee through the agencies of his assistant, Edward Kelley. Kelley's original name was Edward Talbott but, for whatever reasons, he changed it when he went to work for Dee. His job was that of Skryer, or crystal-gazer. Dee himself professed no skills in skrying and so employed others to do the job for him. Kelley claimed to be good at it and got the position after the dismissal of his predecessor, Barnabas Saul.

John Dee believed in angels, and further believed that they would appear in visions and freely give information. Over the many years of "conversing" with them, he kept copious notes on what they said. In 1659, fifty years after Dee's death, Meric Casaubon published some extracts of these "conversations" in a book titled: *A True and Faithful Relation of What Passed between Dr. John Dee and Some Spirits.*

Dee would seat Kelley at a table, before a crystal, and have him gaze into the ball and tell what he saw. Kelley had a checkered background—he had been an apothecary, had searched for the Philosopher's Stone, had dabbled in black magick, and had, on occasion, turned to crime—and it's possible that much of what he related to Dee was from his own vivid imagination. Certainly at the end of their relationship, when he insisted that the angels commanded them to share their wives, there seems to be a strong indication that he was inventing most of what he claimed to receive. But in the earlier days he did produce a great deal of fascinating information. Among it was the Enochian language.

A young spirit/angel, who appeared to be no more than eight years of age, gave her name as Madimi and passed on a system of invocations, or "calls." The calls are supposed to have been dictated backwards to Kelley, since direct communication would have been too powerful. Kelley claimed that these calls were in the angels' own language: Enochian. Richard Deacon (*John Dee*, Muller, London, 1968) suggests that they are part natural magick, part mathematical and astrological, and part pure cryptography. It is certainly a complete language of its own, with its own alphabet, consistent grammar and syntax. There are nineteen Enochian Calls or "Keys." The first two conjure spirit, the next sixteen the elements earth, fire, air, water, and the nineteenth invokes any of the thirty Aethyrs.

—RB

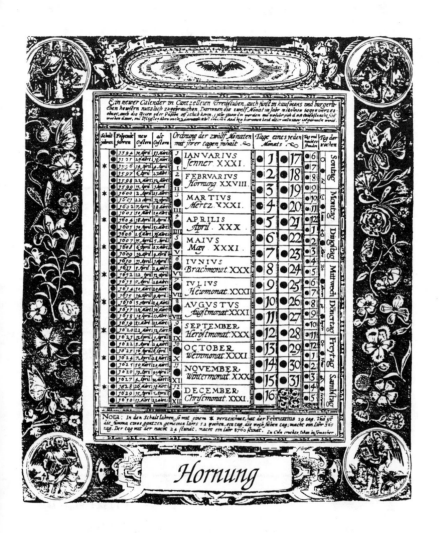

February

Monday

Tuesday

Wednesday

---

1 *Thursday*

Moon Sign: Taurus
Moon Phase: 1st Quarter
Festival: Oimel/Imbolc;
   Brighid's Feast Day
   Eleusinian Lesser
      Mysteries (first day);
   Fire Festival

Tarot Card: Ace of Wands
Herb: Adder's Tongue
Incense: Cinnamon
Mineral: Cape Ruby
Color: Blue
Name of Power: Brighid

2
Friday

Moon Sign: Taurus
Moon Phase: 2nd Quarter
Festival: The Wives' Feast Day;
        Candlemas

Tarot Card: Two of Swords
Herb: Anise
Incense: Frankincense
Mineral: Nephrite
Color: Green
Name of Power: Ceres

3
Saturday

Moon Sign: Gemini
Moon Phase: 2nd Quarter
Festival: Eleusinian Lesser
        Mysteries (last day)

Tarot Card: Three of Wands
Herb: Beechdrops
Incense: Sandalwood
Mineral: Soapstone
Color: Black
Name of Power: Demeter

4
Sunday

Moon Sign: Gemini
Moon Phase: 2nd Quarter

Tarot Card: Four of Wands
Herb: Black Cohosh
Incense: Myrrh
Mineral: Violet Sapphire
Color: Yellow
Name of Power: Agassu

			FEBRUARY			
S	M	T	W	T	F	S
				1	2	3
4	5	6	7	8	9	10
11	12	13	14	15	16	17
18	19	20	21	22	23	24
25	26	27	28			

5   *Monday*

Moon Sign: Cancer
Moon Phase: 2nd Quarter
Festival: Isis Festival

Tarot Card: Five of Wands
Herb: Brooklime
Incense: Jasmine
Mineral: Cat's Eye
Color: White
Name of Power: Isis

6   *Tuesday*

Moon Sign: Cancer
Moon Phase: 2nd Quarter

Tarot Card: Six of Wands
Herb: Carline Thistle
Incense: Benzoin
Mineral: Green Sapphire
Color: Red
Name of Power: Ti-Pété

7   *Wednesday*

Moon Sign: Leo
Moon Phase: 2nd Quarter

Tarot Card: Seven of Wands
Herb: Cinquefoil
Incense: Pine
Mineral: Cornelian
Color: Purple
Name of Power: Bocca

8   *Thursday*

Moon Sign: Leo
Moon Phase: 2nd Quarter
Festival: Brighid Octave

Tarot Card: Eight of Wands
Herb: Cowslip
Incense: Cinnamon
Mineral: Agate
Color: Blue
Name of Power: Brighid

9
Friday

Moon Sign: Leo
Moon Phase: Full Moon
         (Storm)

Tarot Card: Nine of Wands
Herb: Dogwood
Incense: Frankincense
Mineral: Orange Spinel
Color: Green
Name of Power: Frigg

10
Saturday

Moon Sign: Virgo
Moon Phase: 3rd Quarter

Tarot Card: Ten of Wands
Herb: Everlasting
Incense: Sandalwood
Mineral: Red Opal
Color: Black
Name of Power: Semetu

11
Sunday

Moon Sign: Virgo
Moon Phase: 3rd Quarter

Tarot Card: Page of Wands
Herb: Fraxinella
Incense: Myrrh
Mineral: Red Spinel
Color: Yellow
Name of Power: Persephone

FEBRUARY

S	M	T	W	T	F	S
				1	2	3
4	5	6	7	8	9	10
11	12	13	14	15	16	17
18	19	20	21	22	23	24
25	26	27	28			

12
Monday

Moon Sign: Libra
Moon Phase: 3rd Quarter

Tarot Card: Knight of Wands
Herb: Great Burnet
Incense: Jasmine
Mineral: Blue Opal
Color: White
Name of Power:
    Artemis/Diana

13
Tuesday

Moon Sign: Libra
Moon Phase: 3rd Quarter
Festival: Parentalia (1st day)

Tarot Card: Queen of Wands
Herb: Hemp Agrimony
Incense: Benzoin
Mineral: Blue Zircon
Color: Red
Name of Power: Vesta

14
Wednesday

Moon Sign: Libra
Moon Phase: 3rd Quarter
Festival: Valentine's Day;
    Eve of the Lupercalia

Tarot Card: King of Wands
Herb: Horehound
Incense: Pine
Mineral: Star Sapphire
Color: Purple
Name of Power: Gobnata

15
Thursday

Moon Sign: Scorpio
Moon Phase: 3rd Quarter
Festival: Lupercalia

Tarot Card: Ace of Cups
Herb: Indian Turnip
Incense: Cinnamon
Mineral: Leucite
Color: Blue
Name of Power: Lupa

16
Friday

Moon Sign: Scorpio
Moon Phase: 3rd Quarter

Tarot Card: Two of Cups
Herb: Lady's Mantle
Incense: Frankincense
Mineral: Turquoise
Color: Green
Name of Power: Faustina

17
Saturday

Moon Sign: Sagittarius
Moon Phase: 4th Quarter

Tarot Card: Four of Cups
Herb: Loosestrife
Incense: Sandalwood
Mineral: Jasper
Color: Black
Name of Power: Fornax

18
Sunday

Moon Sign: Sagittarius
Moon Phase: 4th Quarter
Sun enters Pisces

Tarot Card: Four of Cups
Herb: Meadow Saffron
Incense: Myrrh
Mineral: Aquamarine
Color: Yellow
Name of Power: Tacita
Tree: Ash

FEBRUARY

S	M	T	W	T	F	S
				1	2	3
4	5	6	7	8	9	10
11	12	13	14	15	16	17
18	19	20	21	22	23	24
25	26	27	28			

19   *Monday*

Moon Sign: Sagittarius
Moon Phase: 4th Quarter

Tarot Card: Five of Cups
Herb: Brandy Mint
Incense: Jasmine
Mineral: Beccarite
Color: White
Name of Power: Hu-Kheru

20   *Tuesday*

Moon Sign: Capricorn
Moon Phase: 4th Quarter

Tarot Card: Six of Cups
Herb: Motherwort
Incense: Benzoin
Mineral: Amber
Color: Red
Name of Power: Deba

21   *Wednesday*

Moon Sign: Capricorn
Moon Phase: 4th Quarter
Festival: Parentalia (last day)
           Festival of the Dead

Tarot Card: Seven of Cups
Herb: Nerve Root
Incense: Pine
Mineral: Cape Ruby
Color: Purple
Name of Power: Mania

22   *Thursday*

Moon Sign: Aquarius
Moon Phase: 4th Quarter
Festival: Charistia (Goodwill)

Tarot Card: Eight of Cups
Herb: Onion
Incense: Cinnamon
Mineral: Coral Agate
Color: Blue
Name of Power: Concordia

23
Friday

Moon Sign: Aquarius
Moon Phase: 4th Quarter

Tarot Card: Nine of Cups
Herb: Peony
Incense: Frankincense
Mineral: Greenstone
Color: Green
Name of Power: Mut

24
Saturday

Moon Sign: Pisces
Moon Phase: New Moon

Tarot Card: Ten of Cups
Herb: Ripplegrass
Incense: Sandalwood
Mineral: Hawaiite
Color: Black
Name of Power: Odin

25
Sunday

Moon Sign: Pisces
Moon Phase: New Moon

Tarot Card: Page of Cups
Herb: Yellow Wood
Incense: Myrrh
Mineral: Imperial Jade
Color: Yellow
Name of Power: Tun-Hat

			FEBRUARY			
S	M	T	W	T	F	S
				1	2	3
4	5	6	7	8	9	10
11	12	13	14	15	16	17
18	19	20	21	22	23	24
25	26	27	28			

26　*Monday*

Moon Sign: Aries
Moon Phase: 1st Quarter

Tarot Card: Knight of Cups
Herb: Gravelroot
Incense: Jasmine
Mineral: Jet
Color: White
Name of Power: Turan

27　*Tuesday*

Moon Sign: Aries
Moon Phase: 1st Quarter

Tarot Card: Queen of Cups
Herb: Euphrasy
Incense: Benzoin
Mineral: Tiger Eye
Color: Red
Name of Power: Mira Bai

28　*Wednesday*

Moon Sign: Taurus
Moon Phase: 1st Quarter

Tarot Card: King of Cups
Herb: Sage
Incense: Pine
Mineral: Mexican Onyx
Color: Purple
Name of Power: Godgifu

FEBRUARY

S	M	T	W	T	F	S
				1	2	3
4	5	6	7	8	9	10
11	12	13	14	15	16	17
18	19	20	21	22	23	24
25	26	27	28			

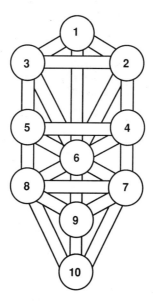

The Tree of Life

Cabalistic Magick

David Godwin

Whenever one mentions cabalistic magick, the usual comment is, "What's cabalistic?" One of the premier forms of magick practiced today, the cabala (also spelled qabalah, kabballah, and any number of other ways) was originally a system of mysticism that flowered among the Jews of Spain in the 14th century. It had its roots in earlier forms of Jewish mysticism, such as the "merkabah riders" and the Essenes, and it was influenced by (or influenced) neo-Platonism and Sufism. But the roots of the system extend back to the *Sepher Yetzirah* (Book of Formation), a book written in the fourth century (according to Gershom Scholem, professor of Jewish Mysticism at Hebrew University in Jerusalem). It is in this book that the idea of the ten *sephirot* was first presented. All subsequent cabalism, up to and including that taught in the western hermetic tradition, has the Tree of Life as its focal point.

The Tree of Life is a diagram showing ten circles arranged in a certain pattern. The circles are connected by lines or "paths." The ten circles represent the *sephirot*—a word that may be translated spheres, numbers, or emanations. They are simply the numbers 1 through 10 considered in their archetypical sense—in the *Sepher Yetzirah*, the means by which God created the Universe by way of successive emanations of divinity. Each *sephira* represents an archetype embedded in the deep unconscious mind—one might almost say in the genes—of every living human being. And each *sephira* has a corresponding name of God, archangel, angelic choir, and (on the material plane) planetary sphere.

The first objection of the skeptic may be that the solar system as we now know it is not well represented by the Tree of Life, which seems to depict the medieval cosmological concept of heavenly spheres. To this one can only gently point out that the planet Venus, for example, as it appears to a naked-eye observer on planet Earth, is a convenient and useful symbol for the unconscious constellated content or archetype called "venus" and corresponds to *netzach*, the seventh *sephira*. The fact that the surface of the physical planet is not a lush forest inhabited by beautiful women wearing Greek tunics (as some sci-fi movies of the '50s would have it), but rather the closest thing to hell in the physical universe, is essentially irrelevant to the unconscious mind—or, if you prefer, to the nature of *netzach* on the higher planes of existence.

The 22 paths connecting the *sephiroth* correspond to the 22 letters of the Hebrew alphabet; also to the twelve astrological signs, seven archetypical planets, and original three elements; and, in modern magickal systems, the 22 trumps of the major arcana of the Tarot cards. The fact that these correspondences, and many others, work out so well in practice is that they are indeed an accurate representation of what the pioneer psychologist C. G. Jung called "the archetypes of the collective unconscious." According to many practitioners they also happen to correspond to a higher reality that is independent of the human mind.

As later developed within the framework of medieval Judaism, cabalistic magick seems to have been concerned mostly with the construction of talismans. However, the tradition soon passed into the rest of Europe and was modified to suit the needs and desires of non-Jews. Ordinarily such an accretion would mean dilution, perversion, and decay—entropy doing its thing. These

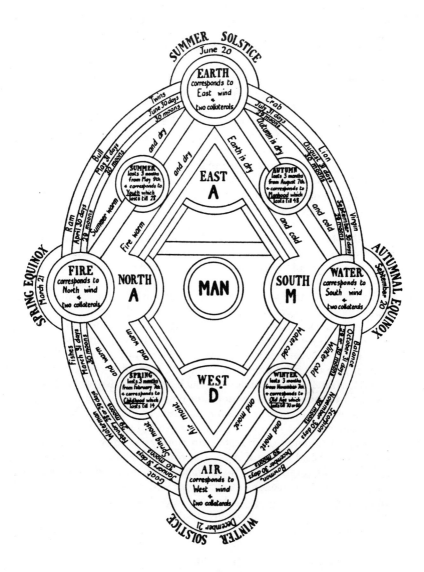

The Macrocosm as conceived in 1011 by Byrhtferth of Ramsey.

forms of the cabala did appear from time to time as the cabala was selectively adopted by dilettantes, would-be Satanists, and mountebanks, but the cabala has such a strong tradition and is so true and apt on the deepest level of the unconscious that it was actually *improved* by all this collective "committee work"—at least as far as magickal working is concerned. The process finally resulted, in the late 19th century, in the most intricate and finely tuned system of magick to be found anywhere, that of the Hermetic Order of the Golden Dawn.

The Order rituals not only retain the Hebrew terminology and nomenclature of the original cabala, insofar as it could be understood at that late date, but they also incorporate elements from the Enochian magick of John Dee and Edward Kelly, as well as from the Egyptian, Coptic, and other elements. They also include the symbolism of the Tarot cards in an ingenious system that is truly a work of art and of deep significance.

The most outstanding feature of Golden Dawn cabalism and its offshoots is that all the gods and spirits that exist are arranged in a very methodical and carefully worked out hierarchy that happens to be psychologically and spiritually right on the mark. Each of the ten *sephirot* has associated with it a name of a God, an archangel, a choir of angels, and a heavenly sphere. Seven of the heavenly spheres correspond, of course, with the seven visible planets, and each planet has a ruling angel, a spirit, and an intelligence. Each sign of the zodiac has an angel ruling three lesser angels of the decanates (ten-degree segments) of that sign, who in turn rule over the angels of the quinances (five-degree segments). There is even an angel for each of the 360 degrees of the Zodiac, but these are not widely known or used.

What this means, in practical terms, is that the cabalistic magician first calls upon the name of God appropriate for the working (for example, a ritual to gain money would be associated with Jupiter, and hence *Chesed*, the fourth *sephira*; the corresponding God name is El). The magician then descends the hierarchy, calling in turn each angel or spirit with the authority of the one above, until reaching the lesser entity that will carry out the work, in this instance probably Iophiel or Hismael or, conceivably, one of the seventy-two spirits of the Goetia of the Key of Solomon. All these hierarchies are very clearly laid out in *The Golden Dawn* by Israel Regardie, and elsewhere, as well as in a slightly more easily referenced form in *Godwin's Cabalistic Encyclopedia.*

A vital part of this working is that each *sephira* has all manner of associations so that the appropriate colors, incense, inscriptions and invoking hexagrams must be used. Another vital point about cabalistic magick is that, according to all reports, it works. "Like a charm," one might say ... *if* you know what you're doing.

Anyone who has ever undertaken magick of any kind knows that you won't get a million dollars simply by burning candles and reading words from a book. Although, if someone has some natural talent in that direction—and many people do, even unknown to themselves—he or she may suddenly come by a few extra dollars or find something at an unexpected bargain price.

But magick, be it cabalistic or that of some other tradition (art magick or natural magick, voodoo or shamanistic magick, Enochian magick or magick based on runes, high magick or low magick, black magick or white magick) requires first of all a good deal of dedicated and occasionally time-consuming *hard work*. In other words, there's no such thing as a free lunch.

Of course, this work is enjoyable and fulfilling; otherwise even fewer people would have anything to do with it than is already the case in the materialistic world. Quite aside from such ordinary goals as raising money, finding love, and so on, the ultimate goal of cabalistic magick is ... what?

There are many terms for this ultimate goal, and none of them is a very adequate description. They fall short; they distort the reality of the experience; but they are the best we have for something that is transcendentally ineffable.

Total realization. Fulfillment. Bliss. Enlightenment. Union with God. Samsara. Nirvana. Moksha. Fana. The pearl beyond price. The grail. The philosopher's stone. The goal of every religion. The only game worth playing.

Perhaps the best approach is that of Aleister Crowley, who called it "the knowledge and conversation of the Holy Guardian Angel"—a phrase that is sufficiently ridiculous, he said, to kill any argument before it starts. He recommended its acceptance as a technical term for what actually happens, which is indescribable in any case.

Quite aside from any such high goal—perhaps taking the attitude that "we're all going to get there anyway, in the end"—even the simplest dedicated practice of this system can turn your life right around. It's the best cure I know for the milder forms of chronic depression. With something like "the power of positive thinking," Emile Coué's formula of "Every day in every way I am getting better and better," or forms of psychotherapy that tell you to "quit telling yourself nonsense," there is always the tendency to think you are a hypocrite because you are telling yourself what you "know" to be bald-faced lies!

In the case of psychotherapy you have a therapist to guide you and keep you on track, but with other such mental systems you have no guide but your own limited perception of yourself and your determination to stick to something even when you think it's ridiculous. Consequently, as often as not, you don't succeed.

In the case of cabalistic magick, you don't tell yourself anything. You start in very simple ways and soon occupy yourself with a simple but frequently practiced ritual wherein you pronounce certain syllables and make certain signs in the air, all accompanied by mental visualizations (no, not at the office or on the street!). In most cases, you will suddenly find, much to your surprise, that your whole attitude is improving. When you feel low, you don't feel quite so low as you did before. You can no longer embrace such nihilistic thoughts as, "Life's a bitch and then you die." You feel as if there might be some hope for you after all.

Circle of Pythagoras *in crude Greek script by an A.S. hand written at Ramsey c. 1110. Above in the circles is written* ZOE MICRA *and* ZOE MEGALE, *below* THANATOS MEGAS *and* THANATOS MICROS *with the numbers of the days of the month.*

This moderate transformation—which, of course, cannot be guaranteed and which does not occur in every case, especially if you don't apply yourself to it adequately—is in no way related to anything that you are telling yourself or not telling yourself. It is not even obviously related to your ritual practice. It just happens.

One difficulty in arriving at an adequate practice is that there is so very, very much material available on the subject and so very, very little of it tells you things you actually need to know. Far and away the best book on the subject of practical, applied, cabalistic magick is *Modern Magick* by Donald Michael Kraig (Llewellyn Publications, 1988). Even if you never get past the first lesson—even if you never get as far as the first simple ritual—your life will be improved.

Another possible problem in working with magick, at least for some people—and I was one of them, some twenty years ago—is that you may have a tendency to pick and choose among all the various available sources—a little of this and a little of that. Even a shotgun approach such as this might be all right, particularly if you are lucky enough to have a brilliant and creative mind, if you would just formulate or arrive at one approach and stick to it instead of scattering your energies.

You can't do an offhand version of the Lesser Banishing Ritual of the Pentagram three days in the first week and then forget about it to try out a ritual you found in a book on shamanistic magick among the natives of Siberia, then a ritual from the Key of Solomon, then one of the Enochian calls, then something you find in Crowley's works, and then decide you are ready for the Bornless Invocation . . .

Another problem that may arise with cabalistic magick might be, as someone once said to me. "Why use all this Hebrew? I'm not Jewish!" Of course, most of the Bible was originally in Hebrew, and any Christian theology student worth his salt has a working acquaintance with it, as well as Aramaic and a healthy dose of New Testament Greek. Nevertheless, it is not uncommon for individuals to be "completely turned off to the whole Judaeo-Christian scene" by virtue of some unfortunate experience, or simply by a certain cast of mind. For a person of intuitive, artistic temperament, the obvious answer is some form of natural magick. The more intellectual type, however—the bookworm, the puzzle solver, the rationalist—may well find the methods of natural magick uncongenial, even more so than a system laden with Hebrew and occasional Christian symbolism.

The obvious solution in such a case is to make substitutions—

using the God names of some other religion or congenial mythology (mythology is a term used here to describe religions that are no longer widely practiced). Thus, one may possibly perform the pentagram ritual mentioned above with the God names Ra, Hathor, Tem, and Khepera, or Zeus, Hades, Poseidon, and Demeter, as opposed to the traditional YHVH, Adonai, Eheyeh, and Agla. The primary difficulties with such an approach are that (1) the ritual is generally not as effective, and (2), as soon as one strays from the Hebrew system, one immediately encounters insurmountable difficulties in maintaining the hierarchies. Only the Enochian system can even begin to approach the sophistication of the cabala when it comes to ordered hierarchies of spirits (angels, gods, whatever). If you use Ares as the God name associated with the sphere of Mars, what are you going to use for the archangelic name? The angelic name? The names of the spirit and intelligence and angelic choir and demonic order and all the rest of it?

It is conceivable that such a system could, with a tremendous amount of effort, be worked out for any given mythology. It would be far easier to accept the cabala as it is. Aleister Crowley had a frightful upbringing by religious extremists, and it drove him so far as to identify himself with the Beast of Revelation. Yet he overcame any resistance he might have had to the cabala so far as to be able to proclaim that the name YHVH has nothing whatever to do with Jehovah of the Old Testament.

Such is the system of magick known as cabalistic. It may appeal to you more than the other forms of magick described in this almanac and, if so, it may be the path for you. No one path is the one and only true path. As Farid ud-Din Attar says in *The Conference of the Bird* (in C.S. Nott's translation of Garcin de Tassy's French translation), "To each atom there is a different door, and for each atom there is a different way . . ." Whatever way you follow, may the end result be the Knowledge and Conversation of your Holy Guardian Angel.

Aleister Crowley

Aleister Crowley and the Star Ruby Ritual

David Godwin

I have read in more than one place that Aleister Crowley's works contain traps for the unwary (the stupid, in his estimation). I don't know what these traps are supposed to be, but it is said they are dangerous. The only example of anything of this nature that I have come across is not really dangerous. It's just one of Crowley's little jokes—if it is a joke. With Crowley, you can never be sure.

In his Star Ruby Ritual, you perform most of the evocations in Greek. For most people, including me, it is an effort to make out the Greek words, especially since he insists on having them in all capital letters. Even then you don't know what they actually mean, unless you know Greek or have a language dictionary handy.

At the beginning of the Golden Dawn Lesser Banishing

Ritual of the Pentagram, which is in wide use today even among non-cabalistic workers, you say: "Atah Malkut ve-Giburah ve-Gedullah le-Olahm. Amen." This is, of course, Hebrew and it means "Thine is the kingdom and the power and the glory forever. Amen." It is related to the Tree of Life, and the accompanying gestures form what is known as the cabalistic cross.

In the Star Ruby ritual, Crowley has substituted "Soi, O phalle, ischuros eucharistos. IAO." Anyone seeing "O phalle" is likely to think, "Oh, some more of Crowley's sex magick." But what the words actually mean is, "To you, O phallus, mighty thankful." Ha ha?

This little phrase might even be valid in a solar-phallic ritual of some sort, but it's his use of *eucharistos* (thankful) instead of something more appropriate such as *endoxos* (glorious) that gives it away as a schoolboy joke—that, and the apparent use of the adjective *ischuros* as a modern English colloquial adverb. Even if you assume that he is giving thanks to a phallic deity, the phrase doesn't quite fit the cabalistic cross or the Tree of Life, as Crowley well knew. He says in a footnote that "The secret sense of these words is to be sought in the numeration thereof." Beyond *phalle* = 666 (by what Crowley called the "Greek cabala"), there don't seem to be any correspondences—at least not in his list of numbers that forms *Sepher Sephiroth*.

The phrase "For thine is the kingdom . . ." and so on might be translated a little more faithfully into Greek as "*Sou e basileia kai e dynamis kai e doxa eis aione. Amen.*" However, I have found that this wording is not nearly so effective—for me—as is the Hebrew.

The Magickal Cabala

Ted Andrews

In each of us the qualities essential for accelerating our growth and empowering our life are innate, but even if we recognize such potentials, we still need a means of unfolding them. The ancient, mystical cabala is that means.

The cabala is one of the most ancient of all mystery traditions. Almost every civilization has utilized aspects of its system. The cabala and its primary symbol—The Tree of Life—is a diagram, a map, leading to all the treasures of the Universe. It is a system rich in rewards for those who know how to use it.

On one level (*refer to the diagram of the Tree of Life on page 56*) it reflects how the Universe was formed through stages of manifestation. Energy condensed itself through ten stages, culminating with physical life and matter. This is comparable to the process of condensing steam into water and then into ice.

On another, more personal level it is a map for opening deeper levels of our consciousness and then unfolding the energies and potentials that lie within each level. It is this tapping and unfolding process that opens higher perceptions and what appears to many to be a magickal existence.

Learning to access these levels of consciousness and release the potentials and energies within is not something highly esoteric or workable by only the "gifted" few. It is simply a matter of learning basic techniques and exercises that facilitate the accessing of these levels. The cabala is rich in mystical and magickal symbolism, colors, fragrances, etc., all of which are tools for unlocking the deeper levels of our consciousness. Learning to utilize the symbols to link our normal everyday consciousness with deeper

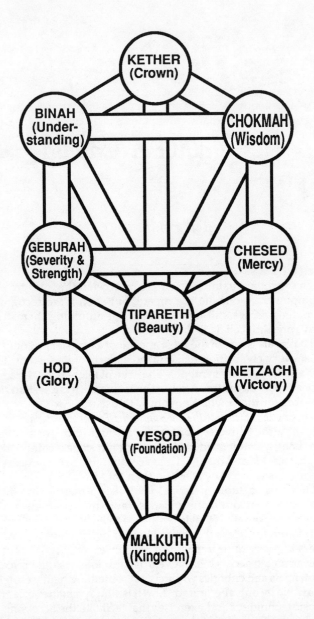

The ten Sephiroth (the ten levels of consciousness) within the map of the Tree of Life and the titles that reflect the character of the energy found at that level.

levels, dimensions, and beings is what the magickal cabala is about.

Each level of consciousness has certain energies that are released into our lives when we learn to access them. Each level can open up communication and assistance from those beings of the angelic hierarchy that work to guide us in our growth. Each level has a "god-Name" which is the highest spiritual and protective force at that level of our consciousness. It is a manifestation of the one Divine Force operating most intimately within and through us at that level of our consciousness. Each level has colors, fragrances, stones and gems associated with it. These—as will be seen in the meditation which follows—provide a means for opening up the levels of our consciousness as depicted within the Tree of Life.

Malkuth, at the bottom of the tree, is that level of consciousness closest to our normal waking state. We have access to the Archangel Sandalphon, who works with the formation of all life. It is a level of consciousness that can open energies that enable us to overcome inertia in our lives, discriminate, awaken greater common sense, overcome greed and laziness. Tapping into it can release greater physical energy and ultimately awaken a Vision of the Holy Guardian Angel.

Yesod is the next deeper level. It is at this level of our consciousness that we can connect with the Archangel Gabriel, who gives the gift of hope. At this level we can open to greater psychic energy and intuition. It stimulates independence and dream activity. It can be used to overcome idleness, impulsiveness and emotional imbalance. It is a level of consciousness that helps us to understand that there is a Divine Plan.

The next level of consciousness is *Hod*. It is a level of creative energies, especially for their expression in art. It releases energies that awaken greater unselfishness, warmth and idealism, and it can reveal insight into relationships. It can assist in overcoming lust, overemotionalism and jealousy. It is a level that can open the nature kingdom. Haniel is the archangel to whom we have access through this level of our consciousness. She is the patroness of the arts, bringing inspiration.

At the heart of the Tree is a level of our consciousness called *Tiphareth*. It is a level of consciousness for healing and compassion. At its deepest level it awakens Christ consciousness. It releases energies into our life for overcoming fear, insecurity and false pride, while awakening devotion and healing. The Archangel Raphael works through this level. He is the Keeper of the Grail and is known as the Healing Angel of God.

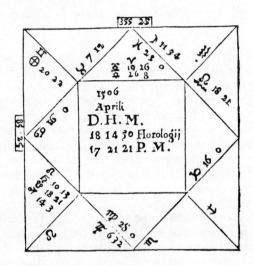

*Specimen of a Genethliac, or Astrological Horoscope,
composed in the Sixteenth Century.*

The next level of consciousness is called *Geburah.* Kamael is
the archangel to whom we have access by learning to tap this level
of our consciousness. He defends the weak and the wronged and
he helps us slay our dragons in life. At this level we can release
energies for overcoming anger, fear, timidness and aggression. It
can awaken courage and strength. It can release energy so we can
initiate change. It assists us in critical judgment, and it awakens us
to the power that is innate within us.

Chesed is a level of our consciousness that can manifest
energies of peace and devotion. It can release greater abundance
into our lives, while helping us to overcome stinginess, self-
righteousness and hypocrisy. At this level of our consciousness,
we begin to truly know that we are called to higher and greater
things. Tzadkiel is the archangel operating at this level of our consciousness. He is the protector of all teachers and brings the
winds of mercy into our lives.

Binah is the next deeper level. It is a level of our consciousness that opens greater understanding of all things. It is a level
that when tapped will release understanding of sacrifices we
have made in our life. It opens higher intuition and understanding of the processes of birth and death. It releases energies into

our life for overcoming fear, insecurity and false pride, while awakening devotion and healing. The Archangel Raphael works through this level. He is the Keeper of the Grail and is known as the Healing Angel of God.

Chokmah is the next deeper level of consciousness. It is a level of our consciousness which opens higher wisdom to us in life. Its energies may manifest in our life in the form of greater initiative and devotion. It awakens strong inspiration and vision. It opens a realization of one's hidden abilities. Its energies help us in overcoming forgetfulness, inefficiency and an inability to manifest things within our lives. Ratziel is the archangel to whom we have access. It is he who helps us to understand how heaven and all of the universe operate within our lives—all according to divine laws.

At the top of the Tree lies *Kether.* Touching this level of our consciousness releases the energies of true creativity into our lives. It is a source of spiritual energy that can be activated to amplify and intensify any aspect of our life. It stimulates creative imagination and the power to transform ourselves. It ignites the spiritual fires within our lives, while manifesting opportunities to overcome illusions, self-denial and negative self-images. Metatron is the archangel operating at this level. It is his task to help sustain humanity through the evolutionary process. Tradition says that it was he who gave us the Cabala so that we could re-attain our former status.

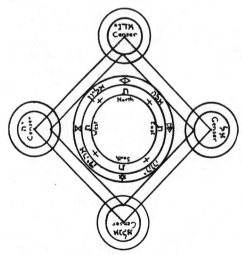

A Magickal Circle

Touching the Powers

When we start accessing deeper levels of consciousness as they are depicted upon the Tree of Life, it is best to start with the level of Malkuth, as it is closest to our normal waking state of consciousness. We can then work our way up the tree. Remember that these are *untapped* levels of consciousness and power within you.

Every level has levels within it, so each time we work with this, we can release greater energy and greater depths of awareness and knowledge into our life. This play of energy does not manifest in our lives in artificially contrived situations, but through the normal life circumstances. When we touch these levels it activates learning by intensifying our life circumstances. It releases the energy that enables us to handle life situations with greater power and control.

In the Table is shown a list of correspondences; these are tools to assist you in accessing the various levels of consciousness and releasing their energies more fully within your life. Candles and incense are two of the easiest and most effective means of inducing the correct altered state of consciousness. Light candles and burn incense associated with the level of consciousness you have chosen to access. By lighting the candle and using the incense, you put the vibrational energy of both into the environment in which you will be working. This triggers resonance within you. The appropriate level of consciousness responds. The tools serve as a doorbell, awakening the appropriate level.

Next, allow yourself to relax. Then following the basic procedure as is outlined in the following meditation ritual, allow yourself to access these temples of consciousness and extract the energies within them and within you.

These temples of consciousness are high and holy places. They are where we unite with all of mankind and life—past, present and future. They are places of tremendous energy and power and, according to the level, once touched the energy is released to manifest in your life on some level. Earlier we discussed how the energy operates at each level, but do not limit your thoughts to that. It manifests itself in many ways more than is outlined here. Discovering these ways is what helps us to grow.

Above the portals of the Ancient Mystery Schools was but one precept: "KNOW THYSELF!" Within each of us are *all* of the energies and forces of the Universe. Within each of us is the

Levels of Consciousness	God-Force	Color	Fragrance	Meditation Stone/Gem	Magickal Image	Magickal Gift
Kether	Eheieh (I AM)	White	Frankincense	Double terminated quartz	Ancient, bearded King in profile	Spinning top
Chokmah	Jah (The Lord)	Gray	Eucalyptus	Fluorite	Bearded male	Sceptre of Power
Binah	Jehovah Elohim (Lord God)	Black	Myrrh	Black tourmaline	Mature woman	Cloak of Concealment
Chesed	El (God)	Blue	Bayberry	Lapis Lazuli	Mighty, throned king	King's Cup
Geburah	Elohim Gebor (God Almighty)	Red	Cinnamon	Garnet	Mighty warrior	Sword
Tiphareth	Jehovah Aloah va Daath (God made manifest in mind)	Yellow	Rose Oil	Rose quartz	Majestic king, sacrificed god, and a child	Crown (too large)
Netzach	Jehovah Tzabaoth (Lord of hosts)	Green	Petuli	Malachite	Beautiful, naked woman	Rose
Hod	Elohim Tzabaoth (God of Hosts)	Orange	Rosemary	Citrine	Hermaphrodite	Caduceus pendant
Yesod	Shaddai el Chai (Almighty Living God)	Violet	Wysteria	Amethyst	Beautiful, strong naked man	Silver slippers and a mirror
Malkuth	Adonai ha Aretz (Lord of Earth)	Black; Olive; Russet; Citrine	Sandalwood	Smokey Quartz	Young woman, crowned & throned	Shafts of wheat and grains of corn

Table of Magickal Correspondences

capability of releasing that infinite potential to manifest greater enlightenment, fulfillment, love, and abundance in all arenas of life. The recognition of this, and then the utilization, is what makes the magick of life.

Magick is not a charm or a spell to manifest a special person or thing in your life. It is not an escape from our day-to-day life circumstances. Magick is the initiation into a higher understanding of our responsibility for the course and circumstances of our existence. It is the utilization of higher awareness to recreate our lives upon a higher realm.

The cabala shows us that the world is one of color and light and joy. It shows us that the world is one that we can fashion to our highest dreams and ideals. It is a world that *all* may enter—but enter with openness and reverence, for this is God's world!

Meditation Ritual

"Awakening the Tree of Life"

Ted Andrews

For this exercise, you will need to use the Table of Correspondences. Everything listed beside the Level of Consciousness will help awaken that level and release that energy into your life. Pay close attention to the events of your life in the days and weeks that follow, for many of the events—great and small—will result from the energy that you release through this exercise.

Preliminaries:

1. *Review the level of consciousness and its associations.*
2. *Find a comfortable place and time.*
3. *Remove the phone and eliminate as many auditory distractions as possible.*
4. *Close your eyes throughout the exercise to eliminate visual distractions.*
5. *Sit with a candle lit on either side of you.*
6. *Light the incense and lightly hold the meditation stone upon your lap.*
7. *Take time to do a progressive relaxation, relaxing each part of your body in turn. This allows you to become more receptive to the energies of the candles, fragrance and stone. It greatly enhances the altering of consciousness.*

As you close your eyes and relax, allow yourself to see/sense the colors of the candles growing brighter around you with each breath. Imagine it. Feel it. See yourself surrounded and permeated by the soft crystalline color. Picture yourself within a spherical temple room of this color.

As with all temples, there is an altar upon which burns an eternal light; it is the light within you that shines perpetually. Alongside of the altar are two massive pillars, one black and one white—reminders to maintain balance in all things and at all times.

Softly (in your mind or audibly) sound the name of the God-force that operates through that level of your consciousness. Use the Hebrew name or its English translation. Sound it slowly, syllable by syllable, as if toning a prayer. See the temple grow brighter and brighter with each utterance. In the case of Malkuth, with each utterance see the light in the temple change from black to olive to russet and then to citrine (sun yellow).

As the temple grows brilliant and radiant with light, the Magickal Image reflects you at that level of your consciousness. Allow the Image to speak to you, telling you about the energies at this level, and how they manifest within your own individual life now that you have touched it. If you have questions, ask. If the answer is within the realm of this level of consciousness, the Image will answer. If not, the Image will inform you.

The Magickal Image then extends to you the magickal gift to take with you to the outer world. Let the Image tell you of the function of this gift and how merely thinking of it, visualizing it, will activate its energies in your life. Let the Image teach you how it is to be used or not used by you.

At this point, the Magickal Image steps forward and embraces you. In the warm, loving embrace, a word, a phrase, a reminder, etc. is whispered into your ear. Then with a shimmering of soft, warm energy, the figure melts into you to become a part of you, to keep that level of your consciousness active within your life.

As you feel the Image within you, the temple scene begins to fade, but you now feel it within. As you breathe deeply, you begin to become aware once more of the room you began this work in. You are surrounded by the fragrance and the color of the candles, the outer reflection of the inner temple.

With this exercise, you begin the process of activating all of the levels of consciousness and bringing the energies out into your normal life. All images, colors, fragrances, etc. reflect archetypal energies within the universe. This process activates them more fully within your own life.

To enhance the effects, perform the exercise three days in a row. Three is a creative number and serves to amplify the effects. Then wait at least one week before awakening the next level. If you touch them too quickly, you will activate so much energy that you won't be able to discern which life situations are the result of which level of consciousness.

It is also recommended that you write down, in a journal of some kind, the meditation experience—at least the final message that was whispered in your ear. This grounds the experience, taking it out of that ethereal mental realm, and sets it into play more quickly upon the physical.

You are awakening the Tree of Life. You are *becoming* the Tree of Life—with your roots in the earth and your limbs and crown in the heavens. You are bridging the two worlds. And when heaven and earth merge—we create the *magickal existence*.

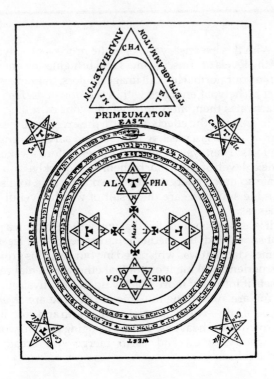

Origins of the Cabala

Raymond Buckland

The word "cabala," or *Kabbalah*, is frequently applied almost
indiscriminately to many different forms or mixtures of theoso-
phy/magick and secret lore, yet actually is peculiar to a particular
body of Jewish doctrines. It comprises a number of different texts
written by various authors at scattered periods in Jewish history.
For the most part these authors were simply putting into writing
what had been carefully guarded knowledge, passed along orally
for many generations, dealing with the nature of God and the
place of Man in God's universe.

The cabala may be viewed as being in two parts: the *Kabbalah
Maasit*, or "practical" cabala, and the *Kabbalah Iynnit*, or "contem-
plative" cabala. Both deal with removing the barriers between
Man and God, though the *Kabbalah Maasit* might be deemed the

more "occult" of the two. Cabalists believe that it is the goal of every human soul to seek unity with the Godhead and that unity will only be possible through perfection.

Teaching of the cabala was originally done on a very secretive level, with the teacher working closely—and frequently in complete hiding—with a single pupil. The Haggidah stated that "It is forbidden to expound the first chapters of Genesis to two men (in other words, more than one person at a time), and it may be expounded only to one by himself . . . (if) he be wise and filled with understanding." It is universally believed that there are many teachings, and objects, too sacred to be casually handled by an unprepared person, one not properly initiated, or prepared, to receive that teaching or object. The strict translation of the word *Kabbalah* is "that which is received."

The cabala, then, was a teaching that was hidden from the uninitiated for centuries. Indeed, the teachings were unknown and unsuspected by most people—and even by some of the rabbis—until the twelfth/thirteenth century, when it surfaced in Spain and the south of France. The reason it did surface was that there was fear of the teachings becoming lost. With various crises that befell the Jews, teachers were being killed before they could complete their work with their students. Rather than lose the cabalistic teachings altogether, they were put into writing. Of course, once that happened there was the opportunity for people, other than the specially selected students, to obtain it. And that is precisely what happened. Over the succeeding centuries the written words have become widely spread, not only among Jews but elsewhere.

The cabala, however, is written in veiled terms, the true meanings of the texts not being immediately apparent. It has been said that the key to the cabala is written in code and that only a Jew can break that code. This is not true, but a student of the cabala certainly does need to be well versed in Hebrew.

Many of the "modern" Magicians (for example, Eliphas Levi, Aleister Crowley) have been strongly influenced by the cabala. In it they see the macrocosm/microcosm: the belief that Mankind is a miniature of the universe and that Man is capable of expansion to become one with God.

Mertz

March

Monday

Tuesday

Wednesday

1

Thursday

Moon Sign: Taurus
Moon Phase: 1st Quarter
Festival: Matronalia

Tarot Card: Ace of Pentacles
Herb: Agave
Incense: Cinnamon
Mineral: Montana Ruby
Color: Blue
Name of Power: Juno Lucina

2
Friday

Moon Sign: Gemini
Moon Phase: 1st Quarter

Tarot Card: Two of Pentacles
Herb: Arnica
Incense: Frankincense
Mineral: Ox-Eye
Color: Green
Name of Power: Spenta-
                    Armaiti

3
Saturday

Moon Sign: Gemini
Moon Phase: 2nd Quarter
Festival: Girls' Festival

Tarot Card: Three of Pentacles
Herb: Belladonna
Incense: Sandalwood
Mineral: Pigeonblood Agate
Color: Black
Name of Power: Munakata-
                    No-Kami

4
Sunday

Moon Sign: Gemini
Moon Phase: 2nd Quarter

Tarot Card: Four of Pentacles
Herb: Black Root
Incense: Myrrh
Mineral: Rainbow Agate
Color: Yellow
Name of Power: Seget-Hra

MARCH

S	M	T	W	T	F	S
				1	2	3
4	5	6	7	8	9	10
11	12	13	14	15	16	17
18	19	20	21	22	23	24
25	26	27	28	29	30	31

5

Monday

Moon Sign: Cancer
Moon Phase: 2nd Quarter
Festival: Ship of Isis

Tarot Card: Five of Pentacles
Herb: Bryony
Incense: Jasmine
Mineral: Rose Kunzite
Color: White
Name of Power: Isis

6

Tuesday

Moon Sign: Cancer
Moon Phase: 2nd Quarter
Festival: Start of Flowering
         Time in Celtic
         calendar

Tarot Card: Six of Pentacles
Herb: Carrot
Incense: Benzoin
Mineral: Rubolite
Color: Red
Name of Power: Mania

7

Wednesday

Moon Sign: Leo
Moon Phase: 2nd Quarter
Festival: Junonalia

Tarot Card: Seven of Pentacles
Herb: Clove
Incense: Pine
Mineral: Star Topaz
Color: Purple
Name of Power: Juno

8

Thursday

Moon Sign: Leo
Moon Phase: 2nd Quarter

Tarot Card: Eight of Pentacles
Herb: Cubeb
Incense: Cinnamon
Mineral: Zebra Stone
Color: Blue
Name of Power: Perpetua

9
Friday

Moon Sign: Virgo
Moon Phase: 2nd Quarter

Tarot Card: Nine of Pentacles
Herb: Dyer's Broom
Incense: Frankincense
Mineral: Aquamarine
Color: Green
Name of Power: Aphrodite

10
Saturday

Moon Sign: Virgo
Moon Phase: 2nd Quarter
Festival: Favardigan (1st day)

Tarot Card: Ten of Pentacles
Herb: Fennel
Incense: Sandalwood
Mineral: Beryl
Color: Black
Name of Power: Ishtar

11
Sunday

Moon Sign: Libra
Moon Phase: Full Moon
    (Chaste)

Tarot Card: Page of Pentacles
Herb: Fringe Tree
Incense: Myrrh
Mineral: Chrysoberyl
Color: Yellow
Name of Power: Sabes

			MARCH			
S	M	T	W	T	F	S
				1	2	3
4	5	6	7	8	9	10
11	12	13	14	15	16	17
18	19	20	21	22	23	24
25	26	27	28	29	30	31

12 *Monday*

Moon Sign: Libra
Moon Phase: 3rd Quarter

Tarot Card: Knight of Pentacles
Herb: Ground Ivy
Incense: Jasmine
Mineral: Alexandrite
Color: White
Name of Power: Hypatia

13 *Tuesday*

Moon Sign: Libra
Moon Phase: 3rd Quarter

Tarot Card: Queen of Pentacles
Herb: Hemp Nettle
Incense: Benzoin
Mineral: Golden Beryl
Color: Red
Name of Power: Diotima

14 *Wednesday*

Moon Sign: Scorpio
Moon Phase: 3rd Quarter

Tarot Card: King of Pentacles
Herb: Horse Chestnut
Incense: Pine
Mineral: Morganite
Color: Purple
Name of Power: Poreskoro

15 *Thursday*

Moon Sign: Scorpio
Moon Phase: 3rd Quarter
Festival: Anna Perenna

Tarot Card: Ace of Swords
Herb: Irish Moss
Incense: Cinnamon
Mineral: Spinel
Color: Blue
Name of Power: Cybele

16

Friday

Moon Sign: Sagittarius
Moon Phase: 3rd Quarter

Tarot Card: Two of Swords
Herb: Larch
Incense: Frankincense
Mineral: Topaz
Color: Green
Name of Power: Melalo

17

Saturday

Moon Sign: Sagittarius
Moon Phase: 3rd Quarter
Festival: Liberalia

Tarot Card: Three of Swords
Herb: Lovage
Incense: Sandalwood
Mineral: Garnet
Color: Black
Name of Power: Libera

18

Sunday

Moon Sign: Sagittarius
Moon Phase: 3rd Quarter

Tarot Card: Four of Swords
Herb: Meadowsweet
Incense: Myrrh
Mineral: Cape Ruby
Color: Yellow
Name of Power: Freyr
Tree: Alder

MARCH

S	M	T	W	T	F	S
				1	2	3
4	5	6	7	8	9	10
11	12	13	14	15	16	17
18	19	20	21	22	23	24
25	26	27	28	29	30	31

19 *Monday*

Moon Sign: Capricorn
Moon Phase: 4th Quarter
Festival: Minerva's Birthday;
           Lesser Panathenaea

Tarot Card: Five of Swords
Herb: Lamb Mint
Incense: Jasmine
Mineral: Almandine
Color: White
Name of Power: Athena

20 *Tuesday*

Moon Sign: Capricorn
Moon Phase: 4th Quarter
Sun enters Aries
Festival: Favardigan (last day)

Tarot Card: Six of Swords
Herb: Mountain Laurel
Incense: Benzoin
Mineral: Spessartite
Color: Red
Name of Power: Iduna

21 *Wednesday*

Moon Sign: Aquarius
Moon Phase: 4th Quarter
Festival: Vernal Equinox
        Persian New Year's
        Day

Tarot Card: Seven of Swords
Herb: Nettle
Incense: Pine
Mineral: Topazolite
Color: Purple
Name of Power: Oestre

22 *Thursday*

Moon Sign: Aquarius
Moon Phase: 4th Quarter

Tarot Card: Eight of Swords
Herb: Orange
Incense: Cinnamon
Mineral: Hyacinth Zircon
Color: Blue
Name of Power: Damballah-
                Wedo

23
Friday

Moon Sign: Aquarius
Moon Phase: 4th Quarter
Festival: Higan Festival

Tarot Card: Nine of Swords
Herb: Periwinkle
Incense: Frankincense
Mineral: Watermelon Tourma-
line
Color: Green
Name of Power: Erzuli

24
Saturday

Moon Sign: Pisces
Moon Phase: 4th Quarter

Tarot Card: Ten of Swords
Herb: Pleurisy Root
Incense: Sandalwood
Mineral: Quartz Crystal
Color: Black
Name of Power: Kali

25
Sunday

Moon Sign: Pisces
Moon Phase: 4th Quarter
Festival: Anunciacíon
        Festival of Joy

Tarot Card: Page of Swords
Herb: Pride of China
Incense: Myrrh
Mineral: Violet Tourmaline
Color: Yellow
Name of Power: Cybele

MARCH

S	M	T	W	T	F	S
				1	2	3
4	5	6	7	8	9	10
11	12	13	14	15	16	17
18	19	20	21	22	23	24
25	26	27	28	29	30	31

26   *Monday*

Moon Sign: Aries
Moon Phase: New Moon
Festival: Fercula

Tarot Card: Knight of Swords
Herb: Purple Boneset
Incense: Jasmine
Mineral: Kunzite
Color: White
Name of Power: Attis

27   *Tuesday*

Moon Sign: Aries
Moon Phase: 1st Quarter

Tarot Card: Queen of Swords
Herb: Red Pimpernel
Incense: Benzoin
Mineral: Smoky Quartz
Color: Red
Name of Power: Ea

28   *Wednesday*

Moon Sign: Taurus
Moon Phase: 1st Quarter

Tarot Card: King of Swords
Herb: Blessed Thistle
Incense: Pine
Mineral: Amethyst
Color: Purple
Name of Power: Theresa

29   *Thursday*

Moon Sign: Taurus
Moon Phase: 1st Quarter

Tarot Card: The Magician
Herb: Senna
Incense: Cinnamon
Mineral: Citrine
Color: Blue
Name of Power: Ogu-Yansan

30
Friday

Moon Sign: Gemini
Moon Phase: 1st Quarter

Tarot Card: High Priestess
Herb: Spikenard
Incense: Frankincense
Mineral: Prasiolite
Color: Green
Name of Power: Janus

31
Saturday

Moon Sign: Gemini
Moon Phase: 1st Quarter

Tarot Card: The Empress
Herb: Witch Hazel
Incense: Sandalwood
Mineral: Aventurine
Color: Black
Name of Power: Luna

MARCH

S	M	T	W	T	F	S
				1	2	3
4	5	6	7	8	9	10
11	12	13	14	15	16	17
18	19	20	21	22	23	24
25	26	27	28	29	30	31

Ancient Rune Magic

Donald Tyson

Runes are the tangible body of the lost art of magic practiced by the ancient Teutonic tribes of northern Europe. Of this potent, complex and unique magical system, only the runes have survived intact. No description detailing the method of rune magic has come down to us, but, by using poetic fragments, relics, brief references in classical writings, and insights into the universal forms of magic, it is possible to reconstruct the technique of rune magic as it was used in the time of Christ, and may still be used today.

Below are the Germanic runes, which are the oldest and purest—all other rune alphabets derive from these. Beside each rune is its phonetic value, its name in Old English (and in parentheses, German), the translation of the name into modern English, and a brief explanation of its meaning. Those wishing a more complete description of all the runes, including the Old English additions to the Germanic rune alphabet, should read my book *Rune Magic* (Llewellyn, 1988).

1)   ᚠ   f; FEOH (FEHU); cattle
   Movable possessions, wealth, servility, bondage.

2)   ᚢ   u; UR (URUZ); aurochs
   Fierceness, virility, power, freedom.

3) Þ   th; THORN (THURISAZ); a devil
Evil, cruelty, baseness, deceitfulness.

4) F   a; OS (ANSUZ); a god
Good, love, nobility, truth.

5) R   r; RAD (RAIDO); journey by horse
Travel, relocation, searching, quest.

6) <   k; KEN (KANO); torch
Firelight, beacon, intelligence, spirit.

7) X   g; GYFU (GEBO); gift
A present, something precious, sacrifice, initiation.

8) Þ   w; WYN (WUNJO); glory
Pride of possession, joy, reward, ecstasy.

9) N   h; HAEGL (HAGALAZ); hail
Winter storms, destruction, hardship, suffering.

10) Ϟ   n; NYD (NAUTHIZ); need
Necessity, resistance, endurance, survival.

11) | i; IS (ISA); ice
Rigidity, glamour, deception, treachery.

12) ⟿   j; GER (JERA); harvest
Cycle of change, revolution, inversion, actualization.

13) ʃ   ei; EOH (EIHWAZ); yew tree
Dependability, strength, solidity, common sense.

14)   p; PEORD (PERTH); apple tree
Abundance, pleasure, gaiety, excess.

15)   z; EOLH (ALGIZ); defense
Warding off, protection, warning, averting evil.

16)   s; SIGEL (SOWELU); sun
Active force, retribution, punishment, sword of justice.

17)   t; TYR (TEIWAZ); the god Tiw
Battle, courage, honor, truth.

18)   b; BEORC (BERKANA); birch tree
Beauty, love, fertility, birth.

19)   e; EH (EHWAZ); horse
Transportation, physical virtues, means, sur-mounting.

20)   m; MAN (MANNAZ); man
Reason, mental virtues, method, realization.

21)   l; LAGU (LAGUZ); water
Secret depths, unconscious, dreams, illusions.

22)   ng; ING (INGUZ); a fertility god
Earth, growth, family, the home.

23)   d; DAEG (DAGAZ); day
Daylight, comprehension, totality, lifespan.

24)   o; ETHEL (OTHILA); homeland
Fixed possessions, birthplace, inheritance, karma.

Two divisions of the rune alphabet must be known by all who intend to use it for magic. Pairs distinguish related runes with complementary or contrasting meanings—these are ᚠ ᚾ ,

ᚦ ᚨ , ᚱ ᚲ , and so on through the alphabet. Families, or *aettir*,

divide the alphabet into three groups of eight consecutive runes, corresponding to the three levels of man: physical, emotional, and mental. Each *aett* takes its name and quality from the rune that begins it. These naming runes are Feoh (physical), Haegl (emotional), and Tyr (mental).

Runes were primarily a magical tool, and only secondarily a medium of written communication. They were seldom used individually, but were combined into series with repeating elements. Scholars have embarrassingly little to say about such inscriptions, except that they must be magical. It has been suggested that such series are contractions where each rune stands for a word. It seems clear, however, that they are based on a system of numerology which probably corresponds in most points with the classical numerology set forth in writings attributed to Pythagoras, Orpheus, Hermes, Plato, and others. For example, the most famous magical use of runes in number series occurs on the Lindholm amulet. It has baffled scholars since its discovery in 1840. The runes read:

ᚠᚠᚠᚠᚠᚠᚠᚠᚱᚱᚱᛣᛣᛣ ? ᛒᛗᚾᛏᛏᛏ

Knowing that eight is the number of realization, and the first "solid" number according to Pythagoras (2 × 2 × 2, which stands for the three spatial dimensions), and furthermore that three is the number of being and identity, and nine the perfect number leading to transition, I would translate the inscription: "Odin, protect my life and lend me courage and warskill as I ride into the

extremity of battle." (ᚠ = Odin; ᚱ = riding, or travel; ᛣ = hardship, or danger; ᛒ = vitality; ᛗ = man, i.e. the possessor of the amulet; ᚾ = valor and battle prowess; ᛏ = war,

and also courage. The ? indicates an indecipherable rune.)

The method of using runes to cause magical change is hinted at in many places in the old writings, and numerous disconnected bits and pieces of information are given. But only in the eddic *Havamal* are the steps of rune magic explicitly listed by Odin, whom the poet makes to say:

> Know how to cut them,
> Know how to read them,
> Know how to stain them,
> Know how to evoke them,
> Know how to send them.

SCRAMASAX FROM THE THAMES *BRIT MUS*

In its simplest sense, knowing how to cut the runes means knowing their shapes. But in magic there is a method to everything. They should be incised or inscribed with strong, simple strokes, moving downward and toward the right, which is the path of the light. Cut them in silence with full concentration upon the act and with solemnity of heart. Never saw back and forth with knife or pen. In writing, use single firm strokes; in carving, use two strokes, one to incise the wood, the second to clear away the groove. Cutting the runes is a ritual act that may be likened to conception. All instruments and surfaces must be purified and consecrated beforehand.

On one level, reading the runes simply involves knowing their names. Odin is saying that no one should copy runes by rote without knowing what they are called. On the occult level, naming a rune brings it from the potential into the actual. It is equivalent to cutting the rune in the mind, even as the hand carves it into the wood. Runes gain form and identity when they are read. In a sense the runes may be said to lie sleeping in the womb, where they await birth; reading may be likened to the entry of the soul into the fetus.

After cutting each rune, look at it intently and form it in the astral, or imaginary, world with as much tangible reality as your skill allows. Speak the name of the rune softly, but let it thunder in your heart, and allow your breath to touch and warm the incised physical rune. The breath is the link between the mentally carved rune and its materially carved counterpart. It is a good idea in carving to keep your head low so that your breath touches the runes, and if your sweat falls upon them, this is also good.

Once you have conceived the runes and given them identity, you must nourish them. In ancient times the runes were stained with blood or red ochre, which magically is the blood of the Earth. Blood feeds the runes and gives them strength. Blood is the life (see Genesis 9:4). The only one who ever truly makes a blood sacrifice is the individual from whose body the blood flows. All other forms of blood sacrifice are various levels of theft and deceit.

If blood is offered to the runes, a small cut should be made in the breast above the left nipple, or in the inside of the left forearm, with a blade cleansed by fire a few moments before. Touch the index finger of the right hand to the cut, and trace each rune in the same order and direction as it was carved, filling all the grooves. If red earth pigment is used, it should be dug by hand from the ground by the rune maker, the impurities separated from it, and reduced to a fine powder with a mortar and pestle. Any reddish clay will do. When used, it should be mixed with fresh saliva to make a thick paste.

I am not for a moment advocating the use of blood in rune magic. If earth pigment is energized rightly it is just as effective. But it would be less than honest to pretend that blood was not used in times past. In fact, its use was universal, and was probably regarded as indispensable by ancient rune masters. Having said this, I sincerely hope there are few readers foolish enough to begin slashing away at themselves, as the shedding of blood by itself is not only useless, but harmful to the soul.

In addition to blood, it may be that other bodily fluids were used to stain the runes for specific magical purposes: sweat for works of building and toil; saliva for works of the spirit and creation; semen (or menstrual blood) for sex magic; tears for devotional works and sacrifices; urine for works of destruction.

The conceived runes, infused by breath with their unique identities or souls, which are defined by the circles of their names and nourished in the magical womb by blood or its substitute, are born into the world through the charm of evocation. In this stage the energies of the runes are actually infused into the material upon which the rune symbols are carved. The runes wake up and become aware.

Although the ancient chants of evocation have been lost, it is possible from the general principles of magic to reconstruct at least their framework. Shamans use rhythmic chants or songs repeated over and over, sometimes for hours, to focus their awareness and call forth spirits. It is probable that Teutonic rune masters employed a similar technique to evoke the runes. The chants would have been short, simple, strongly metrical and alliterative, and perhaps constructed to be chanted in a circle with the end of the verse running back into the beginning. An elaborate exposition of this type of circular poem is William Blake's "The Mental Traveller."

The chant, helped by formal ritual gestures such as the inscription of a tourbillion (or astral vortex) in the air over the runes with the knife, focuses the will and crystallizes the power of the runes. Rhythmic rocking of the body is also good for inducing the semi-trance state through which the powers of the runes, or rune gods, can flow into the material rune symbols. Contemplation on a flame will serve the same purpose. All these devices serve to open a channel between the unconscious, where the runes dwell, and the manifest world.

Once the runes are successfully evoked, they become potent and dangerous. The qualities that distinguish rune magic from all other kinds are its raw, physical power and the difficulty of controlling it. The sooner the runes are applied to their specific purpose, the better. Until this is done they are like a live high-tension electrical wire with a bare loose end blowing in the wind.

Sending the runes is the final step and involves forming a magical link, or bridge, between the runes and the ritual object of desire. The most direct method of sending is to physically put the runes into the possession of the person, or into the place, upon which they are designed to act. For example, one use of runes in ancient times was to assist in childbirth, and for this purpose they were cut into the palms of the woman in labour. Thus the feeding and sending stages were combined, and presumably, while they were being cut, a chant of evocation was spoken over them in which they were named. When sent, the runes should reach as many levels of their object as possible—that is, if sent to an individual he should not only receive them into his hand, but should be aware of their significance. In this way the magical bridge is more complete.

When personal contact is not possible, the runes may be sent through the element most appropriate to the matter of the working. For works of violence, contenting, or high emotion, the runes should be burned. For works of intellect, communication, and formal art such as architecture or acting, the runes should be scattered upon the air. For works of inspired art, illusion, fashion or glamour, cast the runes into running water or the ocean. And for works of construction, physical health, growth and business, the runes should be buried.

In every case, while sending the runes, the will must be concentrated upon the magical object of desire, if possible with the aid of a photograph, personal possession, signature, or other occult link.

The rune ritual that accompanies this article is designed to illuminate the method of rune magic with a practical example. It is hoped this will help the reader make the sometimes difficult jump from theory to practice.

(inside.)

GOLD RING CARLISLE BRIT MUS

A Rune Candle Love Ritual

STONE CROSS
LANCASTER
BRIT MUS

Donald Tyson

This is a ritual for bringing love by the power of the runes through the medium of a candle. Rituals to procure love are best carried out with *love* as their object, rather than a specific individual. If you seek love itself, the right person will naturally appear and become the instrument through which the ritual desire is fulfilled.

The working of the ritual occupies nine days. It is performed in solitude in the bedroom just prior to going to sleep each night. Total concentration is essential. The period of the working must be free from all shocks or disturbances.

Women seeking the love of a man should cut the runes on Friday (Frija's Day) so that the tenth day, the day of realization, will fall on Sunday (Sol's Day). Men seeking the love of a woman should cut the runes on Wednesday (Odin's Day) so that the day of realization falls on Friday.

Select a white candle about half an inch in diameter and cut it to a length of nine inches. For magical purposes, an "inch" is the last joint of your index finger. A smokeless dinner candle is good but it must not taper, or if it does, the tapered section must be the part cut off.

You will need a sharp knife, a clean white cloth, a lighter, and a flat dish. A small table, such as a bedside table, is useful as a support for the cloth, although it is the cloth itself that acts as the altar. It is best to have previously purified all these instruments by sprinkling them with clear water while speaking a cleansing prayer in the name of Odin, father of the northern gods.

On the first night of the working, stand in front of the altar cloth and make the sign ᛏ upon your body for protection, speaking this verse:

> From all hurt guard and protect me,
> By Odin, by Thor, by Tiw,
> So let it be.

As you speak the name Odin, touch with your right index finger your forehead and groin; as you speak Thor, touch your left shoulder and solar plexus; as you speak Tiw, touch your right shoulder and solar plexus. This should be done at the beginning and ending of each ritual period.

Kneel or sit before the altar cloth, and with the purified knife cut eight rings around the candle at one "inch" intervals, dividing it into nine segments. In each segment cut one of the following runes crosswise, so that they read from the top of the candle to the bottom when it is held horizontally:

Top ᛒ ᛏ ᛒ ᚠ ᛜ ᚢ ᛒ ᛗ ᛒ Bottom

After you cut each rune, speak its name so that your breath warms it, and hold in your imagination an image of the rune shimmering with vitality. When all the runes are cut and named, touch the tip of your right index finger nine times to your lips and trace with your saliva the grooves of each rune successively, speaking these words for each rune: "*(name of rune)*, receive this food of sacrifice, blood of my spirit." Visualize your own personal vitality flowing into the runes one after another and nourishing them.

Light the candle, drip a little wax and set it upright on the dish in the middle of the altar cloth. Sit comfortably where you can see the flame without strain (the room should be dark). As the first segment of the candle burns you must focus totally upon your purpose. Imagine your ideal lover coming toward you, gesturing to you in invitation, opening his or her arms to you, laughing with you in perfect harmony.

While you watch the flame and perform this visualization, utter this chant under your breath:

> Upon the earth, upon the sea,
> Upon the air, my lover be;
> Wings of fire, my desire,
> Bring my lover home to me.

Speak the first two lines at one exhalation and the second two lines, after a pause to inhale, on the second exhalation. You must find your own breathing rhythm so that you can keep up this slow dreaming chant, without losing your breath, the entire time the segment of candle is burning.

When the first rune has burned away, blow out the candle, repeat the ᚤ rune across your body and go to sleep with the candle in some place where it will receive your body heat without being accidentally broken. During the day wrap it in the white altar cloth and put it in a safe place. Repeat this procedure eight more times. Fulfillment of the ritual may come any day of the working, or some time after its completion.

It is vital for success that this ritual be the center of your awareness for its nine-day term. You must keep an open mind and heart, be alert for possible communications and budding relationships, and place yourself as much as possible in an environment that will allow such personal communications to occur. In other words, it is no use working this ritual in self-imposed solitary confinement. Such isolation and denial is itself a kind of magic, and a type of ritual.

BONE COMB-CASE LINCOLN BRIT. MUS.

Runes and Divination

An ancient method of divination was to break a small branch from a fruit-bearing tree and slice it into strips. Each strip was marked with a rune. The strips were then cast down onto a white sheet spread out on the ground. The diviner would pick up three of the strips at random and divine from the runes on them. This method of reading the future is described by Tacitus in his *Germania*.

In Early English and related languages, the word *Rune* means "mystery" or "secret." Rather than being used as a normal form of writing, they were only utilized in magickal rituals and for divinatory purposes. There are many variations of Runes (*e.g.* Germanic, Danish, Swedish, Norse, Anglo-Saxon).

Rune Casting

A form of divination that has recently seen a return to favor is Rune Casting. Runes are marked on pieces of wood or stone and drawn out of a bag, or taken from a pile and cast down, their positions then being interpreted.

One method is to draw three runes from a bagful, taking them one at a time and laying them in a line in front of you, right to left. Concentrate on any question while drawing the runes. The first rune represents the situation as it is at present. The second tells what must be done. The third shows the new situation developing.

A second method is to take all the runes, cup them in your hands, then shake them and throw them like dice. Read only those that land face up, and read them in groups of three.

—RB

Deities	Color	Metal	Object	Rune*	Firewood	Jewel
Balder	yellow	gold	bow	⋈	mistletoe	topaz
Heimdall	blue	steel	horn	⌇	yew	sapphire
Loki	mist grey	arsenic	shoes	ᚦ	thorn	opal
Thor	orange	tin	hammer	⌇	oak	jasper
Tiw	red	iron	sword	↑	fir	ruby
Odin	white	mercury	spear	ᚠ	ash	diamond
Frija	green	copper	necklace	ᚴ	apple	emerald
Hel	black	lead	veil	ᛁ	willow	jet
Freyja	purple	silver	cloak	ᛒ	birch	amethyst
Frey	red-brown	bronze	chariot	⋇	pine	tree agate

* The runes are those that most closely approximate the qualities of the gods. They should not be confused with the runes which stand for elemental qualities.

Reprinted from *Rune Magic* by Donald Tyson.

April

Magical Sayings

To keep a cat or dog from running away, chase it three times around the hearth, and rub it against the chimney shaft.

When the crickets sing in the house, things go luckily.

When you've bought a cat, bring it in with its head facing the street and not the house; else it will not stay.

from Grimm's Teutonic Mythology

If a bee alights upon your head and stays there you will be a great person in after years.

It is luck to take a horse through your house.

When you have a new coat do not put it on empty, but put something into the pocket for luck.

When rosemary grows in the garden, the mistress rules the house.

To put on any article of clothing accidentally inside out is regarded by some as an omen of luck; but it is necessary to wear the reversed portion of attire wrong side out till the usual time comes to take it off if one wishes the luck to hold, otherwise the good fortune is immediately lost.

If the bees swarm high upon the trees, it is regarded as an omen that the price of grain will be high, but should they swarm low, the value is likely to be less.

Should a child be born with its hand open it is believed to indicate that it will be of a bountiful disposition in the future.

A bird falling down a chimney is a bearer of good luck, and if a bee flies into a room it is thought to be a harbinger of good news.

In some places it is customary to always place a bed parallel with the boards in the floor, as it is thought unlucky to sleep crossing them.

Country folk in Suffolk say, if a broom is left accidentally in the corner of a room after it has been swept, it is a sign that strangers will visit the house during the day.

—*Folktales and Superstitions of York, Lincoln, Derby,* 7
Nottingham—*1895*

Friday

Saturday

1

Sunday

Moon Sign: Cancer
Moon Phase: 1st Quarter
Festival: All Fools Day;
      Huli Festival

Tarot Card: The Emperor
Herb: Alfalfa
Incense: Myrrh
Mineral: Lapis Lazuli
Color: Yellow
Name of Power: Ceres

APRIL

S	M	T	W	T	F	S
1	2	3	4	5	6	7
8	9	10	11	12	13	14
15	16	17	18	19	20	21
22	23	24	25	26	27	28
29	30					

2   *Monday*

Moon Sign: Cancer
Moon Phase: 2nd Quarter

Tarot Card: The Hierophant
Herb: Arum
Incense: Jasmine
Mineral: Azurite
Color: White
Name of Power: Ti-Jean-Petro

3   *Tuesday*

Moon Sign: Leo
Moon Phase: 2nd Quarter

Tarot Card: The Lovers
Herb: Bennet
Incense: Benzoin
Mineral: Malachite
Color: Red
Name of Power: Nessus

4   *Wednesday*

Moon Sign: Leo
Moon Phase: 2nd Quarter
Festival: Megalesia (1st day);
        Festival of the Great
        Mother

Tarot Card: The Chariot
Herb: Blazing Star
Incense: Pine
Mineral: Silver
Color: Purple
Name of Power: Cybele

5   *Thursday*

Moon Sign: Virgo
Moon Phase: 2nd Quarter

Tarot Card: Justice
Herb: Buchu
Incense: Cinnamon
Mineral: Blue Zircon
Color: Blue
Name of Power: Kwan-Yin

6

Friday

Moon Sign: Virgo
Moon Phase: 2nd Quarter

Tarot Card: The Hermit
Herb: Castor Bean
Incense: Frankincense
Mineral: Hambergite
Color: Green
Name of Power: Res-Hra

7

Saturday

Moon Sign: Virgo
Moon Phase: 2nd Quarter

Tarot Card: Wheel of Fortune
Herb: Club Moss
Incense: Sandalwood
Mineral: Iolite
Color: Black
Name of Power: Ares

8

Sunday

Moon Sign: Libra
Moon Phase: 2nd Quarter

Tarot Card: Strength
Herb: Cucumber
Incense: Myrrh
Mineral: Ivory
Color: Yellow
Name of Power: Agwé

			APRIL			
S	M	T	W	T	F	S
1	2	3	4	5	6	7
8	9	10	11	12	13	14
15	16	17	18	19	20	21
22	23	24	25	26	27	28
29	30					

9 *Monday*

Moon Sign: Libra
Moon Phase: Full Moon
       (Seed)

Tarot Card: The Hanged Man
Herb: Echinacea
Incense: Jasmine
Mineral: Sardonyx
Color: White
Name of Power: Dungi

10 *Tuesday*

Moon Sign: Scorpio
Moon Phase: 3rd Quarter
Festival: Megalesia (last day)

Tarot Card: Death
Herb: Fenugreek
Incense: Benzoin
Mineral: Garnet
Color: Red
Name of Power: Xipe Totec

11 *Wednesday*

Moon Sign: Scorpio
Moon Phase: 3rd Quarter

Tarot Card: Temperance
Herb: Fumitory
Incense: Pine
Mineral: Axinite
Color: Purple
Name of Power: Ceres

12 *Thursday*

Moon Sign: Scorpio
Moon Phase: 3rd Quarter
Festival: Cerealia (1st day)

Tarot Card: The Devil
Herb: Guaiac
Incense: Cinnamon
Mineral: Emerald
Color: Blue

13
Friday

Moon Sign: Sagittarius
Moon Phase: 3rd Quarter

Tarot Card: The Tower
Herb: Henbane
Incense: Frankincense
Mineral: Black Coral
Color: Green
Name of Power: Libertas

14
Saturday

Moon Sign: Sagittarius
Moon Phase: 3rd Quarter

Tarot Card: The Star
Herb: Horseradish
Incense: Sandalwood
Mineral: Epidote
Color: Black
Name of Power: Nannar-Sin

15
Sunday

Moon Sign: Capricorn
Moon Phase: 3rd Quarter

Tarot Card: The Moon
Herb: Ironweed
Incense: Myrrh
Mineral: Moonstone
Color: Yellow
Name of Power: Tellus
Tree: Willow

APRIL

S	M	T	W	T	F	S
1	2	3	4	5	6	7
8	9	10	11	12	13	14
15	16	17	18	19	20	21
22	23	24	25	26	27	28
29	30					

16
Monday

Moon Sign: Capricorn
Moon Phase: 3rd Quarter

Tarot Card: The Sun
Herb: Larkspur
Incense: Jasmine
Mineral: Chalcedony
Color: White
Name of Power: Venus

17
Tuesday

Moon Sign: Capricorn
Moon Phase: 3rd Quarter

Tarot Card: Judgment
Herb: Lungwort
Incense: Benzoin
Mineral: Vesuvianite
Color: Red
Name of Power: Lamashtu

18
Wednesday

Moon Sign: Aquarius
Moon Phase: 4th Quarter

Tarot Card: The World
Herb: Dropwort
Incense: Pine
Mineral: Yellow Carnelian
Color: Purple
Name of Power: Am-Huat-
                      Ent-Pehf

19
Thursday

Moon Sign: Aquarius
Moon Phase: 4th Quarter
Festival: Cerealia (last day)

Tarot Card: The Fool
Herb: Spearmint
Incense: Cinnamon
Mineral: Topaz
Color: Blue
Name of Power: Damballah

20
Friday

Moon Sign: Pisces
Moon Phase: 4th Quarter
Sun enters Taurus

Tarot Card: Ace of Wands
Herb: Mouse Ear
Incense: Frankincense
Mineral: Prehnite
Color: Green
Name of Power: Bel

21
Saturday

Moon Sign: Pisces
Moon Phase: 4th Quarter
Festival: Palilia

Tarot Card: Two of Wands
Herb: Dwarf Nettle
Incense: Sandalwood
Mineral: Turquoise
Color: Black
Name of Power: Pales

22
Sunday

Moon Sign: Aries
Moon Phase: 4th Quarter

Tarot Card: Three of Wands
Herb: Orris Root
Incense: Myrrh
Mineral: Scapolite
Color: Yellow
Name of Power: Astarte

APRIL

S	M	T	W	T	F	S
1	2	3	4	5	6	7
8	9	10	11	12	13	14
15	16	17	18	19	20	21
22	23	24	25	26	27	28
29	30					

23 *Monday*

Moon Sign: Aries
Moon Phase: 4th Quarter
Festival: St. George's Day
       San Jorge Feast Day

Tarot Card: Four of Wands
Herb: Peruvian Bark
Incense: Jasmine
Mineral: Diopside
Color: White
Name of Power: Tanith

24 *Tuesday*

Moon Sign: Taurus
Moon Phase: New Moon

Tarot Card: Five of Wands
Herb: Blackthorn
Incense: Benzoin
Mineral: Beryllonite
Color: Red
Name of Power: Lavinia

25 *Wednesday*

Moon Sign: Taurus
Moon Phase: 1st Quarter

Tarot Card: Six of Wands
Herb: Hagbush
Incense: Pine
Mineral: Brazilianite
Color: Purple
Name of Power: Robigo

26 *Thursday*

Moon Sign: Gemini
Moon Phase: 1st Quarter

Tarot Card: Seven of Wands
Herb: Radish
Incense: Cinnamon
Mineral: African Jade
Color: Blue
Name of Power: Res-Hra

1990 *April* 1990

27 *Friday*

Moon Sign: Gemini
Moon Phase: 1st Quarter

Tarot Card: Eight of Wands
Herb: Red Sedge
Incense: Frankincense
Mineral: Enstatite
Color: Green
Name of Power: Flora

28 *Saturday*

Moon Sign: Cancer
Moon Phase: 1st Quarter
Festival: Floralia (1st day)

Tarot Card: Nine of Wands
Herb: St. Johnswort
Incense: Sandalwood
Mineral: Lazulite
Color: Black
Name of Power: Res-Ab

29 *Sunday*

Moon Sign: Cancer
Moon Phase: 1st Quarter
Festival: Laurentalia

Tarot Card: Ten of Wands
Herb: Seven Barks
Incense: Myrrh
Mineral: Dioptase
Color: Yellow
Name of Power: Vesta

APRIL

S	M	T	W	T	F	S
1	2	3	4	5	6	7
8	9	10	11	12	13	14
15	16	17	18	19	20	21
22	23	24	25	26	27	28
29	30					

30   *Monday*

Moon Sign: Leo
Moon Phase: 1st Quarter
Festival: Oidhche Bhealtaine—
    Beltane Eve

Tarot Card: Page of Wands
Herb: Cypress Spurge
Incense: Jasmine
Mineral: Apatite
Color: White
Name of Power: Lilith

Tuesday

Wednesday

Thursday

DAMBALLAH-WEDO

Voodoo

Raymond Buckland

As with Wicca, Voodoo is first and foremost a religion. The truest form of this religion is found in Haiti and the islands of the Caribbean, though variations can be found in many parts of South America, where it appears under the names *Umbanda*, *Macumba*, *Quimbanda*, and *Candombe*. Other variations are also found in New Orleans and other larger cities of the Southern United States.

As with many forms of religion, magick plays a part. The priesthood certainly needs to have a thorough knowledge of all forms of magick, if only to counteract any problems caused by solitary magickal practitioners. The main such "problem causer" of Haiti is the *Boko*. A few Bokos do work for the good of the community, specializing in healing, fertility and the like. But most people go to the *Hougan* and/or *Mambo* (the Priest and Priestess) for such positive work, so the "black," or negative-working, Bokos are the more common.

The Boko is the one who will sell spells, charms, and curses. Bokos work under the direct "supervision" of the gods of the dead: the *Loa* of the Ghédé family. The main Loa is known variously as Baron Samedi, Baron La-Croix, Baron Cimitière, or The Three Spades (grave-digging tools). Frequently the Boko will work one person against another. For a person with a grievance the Boko will, for a fee, put a curse—known as a *wanga*—onto another person. But he will then offer that cursed person a counterspell (for a fee). He is also not above offering to perform a spell against the originator (for a second fee!).

Wangas are usually small leather bags or pouches, stuffed with an assortment of herbs, feathers, roots, and/or stones, over which the Boko has performed a magickal ritual. Sometimes it is just a single object, such as a black stone. The wanga is placed on the body of the cursed person, or hidden somewhere in his house. Hiding it under the bed or in the roof is a favorite. If a person falls ill and it is believed that a wanga is the cause, the whole house might be pulled to pieces in an attempt to find the offending object.

When talking of Haitian magick, mention must be made of the *zombi* . . . the living corpse. A zombi is, supposedly, a person who has died and then been brought back to life in order to work as a slave for the person resurrecting him. Such a slave needs very little sleep, requires no pay, can be fed on scraps and clothed in rags, and can be literally worked into the ground. For a plantation owner, a work force of zombis would be of great value. A Boko would be well rewarded for providing them. Hollywood used to be enamored of this idea and produced a large number of cheap movies on the theme in the '30s and '40s. But do such things really exist? *Can* a Boko bring a dead person back to life?

The word "zombi" comes from the Congolese *nvumbi*, meaning "a body deprived of its soul." Supposedly there are two ways to create a zombi: magickally and medically. In the magickal method the Boko goes to a graveyard, at dead of night, and performs a ritual at the graveside of a freshly buried corpse. He then performs a ceremony directed by Ghédé. He will take handfuls of meal, flour, or grain, and draw a pattern known as a *vévé* on the ground beside the grave. A circle is drawn, with the meal, around the grave, and a candle placed, and lit, at each of the four cardinal points. The Boko pours liberal libations of rum (favored by the Loa) at the four corners. An assistant to the Boko is usually present and beats out a staccato rhythm on a drum—frequently the "Petro Dance"—which not only aids the Boko in his work but is also heard by the villagers and warns them to keep away.

Part way through the ceremony the assistant will dig into the earth and scrape it away to reveal the bare wood coffin. The lid will be pried off and at the climax of the ceremony, when the Boko calls out the dead person's name, the corpse will sit up, answer, and climb out. The corpse will then follow the Boko, when he walks away from the graveyard, and obey him in all things. It can only be raised from its grave if it answers the Boko's call. Consequently it is common practice for Haitians to have the mouth of their deceased sewn up before burial, to prevent such an answering should a Boko try to make a zombi of that person.

The second, and perhaps more believable, method is to utilize various herbs to bring about a state that seems like death. In Haiti the dead are not embalmed. They are frequently buried without even a death certificate being issued. It seems possible, then, that an unscrupulous person could administer an alkaloid state that could be easily mistaken for death. With the heat and humidity of the country, no time would be lost in getting the resultant "corpse" into its grave. By the night following the burial the drug would have worn off sufficiently for the Boko to rouse the victim and lead him away.

Catalepsy is described as a spasmodic nervous disorder in which there is "a sudden suspension of sensation and volition, with statue-like fixedness of the body and limbs." Similarly, a zombi is said to move in a slow, jerky manner, to be unable to speak or register emotion, to be unable to recognize friends and loved ones.

Cigars and pipes are commonly smoked by both males and females in Haiti. What simpler method to introduce the soporific than by using the dried leaves rolled in the form of a cigar or crushed like tobacco? The drugs that could be used for this purpose are easily obtainable in Haiti. The most obvious ones are *Atropa belladonna, Hyoscyamus niger* and various species of *Datura. Terminalia catappa, Hippomane mancinella,* and *Spondias dulcis* are other easily obtained herbs. All are deadly poisonous if administered incorrectly.

It is interesting that the Criminal Code of the Haitian Republic (Article 248) states that "Murder shall be assumed to include any use made, against others, of substances which, without necessarily causing death, induce a more-or-less prolonged lethargic sleep. And the act of burying the individual to whom such substances may have been administered shall be held to be murder, no matter what the outcome of it."

In New Orleans the word "zombi" is used to refer to the gods, the *loa* of Haiti. There are various priests and priestesses (referred to as "Kings" and "Queens") in New Orleans, but no well-defined religious ceremonies, nor permanent houses of worship to parallel the Haitian *hounfors*. The emphasis is on the magickal side, the commercial magickal side . . . the buying and selling of potions, herbs, powders, washes, candles, incense, and *gris-gris* (New Orleans' version of *wanga*). On almost every street corner of the South Rampart Street area are found street vendors with trays of "novelties."

In the early nineteenth century Voodoo celebrations reached their height with a Queen named Marie Leveau. She was a free mulatto woman who would stage huge dances on the shores of Lake Pontchartrain. The local press would always be advised, in advance, that there was going to be a Voodoo gathering on a certain night, so that they could send along a reporter to cover Queen Marie's spectacle. There were many Queens in the city at that time but, by her skill in organizing spectacular dances/ rituals, and her knowledge of charms and potions, Marie Laveau established herself as *the* Queen.

Marie Laveau had been baptised into the Roman Catholic faith but held it as a mere facade to her real interest. She worshipped daily at the St. Louis Cathedral yet ran her house—given to her by her father on her marriage to Jacques Paris—as a beauty parlor, Voodoo pharmacy, and brothel. Indeed, many of the grand rites she held at the lakeside ended in big sexual orgies. New Orleans Voodoo today is very tame when compared to Marie's day!

In South America, the early Portuguese slave-owners had their charges baptised as Christians—and branded to prove it— but allowed them to continue with their own religious songs and dances. It was felt that this would help prevent revolt. But the vibrant singing, dancing, and drumming actually helped the native religion survive. The predominant group in Brazil was the Yoruba, of southern Nigeria. The second largest group was the Bantus. The Yoruba dealt with the gods, but the Bantus dealt more with the spirits of the dead.

The gods of the Yorubas were known as *Orishas*. Many of them closely parallel the loa of the Haitians. Although the priesthood was originally male, with the men having to work out in the fields of the plantations, the women quickly took over the priestly duties. Working in the houses, the women had the time and opportunity for both the religious practices and the magickal.

They became known as *Iyalorixa*, meaning "Mother of Saints." Followers, initiates, were known as *Iyauo* ("Daughter of Saints"), though this was frequently shortened to *Iao*. Meetings were held in a large building called a *barrack*. This was a wood-framed house with a dirt floor and clay-covered walls. It was kept especially for the purpose, whereas in Macumba the rites could take place practically anywhere out in the open, though preferably close to water.

Although Macumba, Umbanda, Candombé, and Quimbanda retain much of the primitivity of their origins, they are not dying out. Far from it. Even with the ever-increasing literacy in Brazil and the other South American countries, the followers of these different versions of Voodoo are growing in number. The reason is probably the very personal nature of the relationship between worshipper and deity. It may also be because of the availability of practical *magick*, and its power to make life more tolerable.

Haitian Magick

Raymond Buckland

There are bascially two "families" of Gods, or *loa*, in Haitian Voodoo: the *Rada* Loa and the *Petro* loa. "Rada" comes from Arada, the name of a town in Dahomey, in the Gulf of Benin area of West Africa. "Petro" is believed to have come from the name Don Pedro, an eighteenth-century personality who was possibly instrumental in shaping an aspect of the religio-magick. Each family of loa has its own individual drum rhythms, dances, invocations and rituals. Petro Voodoo tends toward the negative side, while Rada Voodoo is decidedly positive.

The main difference between *rada* and *petro* is found in the characteristics of the loa. The rada loa are referred to as the "gentle" deities; they are interested in the family and family harmony. The petro are unyielding and frequently bitter; they are the ones who specialize in magick. All charms and spells come under petro control. It is possible to become rich through dealings with the petro—yet a high price may have to be paid. It is somewhat akin to dealing with the Mafioso!

Many of the petro loa have rada names followed by a second name (*e.g.*, Damballah-flangbo, Erzili-mapyang, Ogoun-yansan). These all have a bad reputation. Some are supposed to have red eyes, which is regarded as a sign of cannibalism and extreme evil. The loa master of charms and spells is Legba-petro. He is invoked at a crossroads and, indeed, is referred to as *Maitre-Carrefour* (Master of the Crossroads). A handful of dirt taken from a crossroads is regarded as a potent magickal tool.

The most feared form of black magick is the "sending of dead," or *l'envoi morts*. A person who has become the prey of dead people, sent against him by a boko, gradually grows thinner and thinner, starts to spit blood, and finally dies. The dead are sent under the auspices of Saint Expedit, and with the "blessing" of Baron Samedi. One way of sending a dead person against someone is to drive two nails into the ceiling beam of a house when a resident of the house dies. The nails prevent the dead person's soul from leaving and cause him, or her, to vent fury on the person named by the boko. Such a sending of the dead can also be done against someone's animals—his cattle, goats, or pigs—causing them to become mad, grow thin, and die.

Many of a Boko's clientele are people wanting to become rich, rich at any price. They are sometimes given a talisman, which will work for them through the agencies of a spirit dwelling within the talisman. This spirit may be a zombi soul or even a loa (such as Ezili-jé-rouge). A general term for these spirits is *baka*, which also covers a whole variety of animal and monster spirits that are said to roam at will through the woods of Haiti. These spirits/monsters can appear to people, causing them to die of fright or be seized by terror.

A person may make a deal with a baka by which his life will be forfeited within a certain number of years in return for the baka bringing fortune during those years. This is very much like the many Satanic pacts that were signed in Europe in the Middle Ages. Also like the dealers in Satanic pacts, the people who accept a baka invariably find that they cannot get out of the pact in any way and, invariably, have taken on far more than they anticipated. When death comes, it is usually accepted gladly.

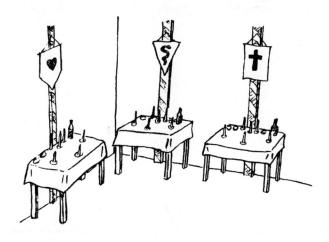

Voodoo and Macumba Magick

The Haitian peasant uses the following technique to work his spell: he takes a charm consisting of two candles in the form of a cross, pierces them with needles, and then hides them where his victim is likely to pass. There is also the macabre system used by some Voodoo Bokos, which is to bury one of the victim's shirts in a coffin along with the corpse. As the corpse gradually decomposes, the unfortunate victim is overcome by a fearful and progressive corruption of his flesh and blood. This is a highly significant example of the old principle of sympathetic magic: what you do to something close to, or part of, a person's body is reflected in the body itself.

Counterspells exist in Voodoo in Macumba, and the trade in them is highly profitable. In Haiti, the most effective of these are called *paquets-congo*. On a less serious note, it might be pointed out that many of the foremost Brazilian football teams have their own resident *macumbeiro*, whose function it is to ensure the victory of his side!

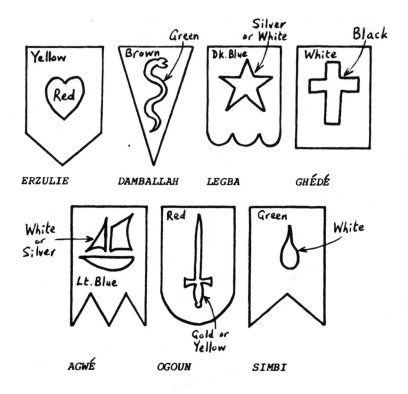

ERZULIE   DAMBALLAH   LEGBA   GHÉDÉ

AGWÉ   OGOUN   SIMBI

The Ritual of Voodoo

Raymond Buckland

Haitian Voodoo ceremonies are not generally held in secret. Everyone is welcome. There are exceptions, of course ... the initiation ceremonies, for instance. But the vast majority of the rites are held in the public *peristyle* with all people—white people included—welcome.

Many whites are surprised, and perhaps amused, at the number of Catholic practices found intermingled with the Voodoo: prayers, chants, Ave Marias, Paternosters. For years the Catholic Church tried its hardest to suppress Voodoo. It was quite unsuccessful; in fact today Voodoo is practiced openly. But one of the ways in which the Voodoo followers were able to continue was by disguising their rites, wrapping them in a cloak of Christianity. The Haitian people also saw that the Church was very powerful.

Consequently they were not averse to adopting segments of the Catholic services. "If these rituals work for the powerful Churchmen, they should also work for us," seemed to be the thinking.

Along with Church influences, there are others. The army, for example, is reflected in the rites. Flags and banners are paraded at the start of a meeting. Every *hounfor* (local "church") has its own identifying flags. *La Place*, the Master of Ceremonies, carries a cavalry sabre, which he flourishes as he directs operations.

Other elements are also present, and can be recognized. Alfred Metraux (in *Voodoo in Haiti*, 1959) suggests: "To grasp its true nature, we should remember that each ceremony is also an opportunity or pretext for profane rejoicing. Certain Voodoo society leaders, anxious to revivify the lustre of the rites they were celebrating, have striven to introduce a vein that was spectacular, almost theatrical. Evincing a genuine talent for showmanship, they turned to good account the darkness, light, processions and dresses, in fact anything which would help to inspire the hearts of the poor, who frequented their *humfo*, with an illusion of magnificence and mystery." Again, this is in imitation of the rites of Roman Catholicism, with incense, music, participants' costumes, asperging, and the rest of the pomp and ceremony.

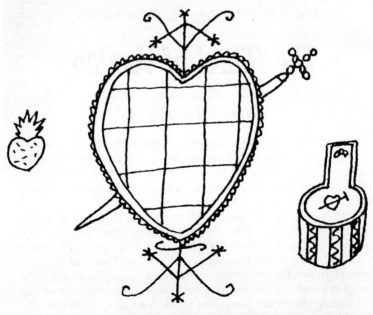

ERZULIE-FREDA-DAHOMEY

May

May

1990 *May* 1990

Monday

1 *Tuesday*

Moon Sign: Leo
Moon Phase: 2nd Quarter
Festival: Beltaine/Caedamh
　　　　　Dea Dia; Fire Festival

Tarot Card: Ace of Cups
Herb: Allspice
Incense: Benzoin
Mineral: Amber
Color: Red
Name of Power: Asherah

2 *Wednesday*

Moon Sign: Leo
Moon Phase: 2nd Quarter

Tarot Card: Two of Cups
Herb: Asarum
Incense: Pine
Mineral: Chalcedony
Color: Purple
Name of Power: Yashodhara

3 *Thursday*

Moon Sign: Virgo
Moon Phase: 2nd Quarter
Festival: Floralia (last day)

Tarot Card: Three of Cups
Herb: Betony
Incense: Cinnamon
Mineral: Sard
Color: Blue
Name of Power: Chloris

4
Friday

Moon Sign: Virgo
Moon Phase: 2nd Quarter

Tarot Card: Four of Cups
Herb: Blind Nettle
Incense: Frankincense
Mineral: Heliotrope
Color: Green
Name of Power: Monica

5
Saturday

Moon Sign: Libra
Moon Phase: 2nd Quarter

Tarot Card: Five of Cups
Herb: Buckbean
Incense: Sandalwood
Mineral: Moss Agate
Color: Black
Name of Power: Ankh-Em-
Fentu

6
Sunday

Moon Sign: Libra
Moon Phase: 2nd Quarter

Tarot Card: Six of Cups
Herb: Catnip
Incense: Myrrh
Mineral: Scenic Agate
Color: Yellow
Name of Power: Legba

MAY

S	M	T	W	T	F	S
		1	2	3	4	5
6	7	8	9	10	11	12
13	14	15	16	17	18	19
20	21	22	23	24	25	26
27	28	29	30	31		

7 *Monday*

Moon Sign: Scorpio
Moon Phase: 2nd Quarter

Tarot Card: Seven of Cups
Herb: Colombo
Incense: Jasmine
Mineral: Striped Jasper
Color: White
Name of Power: Pan

8 *Tuesday*

Moon Sign: Scorpio
Moon Phase: 2nd Quarter
Festival: Flora Day

Tarot Card: Eight of Cups
Herb: Black Currant
Incense: Benzoin
Mineral: Hawk's Eye
Color: Red
Name of Power: Flora

9 *Wednesday*

Moon Sign: Scorpio
Moon Phase: Full Moon (Hare)
Festival: Lémuria

Tarot Card: Nine of Cups
Herb: Elder
Incense: Pine
Mineral: Yellow Jasper
Color: Purple
Name of Power: Lemures

10 *Thursday*

Moon Sign: Sagittarius
Moon Phase: 3rd Quarter

Tarot Card: Ten of Cups
Herb: Fern
Incense: Cinnamon
Mineral: White Opal
Color: Blue
Name of Power: Adum

11
Friday

Moon Sign: Sagittarius
Moon Phase: 3rd Quarter

Tarot Card: Page of Cups
Herb: Galangal
Incense: Frankincense
Mineral: Black Opal
Color: Green
Name of Power: Ashebu

12
Saturday

Moon Sign: Sagittarius
Moon Phase: 3rd Quarter

Tarot Card: Knight of Cups
Herb: Gum Plant
Incense: Sandalwood
Mineral: Fire Opal
Color: Black
Name of Power: Circe

13
Sunday

Moon Sign: Capricorn
Moon Phase: 3rd Quarter

Tarot Card: Queen of Cups
Herb: Henna
Incense: Myrrh
Mineral: Lapis Lazuli
Color: Yellow
Name of Power: Fatima
Tree: Hawthorn

MAY

S	M	T	W	T	F	S
		1	2	3	4	5
6	7	8	9	10	11	12
13	14	15	16	17	18	19
20	21	22	23	24	25	26
27	28	29	30	31		

14 *Monday*

Moon Sign: Capricorn
Moon Phase: 3rd Quarter

Tarot Card: King of Cups
Herb: Horseweed
Incense: Jasmine
Mineral: Jadeite
Color: White
Name of Power: Isis

15 *Tuesday*

Moon Sign: Aquarius
Moon Phase: 3rd Quarter

Tarot Card: Ace of Pentacles
Herb: Jalap
Incense: Benzoin
Mineral: Nephrite
Color: Red
Name of Power: Maia

16 *Wednesday*

Moon Sign: Aquarius
Moon Phase: 3rd Quarter

Tarot Card: Two of Pentacles
Herb: Laurel
Incense: Pine
Mineral: Jade
Color: Purple
Name of Power: Bitoso

17 *Thursday*

Moon Sign: Pisces
Moon Phase: 4th Quarter
Festival: Start of Ripening
           Time in Celtic
           Calendar

Tarot Card: Three of Pentacles
Herb: Madder
Incense: Cinnamon
Mineral: Peridot
Color: Blue
Name of Power: Dea Dia

18

Friday

Moon Sign: Pisces
Moon Phase: 4th Quarter

Tarot Card: Four of Pentacles
Herb: Goatsbeard
Incense: Frankincense
Mineral: Moss Opal
Color: Green
Name of Power: Daghda

19

Saturday

Moon Sign: Pisces
Moon Phase: 4th Quarter

Tarot Card: Five of Pentacles
Herb: Curled Mint
Incense: Sandalwood
Mineral: Tanzanite
Color: Black
Name of Power: Tculo

20

Sunday

Moon Sign: Aries
Moon Phase: 4th Quarter

Tarot Card: Six of Pentacles
Herb: Mugwort
Incense: Myrrh
Mineral: Thulite
Color: Yellow
Name of Power: Okinaga-
Tarashi-
Hime

MAY						
S	M	T	W	T	F	S
		1	2	3	4	5
6	7	8	9	10	11	12
13	14	15	16	17	18	19
20	21	22	23	24	25	26
27	28	29	30	31		

21   *Monday*

Moon Sign: Aries
Moon Phase: 4th Quarter
Sun enters Gemini

Tarot Card: Seven of Pentacles
Herb: New Jersey Tea
Incense: Jasmine
Mineral: Hematite
Color: White
Name of Power: Agassu

22   *Tuesday*

Moon Sign: Taurus
Moon Phase: 4th Quarter

Tarot Card: Eight of Pentacles
Herb: Nightshade
Incense: Benzoin
Mineral: Pyrite
Color: Red
Name of Power: Rhiannon

23   *Wednesday*

Moon Sign: Taurus
Moon Phase: 4th Quarter
Festival: The Rosalia

Tarot Card: Nine of Pentacles
Herb: Pansy
Incense: Pine
Mineral: Feldspar
Color: Purple
Name of Power: Flora

24   *Thursday*

Moon Sign: Gemini
Moon Phase: New Moon

Tarot Card: Ten of Pentacles
Herb: Peyote
Incense: Cinnamon
Mineral: Moonstone
Color: Blue
Name of Power: Janus

25   *Friday*

Moon Sign: Gemini
Moon Phase: 1st Quarter
Festival: Anthea's Day

Tarot Card: Page of Pentacles
Herb: Poison Hemlock
Incense: Frankincense
Mineral: Amazonite
Color: Green
Name of Power: Fortuna

26   *Saturday*

Moon Sign: Cancer
Moon Phase: 1st Quarter

Tarot Card: Knight of Pentacles
Herb: English Cowslip
Incense: Sandalwood
Mineral: Orthoclase
Color: Black
Name of Power: Proserpina

27   *Sunday*

Moon Sign: Cancer
Moon Phase: 1st Quarter

Tarot Card: Queen of Pentacles
Herb: Ragged Cup
Incense: Myrrh
Mineral: Labradorite
Color: Yellow
Name of Power: Diana

MAY

S	M	T	W	T	F	S
		1	2	3	4	5
6	7	8	9	10	11	12
13	14	15	16	17	18	19
20	21	22	23	24	25	26
27	28	29	30	31		

28 *Monday*

Moon Sign: Leo
Moon Phase: 1st Quarter

Tarot Card: King of Pentacles
Herb: Restharrow
Incense: Jasmine
Mineral: Spectrolite
Color: White
Name of Power: Tebherkehaat

29 *Tuesday*

Moon Sign: Leo
Moon Phase: 1st Quarter
Festival: Ambarvalia

Tarot Card: Ace of Swords
Herb: Sandalwood
Incense: Benzoin
Mineral: Rhodochrosite
Color: Red
Name of Power: Ceres

30 *Wednesday*

Moon Sign: Virgo
Moon Phase: 1st Quarter

Tarot Card: Two of Swords
Herb: Shave Grass
Incense: Pine
Mineral: Rhodonite
Color: Purple
Name of Power: Kylin

31 *Thursday*

Moon Sign: Virgo
Moon Phase: 2nd Quarter
Festival: Secula (1st day)

Tarot Card: Three of Swords
Herb: Milk-Spurlane
Incense: Cinnamon
Mineral: Turquoise
Color: Blue
Name of Power: Agau

Women's Spirituality

Diane Stein

The Women's Spirituality movement is an outgrowth of feminism and is the birth/rebirth of a new/old world religion. Archeologists worldwide recognize the universality of Goddess worship and woman-centered culture in civilizations as diverse as Europe, North and South America, China, Japan and Africa. The concept of god as a female is not a new one. It may be fifty thousand or more years old, while the concept of a male God and a male-oriented civilization has perhaps only a five-thousand-year tradition. The Judeo-Christian order submerged the idea and religion of Goddess, which has nonetheless continuously flourished both underground and above. The Shekinah in Judaism and Mary in Christianity are examples and remnants of the idea of a World Mother.

God as female, as Goddess, is a familiar idea in the West. Many of us are raised with some knowledge of Greek and Roman mythology, Egyptian mythology, stories of Hera, Isis, the Chinese Kwan Yin, the African Ymoja Yemaya or Mawu. Since almost all life is born of female wombs, goddess is a logical concept, a recognizable origin for the birth of the world and all life. In a civilization only beginning to reclaim women and women's rights and values after thousands of years of repression, the reawakening of God as female—as Goddess—has major implications. The early first-wave women's rights suffragists understood this and planted the seeds; Elizabeth Cady Stanton's *Women's Bible* (1895) and Matilda Jocelyn Gage's discussions of women's place in religion in *Women, Church and State* (1893) raised questions and opened issues that laid roots for the Women's Spirituality movement of today. Current writers such as Starhawk (*Spiral Dance*), Z. Budapest (*The Holy Book of Women's Mysteries*, Volumes I and II) and Merlin Stone (*When God Was a Woman* and *Ancient Minors of Womanhood*), plus feminist writers of the 1960s and early 1970s like Elizabeth Gould Davis (*The First Sex*), Helen Diner (*Mothers and Amazons*) and Mary Daly (several books, particularly *Gyne/cology*) have caused discussion and examination, and prepared the way for Women's Spirituality as a religion.

When God is female, the psychological implications for women are major. In our current systems of belief—the major religions of the present world—women are often treated as second-class citizens. God is male and women are "not of his image." With this in mind, women in law, education, society and opportunity are often relegated to second place, something the women's and civil rights movements work to correct. With Goddess as divinity, the situation is very different. If Goddess created the world, birthed all life including the life of the planet, women are in Her image and hardly second place at all. The idea is threatening to the status quo, but essential if there is to be true equality between the races and sexes, true civil rights on Earth. A woman who sees herself as Goddess, in the image of divinity and Goddess-within as part of her, takes control of her life and actions, and no longer allows herself to be treated inequitably. She will not tolerate it; she is in the image of the creator of the planet, the Mother of all.

A logical outgrowth of feminism, Women's Spirituality began its most recent resurgence in the late 1970s and is growing rapidly in numbers and scope, inside and outside the United States. It is evident at the national women's cultural festivals, in women's literature, in the practice of thousands of autonomous small groups and circles, and in the individual work of women privately everywhere. Its influence is evident in the peace, antinuke, environmental, civil rights, healing, anti-apartheid, and disability rights movements.

Women's Spirituality is a growing recognition of the Goddess as planet, as the Earth herself, and of women as part of the Earth and Her divine Being. The Goddess is everything creative, everything that exists in nature and in women's lives, including every individual woman in her personal growth and power. She is the circle of birth, growth, maturity, aging and death, the Goddess is the procession of the seasons, the phases of the Moon, the tides, life and time. What each woman does in her life matters; she is Goddess-within. For the first time in thousands of years, Women's Spirituality encourages women to actively be all that they can be, to learn about themselves and their own skills and strengths, and then to join together with others to change the wrongs of the world. All life is respected and affirmed as a part of the Goddess's own. With a worldwide heritage and, cross-culturally, thousands of names for the concept of Goddess, all nations, races, ages and cultures are equally highly valued. Women's Spirituality is worldwide, affirming all in peace, harmony, responsibility, free will and free choice.

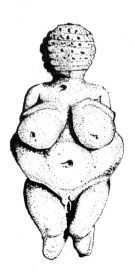

Gravettian Venus *figurine (c. 18,000 BC), found at Willendorf, Austria. (Gerald Luxton, after B. Branston)*

There are few rules or laws in Women's Spirituality, where natural order and natural law are inviolable. "Harming none, do what you will" is a first tenet, as is the Threefold Law that states "Whatever you send out comes back to you." These adages are the roots of the Golden Rule. They are ethically as all-inclusive as the Ten Commandments, but freer and simpler. In the Threefold Law, in which whatever you do comes back to you, and comes back three times as much, the urge to commit a wrong is something to think about. Good sent out to others is good returned to self. Most Women's Spirituality women believe in reincarnation and karma, and deeds follow from one life to the next. Good deeds are much easier to live with.

Another idea of the Goddess religion is that women create their own lives and have choice and freedom to determine what they want their lives to be. Women who help themselves by asking for what they want and working for it receive the help of the Goddess, and the power of this in action can be awesome. Choice is a central issue and idea. Another Goddess adage is the wry warning, "Be careful what you ask for, you may get it." All choices involve free will but not the manipulation or violation of the free will of others.

Women everywhere are discovering and joining the Women's Spirituality movement. No coercion or attempts at conversion are ever made. This is a uniquely women's form of religion, highly ethical and moral, affirming of women's lives, highly creative and filled with eagerness and joy. Many of us watching the movement believe that we are watching the rebirth of a major world religion. With the Goddess's gentle blessing, so may it be.

Self-Blessing: A Women's Ritual

Diane Stein

Standing on salt sprinkled on the floor or on a sheet of white paper, the woman wets her fingers with a few drops of water (wine, oil or menstrual blood can also be used) from her altar chalice and touches them to the top of her head, the crown chakra, *kopavi* of Spider Woman. Visualizing the chakra's clear violet color, she says,

"Bless me, mother, who am your child."

She dips her fingers into the water again and touches her third eye, the indigo chakra between and just above the eyes, and visualizing the color says,

"Bless my mind's eye that I may think of you and see you clearly."

She wets her fingers again and touches her throat chakra, visualizing its healing, sky-blue color, saying,

"Bless my throat that I may speak well and speak of you."

She touches her breastbone, the green-colored heart chakra, and says,

"Bless my heart that it be open to your essence."

She touches drops of water to her solar plexus, the navel chakra, imagining its bright yellow color, and says,

"Bless the center of my energy, that I am centered in your Earth."

She touches her lower abdomen, the orange belly chakra of her womb and ovaries, and says,

"Bless my womb that creates new children, new ideas in your name."

She touches her genitals with the chalice water, visualizing the clear red root chakra spiraling with energy, and says,

"Bless my vagina, gateway of life and pleasure, sipapu

of emergence, the labyrinth."

She touches the water to the palm of each hand, saying,

"Bless my hands that I may do your work and healing," and touches the sole of each foot, saying,

"Bless my feet, that I may walk in your paths."

To complete the ritual, the priestess says,

"Bless me mother, who am a part of you," and she takes a sip of water from the chalice. She meditates on the chakras and senses as she does the ritual on herself as a part of the Goddess, interconnected with all of life. Looking in the mirror at the center of her altar, she sees Goddess and herself, and knows that the two are one Being.

Kwan Yin

[1]From Diane Stein, *The Women's Spirituality Book*, Llewellyn Publications, 1987, pp. 112-113.

How Diana Made
The Stars and the Rain

A Witch Sorcery Tradition

"Diana was the first created before all creation; in her were all things; out of herself, the first darkness, she divided herself; into darkness and light she was divided. Lucifer, her brother and her son, herself and her other half, was the light.

"And when Diana saw the light was so beautiful, the light which was her other half, her brother Lucifer, she yearned for it with exceeding great desire. Wishing to receive the light again into her darkness, to swallow it up in rapture, in delight, she trembled with desire. This desire was the Dawn.

"But Lucifer, the light, fled from her, and would not yield to her wishes; he was the light which flies into the most distant parts of heaven, the mouse which flies before the cat.

"Then Diana went to the fathers of the Beginning, to the mothers, the spirits who were before the first spirit, and lamented unto them that she could not prevail with Lucifer. And they praised her for her courage; they told her that to rise she must fall; to become the chief of goddesses she must become a mortal.

"And in the ages, in the course of time, when the world was made, Diana went on Earth, as did Lucifer, who had fallen, and Diana taught magic and sorcery, whence came witches and fairies and goblins—all that is like man yet not mortal.

"And it came thus that Diana took the form of a cat. Her brother had a cat whom he loved beyond all creatures, and it slept every night on his bed, a cat beautiful beyond all other creatures, a fairy: he did not know it.

"Diana prevailed with the cat to change forms with her; so she lay with her brother, and in the darkness assumed her own

form, and so by Lucifer became the mother of Aradia. But when in the morning he found that he lay by his sister, and that light had been conquered by darkness, Lucifer was extremely angry; but Diana sang to him a spell, a song of power, and he was silent, the song of the night which soothes to sleep; he could say nothing. So Diana with her wiles of witchcraft so charmed him that he yielded to her love. This was the first fascination; she hummed the song, it was as the buzzing of bees (or a top spinning round), a spinning-wheel spinning life. She spun the lives of all men; all things were spun from the wheel of Diana. Lucifer turned the wheel.

"Diana was not known to the witches and spirits, the fairies and elves who dwell in desert places, the goblins, as their mother; she hid herself in humility and was a mortal but by her will she rose again above all. She had such passion for witchcraft, and became so powerful therein, that her greatness could not be hidden.

"And thus it came to pass one night, at the meeting of all the sorceresses and fairies, she declared that she would darken the heavens and turn all the stars into mice.

"All those who were present said:

' "If thou canst do such a strange thing, having risen to such power, thou shalt be our queen.'

"Diana went into the street; she took the bladder of an ox and a piece of witch-money, which has an edge like a knife—with such money witches cut the earth from men's foot-tracks—and she cut the earth, and with it and many mice she filled the bladder, and blew into the bladder till it burst.

"And there came a great marvel, for the earth which was in the bladder became the round heaven above, and for three days there was a great rain; the mice became stars or rain. And

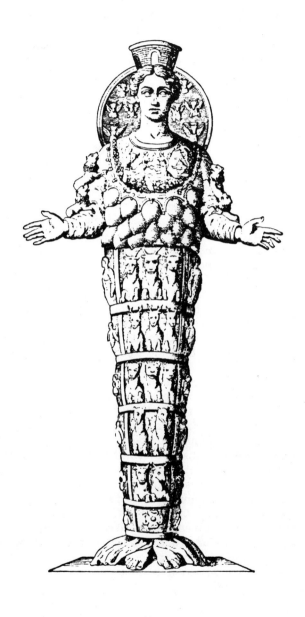

Diana of Ephesus

having made the heaven and the stars and the rain, Diana became Queen of the Witches; she was the cat who ruled the star-mice, the heaven and the rain."

Commentary
Here a reflection occurs which is perhaps the most remarkable which all this Witch Evangel suggests. In all other scriptures of all other races, it is the male, Jehovah, Buddha, or Brahma, who creates the universe; in Witch Sorcery it is the female who is the primitive principle. Whenever in history there is a period of radical intellectual rebellion against long-established conservatism, hierarchy, and the like, there is always an effort to regard Woman as the fully equal, which means the superior sex. Thus in the extraordinary war of conflicting elements, strange schools of sorcery, Neo-Platonism, Cabala, Heretic Christianity, Gnosticism, Persian Magism and Dualism, with the remains of old Greek and Egyptian theologies in the third and fourth centuries at Alexandria, and in the House of Light of Cairo in the ninth, the equality of Women was a prominent doctrine. It was Sophia or Helena, the enfranchised, who was then the true Christ who was to save mankind.

When Illumination or Illumine-ism, in company with magic, mysticism, and a resolve to regenerate society according to extreme free thought, inspired the Templars to the hope that they would master the church and the world, the equality of Woman, derived from the Cairene traditions, again received attention. And it may be observed that during the Middle Ages, and even so late as the intense excitements which inspired the French Huguenots, the Jansenists and the Anabaptists, Woman always came forth more prominently or played a far greater part than she had done in social and political life . . . These remarks are appropriate to my text and subject, because it is in studying the epochs when woman was influential that we learn what the capacities of the female sex truly are. Among these, that of Witchcraft as it truly was—not as it is generally quite misunderstood—is as deeply interesting as any other.

—*Aradia, Gospel of the Witches of Italy*
Charles Godfrey Leland, 1899

To Diana

Lovely Goddess of the bow!!
Lovely Goddess of the arrows!
Of all hounds and of all hunting
Thou who wakest in starry heaven
When the sun is sunk in slumber
Thou with moon upon thy forehead,
Who the chase by night preferrest
Unto hunting in the daylight
With thy nymphs unto the music
Of the horn—thyself the huntress,
And most powerful: I pray thee
Think, although but for an instant,
Upon us who pray unto thee!

—Aradia
C.C. Leland

Isis, Goddess and Magickal Healer of Ancient Egypt

Isis in original conception did not differ much from Hathor, with whom she was sometimes identified by the Greeks and from whom, even in the monuments, it is often difficult to distinguish her. She was called the mother, as well as the wife and sister, of Osiris. It is, however, as his wife and sister that she is chiefly presented to us. The part assigned to her in "The Myth of Osiris" constitutes the main feature in all the longer notices of her which occur in the inscriptions. Thus, in the "Tears of Isis," we have her lamentations over her brother when slain and her joyful address to him upon his reappearance. In "The Book of Respirations" we hear of the "sighs of Isis for her brother Osiris, to give life to his soul, to give life to his body, to rejuvenate all his members, that he may reach the horizon with his father, the sun; that his soul may rise to heaven in the disc of the moon; that his body may shine in the stars of Orion on the bosom of Nut." A hymn to Osiris tells us how "his sister took care of him by dispersing his enemies," how she "unrepiningly sought him, went around the world lamenting him, shadowed him with her wings, made the invocation of his burial, raised his remains, and extracted his essence." Thenceforth, as a reward for her fidelity and love, Isis ruled with Osiris in the Amenti, assisted him in judging the dead, and received in common with him the principle worship of the departed.

The name of Isis is expressed by the hieroglyph supposed to represent a throne, followed by the two feminine signs of the half-circle and the egg, to which is sometimes added the hatchet, neter, or the form of a sitting goddess. She is figured commonly as a female with a so-called throne upon her head, either simply or above the horns and disc which are also characteristic of Hathor. She frequently has in her hands the ankh and the female sceptre. Occasionally she is sitting nursing Horus.

Her most frequent title is "defender" or "avenger of her brother," but she is also called the "goddess mother," "the mistress of the two worlds," and "the mistress of Heaven." She was worshipped more or less in every part of Egypt but her most remarkable temples were those at Philae and Coptos. The Egyptians connected her with Sothis, the Dog-Star, and also with a goddess called Selk, or Serk, whose special emblem was the scorpion.

Isis was also known as a great healer; as "a woman who possessed words of power." She it was who healed Ra and, in the process, learned his most secret name, thus ensuring her own divinity.

—*History of Ancient Egypt*
George Rawlinson, 1880

Isis, bas-relief in gold from the tomb of Amenophis II, XVIII Dynasty

Diana as Goddess of the Hunt

Hymn to Diana

Queen and huntress, chaste and fair,
Now the sun is laid to sleep,
Seated in thy silver chair
State in wonted manner keep;
Hesperus entreats thy light,
Goddess excellently bright.

Earth, let not thy envious shade
Dare itself to interpose;
Cynthia's shining orb was made
Heaven to clear, when day did close;
Bless us then with wishéd sight,
Goddess excellently bright.

Lay thy brow of pearl apart
And thy crystal-shining quiver,
Give unto the flying hart
Space to breathe, how short soever;
Thou that mak'st a day of night,
Goddess excellently bright.

—Ben Jonson (1573-1637)

The Ancient Wise Women

.

The earliest antiquity attributed magick pre-eminently to women. The cause of this lay in outward circumstances. To women, and not to men, were confided the selection and preparation of powerful medicines, even as the preparation of food belonged to them. To prepare ointments, to weave linen, to heal wounds, seemed best to suit their gentle and soft hands. The art of writing and reading letters was in the most ancient times chiefly committed to women. The unquiet career of the life of man was occupied with war, hunting, agriculture, and the mechanical arts. To woman all the facilities for sorcery were furnished by experience. The imaginative power of woman is more ardent and more susceptible than that of man, and from the most remote time homage was paid to the inward and sacred strength and power of divination existing in them. Women were priestesses and soothsayers; the German and Scandinavian traditions have handed down to us their names and their fame. According to the different popular opinions they were Nornor and Valor, Valkyrior and Swan-maidens, with a divine life, or they were sorceresses. Upon a mixture of all this, of natural legendary and imaginary circumstances, are found the ideas of the Middle Ages regarding witchcraft. Fantasy, tradition, the knowledge of curative means, poverty, and laziness converted old women into witches; and the three last circumstances created sorceresses out of shepherdesses and herds-maidens. Christianity then modified these ideas.

The witches of Shakespeare came together to cook; but they may be placed together with the ancient prophetesses of the Cimbri. There are other connecting points between ancient and

modern nations. Salt-springs stand in direct connection with modern witchcraft (see Tacitus, *Ann*. B. 57). There were undoubtedly such salt streams at that period in Germany flowing out of mountains in the sacred woods. Their produce was regarded as the immediate gift of the present godhead; the obtaining and distribution of salt was deemed a sacred employment; possibly sacrifices and popular festivals were connected with it. These wise women priestesses managed the preparation of the salt; when the salt pan was placed under their care we have a direct connection between these salt-boilings and the later notions of witchcraft. On certain days of festivity the witches took their station on the hill in the sacred wood, where the salt wells spring forth, with cooking apparatus, spoons and forks, and their saltpan glowed in the darkness of the night.

It is well known that annually in Germany there was a general expedition of the witches on the night of the first of May—Walpurgisnacht—that is, at the time of the sacrificial feast of the ancient assembly of the people. On the first of May, through many ages, were held the unsummoned tribunals, and on this day were celebrated the merry May games, that is, the riding of summer into the country. Such May games in the ancient Danish and Swedish chronicles are frequently spoken of; they were a great gathering of the nobility for sport. Nobility and royalty frequently took part in them. The young men rode first; then the May-Earl with two wreaths of flowers on each shoulder; the rest of the people only with one. Songs were sung; all the young maidens formed a circle round the May-Earl and he chose a May-Countess by throwing at her a garland. The first of May is one of the most distinguished festivals of the pagans. But if we men tion two or three witch feasts, that of Walpurgis, St. John's, and St. Bartholomew's days, we are reminded by them of all the prosecutions of the Middle Ages. The people would not have given up their honorable days of assembly to the witches had not these been in their hereditary possession.

A part of Carpathia between Hungary and Poland is called in Polish *Babia gora*—the Old Women's Mountain. The witches succeeded to the dethroned goddesses, and the manner in which it took place was this. When the populace went over to the new faith, there were a few who hung back, and for a long time clung to the ancient belief, and in secret continued to practice their rites. From this state of things, the "demonology" of the ancients mingled itself imperceptibly with Christianity, and from a union of actuality and imagination arose the representation of the nocturnal flights of witches, in which all of ancient paganism was perpetuated. How near to the Greek Diana, or the Jewish Herodias, lay the Frau Holda—a Keltic Abundia. This agrees curiously with the tradition that the Thuringian Horselberg was simultaneously possessed by Holda and her host, and by the witches. Kiersersberg makes the night-traveling witches proceed to no other place than Venusberg—Frau Venus with her train—where there is good eating, dancing and leaping. These nocturnal women, white mothers—*dominae nocturne; bonne dames; lamiae sive geniciales feminae*—were originally demoniac, elfish women, who appeared in female shape, and showed kindness to men. The nocturnal women, good, social servants, who went with the witches on their expeditions, brought good luck, performed various little offices, examined the furniture of the house, blessed the children in the cradle.

—*The History of Magic,* Joseph Ennemoser, 1854

Mother Earth
to the Greeks and Romans

In ancient Greece the worship of Earth as a goddess was not an important element of the national religion, unless indeed we regard Demeter as an Earth-goddess, for unquestionably Demeter was one of the most important, as well as among the most stately and beautiful, figures in the Greek pantheon. But she was a goddess of the corn rather than of the Earth. The true Greek goddess of the Earth was Gaia or Ge, whose name means nothing but the actual material earth, and is constantly used in that sense by Greek writers from the earliest to the latest times. Hence in her case the personification is open and unambiguous; the veil of mythic fancy is thin and transparent to conceal the physical basis of the goddess.

But if the Earth-goddess never received a large share of Greek worship, she played an important part in the scheme of Greek mythology as expounded by the poet Hesiod in his Theogony. According to him, Broad-bosomed Earth, as he calls her, was that first being that came into existence after the primeval chaos. She was older than the sky, indeed she gave birth to the starry sky, he was her first-born; and afterwards she brought forth the mountains and the sea. All these, apparently, she was thought to have produced of herself without the assistance of any male power. But thereafter, she mated with the Sky, her own offspring, and from their unison was born Ocean and the Titans. Hesiod appears to have felt little tenderness or respect for the Earth-goddess. Certainly he represents her in a very unamiable light as hard, cruel, and treacherous.

A far more favorable portrait of the Earth-goddess, and one

which probably harmonized better with Greek notions and sentiments about her, is painted by the author of the Homeric hymn addressed to "Earth, the Mother of All." In English it runs thus:

> "I'll sing of Earth, Mother of All, of her
>   the firm-founded,
> Eldest of beings, her who feeds all that in
>   the world exists;
> All things that go upon the sacred land and on the sea,
> And all that fly, all they are fed from thy bounty.
> By thee, O Queen, are men blessed in their children,
>   blessed in their crops;
> Thine it is to give life and to take it back
> From mortal man. Happy is he whom thou in heart
> Dost honor graciously; he hath all things in plenty.
> . . . Hail, Mother of Gods, Spouse of the Starry Sky,
> And graciously for this my song bestow on me
> Substance enough for heart's ease.
> So shall I not forget to hymn thee in another lay."

Hundreds of years later a like feeling of reverence and affection for the Earth Goddess was expressed by Plutarch with that simple piety and transparent sincerity which characterize all the writings of that excellent man.

The ancient Romans, like the Greeks, personified and worshipped the Earth as a Mother Goddess; but though her worship was doubtless very ancient, the evidence for its observance in Rome and Italy is very scanty; the goddess would seem to have been pushed into the background by other and more popular deities, above all by the Sky God Jupiter, and by the Corn-goddess Ceres, with whom she was often confounded. Her proper name was Tellus, which is also a common Latin noun signifying "earth"; but in later times she was more usually invoked under the name Terra or Terra Mater, that is, "Mother Earth," *terra* being practically synonymous with *tellus* in the sense of "earth." Apparently she personified not so much the whole Earth as, primarily, the fruitful field to which men owe their food and therefore their life and, secondarily, the burial ground which receives their bodies after death. The poet Lucretius sums up the conception of the Earth-mother in her double aspect in a striking phrase by saying that she is thought to be "the universal parent and the common tomb." So the older poet Ennius said that the Earth "gave birth to all nations and takes them back again."

—*The Worship of Nature*
Sir James G. Frazer, London, 1926

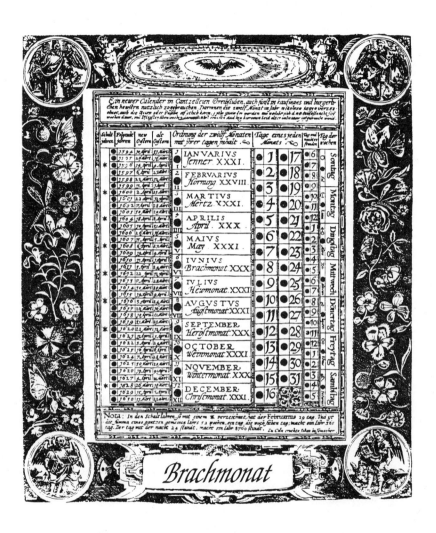

Brachmonat

June

The Full Moon in June is known as the Mead Moon. It was also known as the Honey Moon in ancient times because honey was gathered and the mead was made from honey.

Here are two recipes for mead taken from Buckland's Complete Book of Witchcraft.

Mead

Dissolve four pounds of honey in a gallon of water and add an ounce of hops, half an ounce of root ginger and the pared rind of two lemons. Boil this for three-quarters of an hour, pour it into a cask to the brim and, when it is still lukewarm, add an ounce of yeast. Leave the mead to ferment and when this has ended, put in a quarter of an ounce of *isinglass* (obtainable from wine-making supply stores) and bung the cask tightly. In six months it should be bottled.

Sack Mead

Requirements: a wooden vessel in which to mix the honey and water and carry out the fermentation; a small barrel in which to place the fermented liquor to mature for two to three years; and a smaller container (such as a glass jar), with adequate seal to hold some of the original fermented liquor. This will be used from time to time to top up the liquor in the barrel. In the course of two to three years in the barrel, the liquor shrinks, so surplus liquor is needed to keep the barrel full and so exclude air. This surplus liquor should be put aside after the first month's fermentation, and should be about 10% of the whole.

Mix five-and-a-half pounds of honey to each gallon of warm water until the honey is dissolved. Prepare the yeast by putting it in a small glass vessel and adding small quantities progressively (over several days) of a weak solution of honey and water. Keep the yeast at about 60°F until the yeast has started to ferment, then add this to the dissolved honey and water when the latter is at about 70°F. Cover the fermenting vessel with a loose cover and cloth so that air can reach the fermenting honey and water mixture without allowing insects and dust to penetrate. After about a week, the liquor should be fermenting, and at the end of a month the fermentation should have ceased. The liquor should be strained off carefully, leaving all lees aside, and placed in the barrel which should then be firmly sealed and only opened occasionally to top up, as explained.

To avoid vinegration, first boil the honey and water for about 15 minutes. This kills any wild ferments and ensures a relatively sterile "must," to which to add the yeast. The barrel and the original fermenting vessel should also have been sterilized.

1   *Friday*

Moon Sign: Libra   Tarot Card: Four of Swords
Moon Phase: 2nd Quarter   Herb: Almond
Festival: Carna   Incense: Frankincense
                                Mineral: Black Coral
                                Color: Green
                                Name of Power: Carna

2   *Saturday*

Moon Sign: Libra   Tarot Card: Five of Swords
Moon Phase: 2nd Quarter   Herb: Asparagus
                                Incense: Sandalwood
                                Mineral: Kyanite
                                Color: Black
                                Name of Power: Proserpina

3   *Sunday*

Moon Sign: Libra   Tarot Card: Six of Swords
Moon Phase: 2nd Quarter   Herb: Bilberry
                                Incense: Myrrh
                                Mineral: African Jade
                                Color: Yellow
                                Name of Power: Bellona

| JUNE | | | | | | |
S	M	T	W	T	F	S
					1	2
3	4	5	6	7	8	9
10	11	12	13	14	15	16
17	18	19	20	21	22	23
24	25	26	27	28	29	30

4 *Monday*

Moon Sign: Scorpio
Moon Phase: 2nd Quarter

Tarot Card: Seven of Swords
Herb: Bird's Tongue
Incense: Jasmine
Mineral: Green Feldspar
Color: White
Name of Power: Agwé-Taroyo

5 *Tuesday*

Moon Sign: Scorpio
Moon Phase: 2nd Quarter

Tarot Card: Eight of Swords
Herb: Bloodroot
Incense: Benzoin
Mineral: Smithsonite
Color: Red
Name of Power: Damna

6 *Wednesday*

Moon Sign: Sagittarius
Moon Phase: 2nd Quarter

Tarot Card: Nine of Swords
Herb: Buckthorn
Incense: Pine
Mineral: Fluorite
Color: Purple
Name of Power: Akentauk-Ha-Kheru

7 *Thursday*

Moon Sign: Sagittarius
Moon Phase: 2nd Quarter

Tarot Card: Ten of Swords
Herb: Cat's Foot
Incense: Cinnamon
Mineral: Fluorspar
Color: Blue
Name of Power: Vesta

8
Friday

Moon Sign: Sagittarius
Moon Phase: Full Moon (Dyad)

Tarot Card: Page of Swords
Herb: Colt's Foot
Incense: Frankincense
Mineral: Jet
Color: Green
Name of Power: Mens

9
Saturday

Moon Sign: Capricorn
Moon Phase: 3rd Quarter
Festival: Vestalia

Tarot Card: Knight of Swords
Herb: Cyclamen
Incense: Sandalwood
Mineral: Bonamite
Color: Black
Name of Power: Oro-Ibah-
                            Aozpi

10
Sunday

Moon Sign: Capricorn
Moon Phase: 3rd Quarter

Tarot Card: Queen of Swords
Herb: Elecampane
Incense: Myrrh
Mineral: Diamond
Color: Yellow
Name of Power: Bakulu

			JUNE			
S	M	T	W	T	F	S
					1	2
3	4	5	6	7	8	9
10	11	12	13	14	15	16
17	18	19	20	21	22	23
24	25	26	27	28	29	30

11 *Monday*

Moon Sign: Aquarius
Moon Phase: 3rd Quarter

Tarot Card: King of Swords
Herb: Ferula
Incense: Jasmine
Mineral: Cerussite
Color: White
Name of Power: Matuta

12 *Tuesday*

Moon Sign: Aquarius
Moon Phase: 3rd Quarter

Tarot Card: Ace of Wands
Herb: Garden Violet
Incense: Benzoin
Mineral: Cape Ruby
Color: Red
Name of Power: Kwan-Ying

13 *Wednesday*

Moon Sign: Aquarius
Moon Phase: 3rd Quarter
Festival: Tibetan All Saints Day
San Antonio de Padna

Tarot Card: Two of Wands
Herb: Hawthorn
Incense: Pine
Mineral: Serpentine
Color: Purple
Name of Power: Minerva

14 *Thursday*

Moon Sign: Pisces
Moon Phase: 3rd Quarter

Tarot Card: Three of Wands
Herb: Hepatica
Incense: Cinnamon
Mineral: Garnet
Color: Blue
Name of Power: Aplu

15 *Friday*

Moon Sign: Pisces
Moon Phase: 4th Quarter

Tarot Card: Four of Wands
Herb: Hound's Tongue
Incense: Frankincense
Mineral: Tiger's Eye Matrix
Color: Green
Name of Power: An-Hra

16 *Saturday*

Moon Sign: Aries
Moon Phase: 4th Quarter

Tarot Card: Five of Wands
Herb: Jasmine
Incense: Sandalwood
Mineral: Datolite
Color: Black
Name of Power: Ahura-Mazda

17 *Sunday*

Moon Sign: Aries
Moon Phase: 4th Quarter

Tarot Card: Six of Wands
Herb: Lavender
Incense: Myrrh
Mineral: Colemanite
Color: Yellow
Name of Power: Eurydice

			JUNE			
S	M	T	W	T	F	S
					1	2
3	4	5	6	7	8	9
10	11	12	13	14	15	16
17	18	19	20	21	22	23
24	25	26	27	28	29	30

18 *Monday*

Moon Sign: Taurus
Moon Phase: 4th Quarter

Tarot Card: Seven of Wands
Herb: Magnolia
Incense: Jasmine
Mineral: Magnetite-Jade
Color: White
Name of Power: Anna

19 *Tuesday*

Moon Sign: Taurus
Moon Phase: 4th Quarter

Tarot Card: Eight of Wands
Herb: Mexican Damiana
Incense: Benzoin
Mineral: Gold
Color: Red
Name of Power: Brisé

20 *Wednesday*

Moon Sign: Gemini
Moon Phase: 4th Quarter

Tarot Card: Nine of Wands
Herb: Cross Mint
Incense: Pine
Mineral: Silver
Color: Purple
Name of Power: Alako

21 *Thursday*

Moon Sign: Gemini
Moon Phase: 4th Quarter
Sun enters Cancer
Festival: Summer Solstice;
        Feast of San Aloisio

Tarot Card: Ten of Wands
Herb: Black Mulberry
Incense: Cinnamon
Mineral: Watermelon Tour-
        maline
Color: Blue
Name of Power: Oraea

22   *Friday*

Moon Sign: Cancer   Tarot Card: Page of Wands
Moon Phase: New Moon   Herb: Bittersweet
                             Incense: Frankincense
                             Mineral: Tufa
                             Color: Green
                             Name of Power: Cerridwen

23   *Saturday*

Moon Sign: Cancer   Tarot Card: Knight of Wands
Moon Phase: 1st Quarter   Herb: Heartsease
Festival: Midsummer Eve;   Incense: Sandalwood
        Noche de San Juan   Mineral: Onyx
        Bautista   Color: Black
                             Name of Power: Ishtar

24   *Sunday*

Moon Sign: Leo   Tarot Card: Queen of Wands
Moon Phase: 1st Quarter   Herb: Pilewort
Festival: Midsummer Day   Incense: Myrrh
                             Mineral: Tektite
                             Color: Yellow
                             Name of Power: Neith

JUNE						
S	M	T	W	T	F	S
					1	2
3	4	5	6	7	8	9
10	11	12	13	14	15	16
17	18	19	20	21	22	23
24	25	26	27	28	29	30

25 *Monday*

Moon Sign: Leo
Moon Phase: 1st Quarter

Tarot Card: King of Wands
Herb: Pokeweed
Incense: Jasmine
Mineral: Alabaster
Color: White
Name of Power: Metes-Hra-
Ari-She

26 *Tuesday*

Moon Sign: Virgo
Moon Phase: 1st Quarter

Tarot Card: The Magician
Herb: Butter Rose
Incense: Benzoin
Mineral: Meerschaum
Color: Red
Name of Power: Zom

27 *Wednesday*

Moon Sign: Virgo
Moon Phase: 1st Quarter

Tarot Card: High Priestess
Herb: Compass Plant
Incense: Pine
Mineral: Coral
Color: Purple
Name of Power: Aestas

28 *Thursday*

Moon Sign: Virgo
Moon Phase: 1st Quarter

Tarot Card: The Empress
Herb: Rhatany
Incense: Cinnamon
Mineral: Ivory
Color: Blue
Name of Power: Exú

29   *Friday*

Moon Sign: Libra
Moon Phase: 2nd Quarter

Tarot Card: The Empress
Herb: Sanicle
Incense: Frankincense
Mineral: Ruby
Color: Green
Name of Power: Fatras

30   *Saturday*

Moon Sign: Libra
Moon Phase: 2nd Quarter

Tarot Card: The Hierophant
Herb: Shepherd's Purse
Incense: Sandalwood
Mineral: Emerald
Color: Black
Name of Power: Llwy

Sunday

JUNE

S	M	T	W	T	F	S
					1	2
3	4	5	6	7	8	9
10	11	12	13	14	15	16
17	18	19	20	21	22	23
24	25	26	27	28	29	30

Dressing With Power

Scott Cunningham

(*Scott Cunningham defines magic as "the projection of natural but subtle energies to produce needed change." This article is the result of his ongoing investigation into the ways that we can bring magic into our daily lives.*)

These days there's much talk about "power lunches," "power cars" and "power colors" for clothes. The premise behind this—the image you present will help you move up in the world—has nothing to do with this article. Power, here, is seen as the real thing—the juice that fuels magic. All things that exist, including color, contain energy. Because clothing is colored it can be used for magical purposes just as can crystals, herbs, music, food and virtually anything else.

This is an age-old practice. An excellent example of the special uses of clothing today are the robes worn by some ritual magicians and Wiccans (Witches). These are usually hooded, of natural fibers, and are worn solely for ritual purposes. They may be embroidered with specific designs or left plain. Such robes are usually donned to awaken the "magical personality" of the practitioner, to prepare his or her consciousness at every level for the rite about to be performed.

That's all very well and good, but our everyday clothing presents us with powerful possibilities for improving our lives, for shaping our future into more positive experiences. Anyone can practice clothing magic and, indeed, the art of dressing can be a magical one.

First, the color of the clothes we wear—both those that can be seen by others as well as those that cannot—is of vital importance. Just as colors in our environment affect us, so too do the colors of our apparel. Some general ideas regarding the colors of clothing and their magical effects follow, but a few words are appropriate here:

• To bring a specific color's influence into your life, be aware of it. Look at your clothing during the day and feel its energy seeping inside you. Make dressing itself a ritual. As you slip on the first garment of the color you've chosen to help you, see yourself (visualize) that power becoming a part of you. Accept it.

• You needn't wear an entire outfit of a single color. As long as some of your clothing is of the needed color it can work its magic. (If, for example, a man would feel uncomfortable wearing pink, simply wear it where it won't be seen—undershirts, socks etc.)

• When you've accomplished your goal, move on to a new color and a new goal. Continuing to wear one color day after day may cause imbalances—three months of wearing nothing but blue may make you depressed; too much red can make steam boil out of your ears! Keep it in balance.

• Dirty clothing won't work properly. If you decide to use clothing as tools of magic, "ritually" prepare them by washing at frequent intervals.

• Remember to *allow* the color's energy to affect you. Invite it inside—don't just put on a red shirt and expect it to do all the work. Prepare yourself for the coming change.

• As will be seen in the following discussion, specific colors of clothing can be worn during specific magical acts to enhance their effectiveness.

The Colors

Wear *white* clothing for purification. This is excellent for ridding yourself of depression, for removing doubt, for freeing yourself from past negative habits. White clothing is, of course, also fine for use during all rituals of purification. It's a natural at the time of the full moon. Wear it to find peace within yourself.

Pink clothing promotes love. If you tend to go through your day (at work or at play) with an aggressive, negative approach, pink clothing soothes you and produces a more pleasant personality. It is also ideal when relaxing with a loved one or when looking for an interpersonal relationship.

To attract attention and objects to yourself, *orange* is an excellent color. This color is a powerful drawing force. It is also fine to wear during solar rituals, for notice in a crowd and also for asking for promotions.

Red clothing produces physical energy. If you need to work long hours to accomplish something, if you just can't seem to wake up in the morning, put on some red clothing and let its energy get you started and keep you going until the task is completed. At one time red clothing was thought to keep "evil demons" at bay, and in China red clothing was thought to protect children. Today we see it as a protective color because its energies are strong enough to deflect outside influences. This isn't an appropriate color for very outgoing, aggressive people—they don't need red.

To improve your mind wear *yellow* clothing. This color stimulates the conscious mind and may be of help while studying, memorizing or trying to absorb new information. If you're forgetful, try putting on something yellow. Hats would, of course, be very appropriate.

Green clothing was once thought to be unlucky—especially for brides. In Ireland the color itself was long considered to be taboo due to its connections with the fairies. Even green foods weren't eaten. However, green is an excellent color to wear to expand your ability to receive money, to promote spiritual as well as physical fertility and, according to some traditions, for maintaining good health.

Blue is considered to be a fortunate color for clothing nearly all around the world. One old rhyme says:

"Always wear threads of blue,
Keep danger far from you."

It was once thought to protect its wearer from insults. From a magical perspective, blue clothing awakens psychic consciousness and so is excellent for promoting intuition. It is worn when seeking psychic information. Blue is also a healing color suitable for resolving physical, mental and emotional problems.

Violet or *lavender* clothing is ideal for slipping into meditative states—which isn't the best thing if you happen to be driving! At home however, violet clothing (even just a t-shirt) can be worn for times of quiet contemplation or for spiritual activities.

When performing magical rituals, *purple* is the color of choice, for this hue is linked with Akasha, the power of the universe. Its other association with riches may have something to do with its recent stint as the power color among men in the corporate world.

Brown clothing is suitable for peaceful moments. It blends into the Earth and is comforting and nourishing. Animals respond favorably to this color, but this won't necessarily halt attacks of vicious dogs.

Gray is a neutral color with little magical effect. It is suitable for general clothing.

Black clothing still frightens many. The heroes in old movies wore white while the "bad guys" wore black (symbolizing evil). However, black is no more evil than the night. For many, black clothing acts as a shield which guards the wearer from outside influences and energies. It is a color of protection. Wear it when you don't wish to be unduly noticed by others. Many ritualists wear black robes during magical workings because of its links with outer space and the deities who created all that exists.

The magical effects of *multi-colored* clothing depend, of course, on the colors used in the material. Harsh slashes of bright red across cool blue may produce magical chaos for some while others will feel no ill effects at all. Still, this confusing pattern may be protective. Experiment with clothing of this kind (if you already have it) to find out how it affects you.

Plaids, the generic tartans that continue to be used in clothing for men and women, are long-time protective patterns. Those incorporating red into the design are excellent for this use. The intersecting lines bind and guard the wearer.

As to the type of materials: to put it bluntly, swear off polyester and all other synthetic fabrics, at least for outerwear. I have no desire to walk around in a plastic bag, which is just what these things are. Synthetic materials are, after all, synthetic—and not useful in magic.

Cotton, linen and wool, while being more expensive, are ideal materials for magic. In the past, wool was thought to lead to sexual desires and so its use was restricted from those on spiritual quests. This may also be the reason why linen became so popular among the Western clergy. All I've noticed from wool in general—leaving color aside for a moment—is that it's scratchy. Cotton is the best material to use for virtually all your magical clothing.

If you have success with clothing magic the horizons are unlimited. You may decide to dye your own clothing to produce the exact shade desired. Tie-dyeing produces a look which is once again popular, and these designs are protective. Those who embroider can sew symbols onto their clothing for specific purposes. Personal "luck" signs, runes and planetary symbols are all appropriate.

Virtually every article of clothing, from shoes and socks to scarves and hats, is infused with ancient magic. For example, did you know that high-heeled shoes are thought to be protective? (They may be, but they kill the feet!) Those waiting for a complicated matter to be brought to a conclusion were once directed to blow up a sleeve. And did you ever wonder why some dark-colored socks have white toes? They were originally made this way to protect the wearer from being tripped by elves.

Superstitions regarding clothes abound. Don't put hats and shoes on the bed. Tie knots in a piece of your mate's underwear to ensure fidelity. If you accidentally put on an article of clothing inside-out, you should wear it that way for good luck. Or, if you're having a bad day, take off your clothing and put it on inside-out to bring positive changes. Such popular beliefs are half-remembered survivals of rituals performed long ago. They point to the power which earlier humans saw in clothing.

Granted, this magic isn't for those who follow the dictates of high fashion, who allow others to say what's "in" and what to wear. It is for true individualists who are willing to take control of their clothing and their lives.

So the next time you look at your wardrobe and sigh to yourself, "What should I wear today?," think about this article—and dress with power!

Natural Elements

Deborah Lipp

There is a conventional way of looking at the four elements of Earth, Air, Fire and Water. When we learn to do magick, or to meditate, or to cast a circle, we use visualizations of the elements as focal points. We use them for protection and to draw on their power to eliminate the obsessions in our lives that cluster around one or another of them. We learn about the elements early on, that they have correspondences to the directions North, East, South and West, to the magickal tools, to the suits of the Tarot and to the signs of the zodiac. Like any good magickal technique, these basics become second nature, and thus can become stagnant. When was the last time you really *looked* at the elements you invoked?

This summer, I spent several weeks traveling: driving through the Midwest, Southwest and California from the Mexican border to the Sierras. I saw deserts, mountains, seashore, farmland and forest, experiencing life (and lifelessness) in a startling new way. Through the range and novelty of this journey, I began to contemplate the elements. I was struck by the variety present in the world. The richness of Air, Fire, Water and Earth was much greater than I generally visualized, or than the visualizations generally recommended in most magickal texts and study groups.

Look to the East and imagine air. Imagine the Grand Canyon. See a raven—black and strong, her powerful wings carrying her thousands of feet above the Earth—and notice that she is still hundreds of feet below where you stand. *That* is the glory of Air. Feel the dizzyness. Feel the pain as your ears pop from the altitude. Look far, far below you, to what you believe is the ground, and realize that it is a cliff top. See the ground below it, and realize that it too is a cliff top.

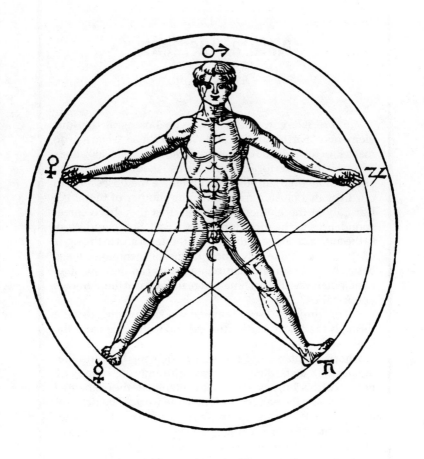

The ground cannot be seen. Sway; feel the threat of falling, and the desire to fall.

Stand in the Sierras and look up. The lush green trees tower above you. The sky is made invisible by the incredible height. Close your eyes and learn air's method of communication. Smell pine. Smell a coming rainstorm. Smell manure. Hear the birdsong. Sound flies on the wind. Know where you are, without seeing and without moving through the medium of air.

Look to the South and imagine fire. The desert sun brings endless heat. The wind comes but does not cool. Imagine the fire that comes from the earth, from plants whose lives are twisted by its driving will, the fire that exhausts and drains and saps the will. Imagine sweltering heat hours past sunset.

See fire in the blankets that you layer over you on a cold Midwestern night. See fire in the arms of your lover next to you, who will warm you against the chill. See the fire that cooks when you're hungry, that burns when you're careless. See, instead of a highly symbolized salamander, a lizard racing at incredible speed across the desert floor. Let the sweat drip down your forehead; taste salt on your upper lip. Feel the itching pain of sunburn and the delirium of fever.

Look to the West and imagine water. Stand beneath Yosemite Falls: towering, crashing water, endlessly moving yet endlessly unchanged, violently rapid yet ever still; feel the power of water to entrance, to enchant. Feel the icy pain of the pools at its base, the luscious relief of it on your lips and in your throat. Wipe your brow with it; wash a cut with it.

At Sea World you can feed fish to dolphins and baby whales; they accept and enjoy your caresses. Their touch communicates the consciousness of water: fluid, loving and serene. The sour stink of fish and brine is in your lungs.

See a dry riverbed. Water is nowhere in sight, but the large, smoothly rounded stones, the shape of the trail they make, the kind of trees that grow and the way their roots are formed, everything you see is a creation of water. A dry stream is still a stream; see the power that lies dormant there. Now imagine the coming spring, when the stream is awash with water's magnetic life. Cast your mind back to the desert and see a dry stream there, a frightening, scar-like place where Death seems to have passed. How rich is life where water is present; how life struggles where it is not!

Now let the floods come. The telephone poles, power lines, picket fences are submerged; the highway is a bare strip of mud. Water has brought silence, sleep. See a house built on the edge of the sea. The huge, broken slabs of concrete were on its pier; never forget that water can destroy.

Look to the North and imagine earth. Enter a cave; bats, hundreds of them, come rushing out. Feel the living rock as the air about you cools; earth's breath is cold. Deep in a cavern, earth is above, below, all around you; it is everything. Stalactites and stalagmites long for each other, reach to each other, taking hundreds of years to finally caress each other. Pools beneath the earth are so clear they're invisible. Shadows and crevices call you to their hidden realms, offering comfort, peace and secrecy. A cave is a womb made of rock.

Snow-capped mountains, or painted mountains, or tree-covered mountains, or mountains barren of life—the earth rises above to observe with patience and love. Wearing a variety of colors, earth houses and encompasses infinite possibility; everything that lives is approved. The earth gives foundation to all.

When air dizzies, or water threatens to drown, or fire to burn, we cling to the earth for support. Feel the security of the rock and roots that hold back danger and offer a place to rest. A stone cliff hundreds of feet tall rises startlingly straight above you. The earth takes your breath away with magnitude and respect. Seared by fire, eroded by water, shifted by air, it is the earth that remains.

Your memories hold the taste and feel of Air, Fire, Water and Earth, more poignant and real than any "symbol system." Use them, call them forth, and feel your own power increase a thousand-fold.

Bell, Book, and Briefcase

Kathleen Wilder

At first glance the combination of witchcraft and the work-place may seem to be an unlikely one. "No!" you may think, "I can't let anyone at work know I'm a witch—I'll be fired!" I'm not suggesting that you take to burning candles at your desk at lunchtime or start wearing dangling pentagram necklaces that catch in the typewriter. But nonetheless, there are many easy, subtle, magickal techniques you can employ that might make the difference between being hired or fired.

Of course, just as in love spells, you will want to use these methods with an understanding of the personal freedom that is a right of every human soul. Using magick to coerce someone against his or her feelings is not only bad business, it's bad magick and will boomerang against you. If you use a spell to get a raise you do not deserve, the very least that will occur is that you will at some point be passed over for several that you genuinely deserve. Good, positive magic is like money in the bank, collecting interest; bad, negative magic is like an unpaid bill that will suddenly come due, payable in full immediately. Not a very relaxing feeling, is it?

As you are probably aware, magickal symbols and the work-ing environment do not mix well unless you are fortunate enough to work in a business operated by like-minded or at least *open*-minded people. Even so, you have no control over the prejudices of your coworkers. There are several ways you can still proclaim your faith quietly. Many people look askance at pentagrams, but no one would think anything of a small gold starfish charm worn on a chain around your neck. Necklaces, including natural objects such as seashells or tumbled crystal beads, are also a positive way of showing your reverence for the deities of nature. With the flood of interest in things Egyptian since the Tutankhamen exhibits, images of Egyptian deities will often be thought of as merely a pretty bit of jewelry. However, I have on more than one occasion had a casual observer assume my winged Isis necklace and ring were the winged Harley-Davidson motorcycle emblem instead! In the same way, when I wore a pentagram some have assumed I am Jewish, mistaking the five-pointed pentagram for the six-pointed Star of David.

Osiris

It is not necessary to see or feel the symbols of our religion for them to exert a protective and inspirational effect. Try painting a symbol of a force you wish to be with you in your workplace in clear nail polish over your usual manicure; the act of drawing the symbol will invoke its presence and, as the nail polish dries, the energy will be sealed until you remove it or it chips away. Appropriate signs might be the astrological sigil of Mercury in his aspect as a god of eloquence. Wear it on the day you plan to ask for that well-deserved raise. Or wear the sign of Venus, if you want others to relate well to you emotionally. Any simple symbol will work. For instance, you might want to paint a dollar sign on another nail in addition to the sign of Mercury. This is one way of openly practicing your magick—after all, your fingers are visible to everyone, but in an invisible way known only to you.

Another way you can bring magickal influences into work is through the use of scent, though here again subtlety and appropriateness are the keys to effectiveness. I've used *ylang-ylang* oil many times, delicately applied, to get through difficult employer situations. Too much of this oil, however, is overpowering and will drive people away from you. Remember, the purpose of magic in the workplace is to help your employers realize that they like you, like your work, and want to hire or continue employing you. It's difficult for them to do this if they are cowering in a corner hiding from a cloud of scent!

Many of us have personal oil blends that we use to attune with our deities, and often these personal oils will be perfectly appropriate to wear at work. It's a good idea to make up a special batch of these oils purely for the times you wear them to the office. Change the recipes slightly, otherwise you may find that some of the oil's power diminishes as you become used to smelling it daily and in mundane surroundings.

Many people have a telephone answering machine. Your taped message could be the first contact a potential client has with you, and his or her impression of you may be formed based on that fifteen or twenty seconds. This is a perfect opportunity to maximize your potential by creating a message that tells the listener that this is a competent, creative, valuable individual, one whom she or he is very fortunate to have contacted.

To do this, sit down by yourself in a quiet place, with your answering machine hooked up and ready to work. Unplug the phone itself, since nothing could be more jolting to your magick than to have it suddenly ring twelve inches away. Stretch your arms and legs and take several deep breaths. Feel the air circulating in your lungs; visualize it as liquid light entering your body. Smile as you do this, a smile of genuine confidence in yourself and in your abilities to do the work you have chosen. Write down what you want to say, and read it out loud. Let your voice emanate from your stomach and chest as well as through your throat and mouth. Make any changes you wish in your script and read it through until you like your delivery. Then record your message. An additional benefit to this bit of magick is that, like all spells, it works two ways. You are presenting to others an image of you at your most positive; at the same time, you are making that image more real to yourself. You are invoking into your soul the qualities of confidence and competence, and these will continue to expand and grow.

If you are between jobs, this is an ideal time to do work spells, because all of the potentials exist and are not limited by the conditions of a current job. What is hardest to do is to invoke for a job that will really fill your needs, and not just bring in a paycheck on time for next month's rent. Too often, the job you take "just for a few weeks" will be the job you still have (and still hate) two years from now. If finances are an urgent problem, try taking work that is temporary in nature, such as a type of seasonal work or fill-in work through an employment agency. Then when the job that is meant for you is ready for you, and you are ready for it, you'll be able to accept it without being torn between the familiar rut of your old job and the sometimes frightening challenges of a new one.

A simple spell to find a new job can be done using the employment section of the newspaper, green or gold candles, and the tools or symbols of your profession. Or you may want to use a divination method to find a type of job you would be good at, or you may simply request that the ideal job, one that supports you comfortably and makes you content, be found for you. A construction worker might want to put a small toy building on the altar area, or cut out pictures of buildings under construction. Writers might do this spell at the desk beside the typewriter. A secretary might include a steno pad, pens, and a computer manual. Anything that means your job to you, and that has a positive connotation for you, can be used. If you find these things depressing, or they are reminders of frustrating experiences for you, you may want to ask yourself why you are trying to find more work in that field. Are all your bad job experiences the result of unreasonable bosses, or are you not happy in your present line of work, which causes you to sabotage yourself? Again, you may want to use a divination method to discover the truth, or have a friend who is not so deeply involved do a reading for you.

To work the spell, take the newspaper and cut out individual want ads. They don't have to be in the line of work you are pursuing. Cut them out as neatly as possible. When you have a good number of them, say fifty or sixty, play with them as you would a deck of cards, stacking them, cutting them, laying them out and mixing them up. As you do this, say aloud the following: "Jobs, jobs, jobs, so many under the sun; Jobs, jobs, jobs, and all I need is one." Say this until you feel silly, because that is when you will begin to relax and become receptive to the energy this spell is creating for you. Play with the job slips. You may even find one just right for you that you overlooked, or that was listed under a category you never would have dreamed of looking under. Finding these missed notices is not strictly the intention of this spell, but if it gets you the job, we won't quibble.

After you have broken through to your own sense of silliness and playfulness, enjoy the feeling for a while. In a few moments you will begin to feel calmer and ready for the final phase of the spell. Arrange your tools and job symbols on your altar. If you have no symbols or tools, simply arrange the job slips in a pattern that pleases you. Set the candle in front of you, breathe deeply, and light it, saying "Bountiful Universe, I am ready and willing to labor in the sphere of the created world. I have been blessed with my abilities, which flow from the highest source; let me use my talents to fulfill my needs, my desires, and my obligations that I may flourish and help others to do the same. So be it!" As you bend to blow out the candle, say, "Blow, winds of prosperity, blow prosperity to me." If possible, leave your altar set up where it is, and repeat the spell daily from the point where you light the candle. By the way, if you plan to do this spell only once, a cloth-draped briefcase makes an excellent small altar. However, if your job could require a briefcase, you don't want to leave the altar set up on top of it. It, and all the rest of your business supplies, should be cleaned out and ready to go. A small drop of money-drawing oil, either commercially made or created from the prosperity-oriented recipes in books such as Scott Cunningham's *The Complete Book of Incense, Oils, and Brews,* can be placed inside each corner of your briefcase. Again, subtlety is the key and the closed area of a briefcase will tend to keep scents stronger than you might expect.

For businesses experiencing financial difficulties, a healing ritual performed over a business card can work wonders in a short time. Take the business card, along with any products or current business literature, and place them on your altar or magick-al working space. Burn green candles, since green can be a color of healing as well as finance. Sprinkle over the items healing herbs, singly or in combination. Herbs with healing properties that retain a strong gold or green color are best, such as hyssop. If you can find a healing herb whose name creates a link with the company name or product, that's even better. Goldenseal, with its golden color, would be doubly excellent for "Goulden Truck-ing, Inc."; rosemary could be used for a gardening service that tends roses, or one owned by a woman named Rose or Mary. These linguistic links are not necessary, but they can add extra power to the working.

As you sprinkle the herbs, concentrate on the image of the business thriving, gaining new strength, growing in reputation. If you are doing this spell for someone else, picture the owner of the business smiling and happy as he or she goes over paperwork. You might also visualize the hiring of new employees and imagine the increased prosperity that they also would enjoy. You can say aloud any healing spell that you know, or say something like the following:

> "Thrive, thrive, my company,
> Bring increased prosperity
> With great alacrity.
> Heal, heal, my company."

Blow out the candles with the same words you used in the job-finding spell.

The elephant-headed Hindu god Ganesha is particularly

efficient when invoked for business matters. If you can't find a statue or drawing of him, try using a picture of an elephant and write the name "Ganesha" along the edge of the picture. Then put the picture where you can see it as you attend to business at home. As an unobtrusive symbol at the workplace, a ceramic or stone elephant paperweight or even a coffee cup with an elephant on it can work well. The traditional *mantra*, or chant, to Ganesha to bring prosperity is very simple: "Jaya Ganesha, Jaya Ganesha," repeated over and over. For best results, it should be spoken aloud as you think of the elephant god. Try saying it as you ride alone in an elevator on your way to an important business appointment.

This last spell is the only financially dangerous one, since it requires a certain amount of good judgment as to its timing and frequency of use, but it has worked so many times that it should be included here. When finances seem particularly dire, purposefully indulging in an extravagance can sometimes break through the monetary doldrums and remind the universe that you truly do have faith that your needs will be answered and your financial situation will improve. But the purchase has to be made fearlessly, and when your mind is tied up with money problems, that is difficult to do. For this reason, next time you feel a spur-of-the-moment impulse to spend money, just enjoy yourself. It has to be a positive purchase, one that makes you feel good, and if it is for an object you can use magickally, that's even better, since such a purchase is in effect an offering to the deities you worship. Also, the object must be paid for in cash—credit cards won't work, though it is acceptable to write a check if there are funds in the bank to cover it at that instant (not three days from now).

Color Treasure Maps

There is a magickal technique used to help in creating your own reality. It is the Treasure Map. Through the Treasure Map it is possible to manifest virtually anything that you desire. As a road map shows you how to get to your destination, so a Treasure Map helps you achieve your goals. It can be large or small, with or without elaborate pictures. Whatever its composition, it is a means of keeping your intent on your goal, of keeping you always moving forward towards what you desire.

The very act of making a Treasure Map is a ritual for success. When making a magickal talisman you put "power," or *mana*, into it by working on it personally, by directing your energies into it. So with the Treasure Map. And by incorporating color in its construction, you can really create an abundance of power, as you will see.

Many people feel that they are "not worthy" of the good things of life. Or perhaps, through ingrained Christian or other religious training, feel that it is somehow "wrong" to have material possessions and/or wealth. Nothing could be further from the truth. We are all worthy of, and fully entitled to, the Universal Abundance. It is as much right for *you* to have what you want as it is for anyone else to. The more you keep that thought in mind, the sooner you will achieve your desires. And the Color Treasure Map will make it happen.

It may seem unbelievable that simply by drawing and coloring pictures you can get what you want. It seems especially so when you can't draw too well and your efforts look like those of a nine-year-old! But don't despair, nine-year-olds generally have a *lot* of psychic energy.

Your map should be as simple as possible, with clear vivid pictures (we'll consider the pictureless ones later). At the top center you need a picture of the "Source" of all things. This could be a God- or Goddess-like figure, or a symbol (such as the Infinity sign, the Chinese Yin-Yang, a Pentagram, Cross, Star of David), or anything which to you personally is indicative of The Source.

Now show (draw) what you want, coming from this Source to you. Suppose, for example, you want enough money to buy a car. Then you might draw a Treasure Map something like that shown in the illustration.

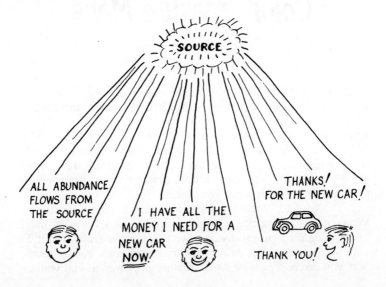

As you see, everything comes from the Source to *You*. I find it good to work in three steps—(i) (*on the left of the Treasure Map*) acknowledgment that everything comes from The Source. (ii) (*center*) affirming that I have what I want, *and that I have it now*. (iii) (*right of the Treasure Map*) giving thanks for receiving what I wanted.

The standard of drawing is not important. In fact I would go so far as to say that the more basic it is, the better. Almost make it a caricature. In other words, don't try for photographic realism. And—most important—*use lots of bright colors*. If you are a blonde, for example, draw yourself with bright yellow hair. Let The Source—be it God, Goddess, Jesus, Ankh, Pentagram, or what/whomever—be surrounded with *all* the colors.

Some people suggest that you find appropriate pictures in magazines and cut them out, pasting them on to make your Treasure Map. I think you'll find it much more effective to do all the illustrating yourself. This way there are far more of your energies going into the map, plus it is *exactly* what you want, and not a compromise of any sort.

A pictureless Treasure Map *can* be made, if you really feel that you can't draw at all. Instead of the pictures, then, you simply write out, in plain, simple terms, exactly what it is you want. Use as few words as possible and, again, use bright colors for writing them. But I would again emphasize that artistic skills are not important. It will be *far* better to draw—however simply, however crudely, than to spell out.

What do you do with the map after it's made? Hang it somewhere where you will see it frequently. Tape it to the refrigerator door, to the side of a filing cabinet, to your bedroom wall. Put it somewhere where you can keep looking at it and keep going over, in your mind, all that it shows. Get to where you can see it in your mind's eye when you are riding the bus or train to work, when you are jogging, when you are sleeping. Constantly seeing and repeating what the Treasure Map shows will take you to your destination. It won't happen overnight, but it will happen.

Treasure Maps can be done for possessions, for jobs, love, health, business success, spiritual advancement . . . for anything. They are fun to do but, most importantly, they work. Remember—*basic drawing* and *bright colors*.

Incorporate color correspondences (*see the following page*) into your map. For instance, if you are working for money, draw your map on green paper. Working for love? Use pink paper. Tranquillity? Blue paper, and so on.

Hewmonat

July

The Meanings of Flowers

Rose Acacia . . . . Friendship
Amaryllis . . . . Beautiful but timid
Blue Bell . . . . Constancy
Buttercup . . . . Riches; Memories of childhood
Camellia . . . . Gratitude, Perfect loveliness
Carnation . . . . Pure and deep love
White Clover . . . . I promise
Four Leaved Clover . . . . Be mine
Red Columbine . . . . Anxious and trembling
Dahlia . . . . Dignity and eloquence
Daffodil . . . . Unrequited love
Garden Daisy . . . . I share your feelings
Single Field Daisy . . . . I will think of it
Dandelion . . . . Oracle; Coquetry
Foxglove . . . . Insincerity; Occupation
Rose Geranium . . . . I prefer you
Honeysuckle . . . . Devoted love; Fidelity
Hyacinth . . . . Constancy; Benevolence
White Jasmine . . . . Amiability
Jonquil . . . . Desire; Affection returned
Lavender . . . . Mistrust
Purple Lilac . . . . First emotions of love
White Lily . . . . Majesty; Purity
Lily of the Valley . . . . Return of happiness
Lupine . . . . Dejection
Magnolia . . . . Love of nature
Marigold . . . . Sacred affection
Garden Marigold . . . . Grief; Chagrin
Mignonette . . . . Your qualities surpass your charms
Morning Glory . . . . Coquetry; Affection
Myrtle . . . . Love in absence
Purple Pansy . . . . You occupy my thoughts
Periwinkle . . . . Sweet memories
Phlox . . . . Our hearts are united
Pimpernel . . . . Rendezvous; Change
Primrose . . . . Modest worth; Silent love
Rhododendron . . . . Agitation
Rosebud . . . . Confession of love
Red Rose . . . . I love you
White Rose . . . . Silence

Friday

Saturday

1

Sunday

Moon Sign: Scorpio
Moon Phase: 2nd Quarter

Tarot Card: The Lovers
Herb: Aloe
Incense: Myrrh
Mineral: Agate
Color: Yellow
Name of Power: Neshtu

			JULY			
S	M	T	W	T	F	S
1	2	3	4	5	6	7
8	9	10	11	12	13	14
15	16	17	18	19	20	21
22	23	24	25	26	27	28
29	30	31				

2
Monday

Moon Sign: Scorpio
Moon Phase: 2nd Quarter

Tarot Card: The Chariot
Herb: Balm
Incense: Jasmine
Mineral: Amber
Color: White
Name of Power: Azaka-Si

3
Tuesday

Moon Sign: Scorpio
Moon Phase: 2nd Quarter
Festival: Dog Days begin

Tarot Card: Justice
Herb: Birthroot
Incense: Benzoin
Mineral: Amethyst
Color: Red
Name of Power: Sothis

4
Wednesday

Moon Sign: Sagittarius
Moon Phase: 2nd Quarter

Tarot Card: The Hermit
Herb: Blue Cohosh
Incense: Pine
Mineral: Beryl
Color: Purple
Name of Power: Pax

5
Thursday

Moon Sign: Sagittarius
Moon Phase: 2nd Quarter

Tarot Card: Wheel of Fortune
Herb: Burdock
Incense: Cinnamon
Mineral: Bloodstone
Color: Blue
Name of Power: Anston

6
Friday

Moon Sign: Capricorn
Moon Phase: 2nd Quarter

Tarot Card: Strength
Herb: Cayenne
Incense: Frankincense
Mineral: Carnelian
Color: Green
Name of Power: Metes-Sen

7
Saturday

Moon Sign: Capricorn
Moon Phase: Full Moon (Mead)
Festival: Tanabata

Tarot Card: The Hanged Man
Herb: Columbine
Incense: Sandalwood
Mineral: Chrysolite
Color: Black
Name of Power: Chin-Nu

8
Sunday

Moon Sign: Aquarius
Moon Phase: 3rd Quarter

Tarot Card: Death
Herb: Dandelion
Incense: Myrrh
Mineral: Ruby
Color: Yellow
Name of Power: Arsinoe

JULY

S	M	T	W	T	F	S
1	2	3	4	5	6	7
8	9	10	11	12	13	14
15	16	17	18	19	20	21
22	23	24	25	26	27	28
29	30	31				

9 *Monday*

Moon Sign: Aquarius
Moon Phase: 3rd Quarter

Tarot Card: Temperance
Herb: Elm
Incense: Jasmine
Mineral: Coral
Color: White
Name of Power: Hevieso

10 *Tuesday*

Moon Sign: Aquarius
Moon Phase: 3rd Quarter

Tarot Card: The Devil
Herb: Asafetida
Incense: Benzoin
Mineral: Quartz Crystal
Color: Red
Name of Power: Godgifu

11 *Wednesday*

Moon Sign: Pisces
Moon Phase: 3rd Quarter

Tarot Card: The Tower
Herb: Garlic
Incense: Pine
Mineral: Diamond
Color: Purple
Name of Power: Cerreton

12 *Thursday*

Moon Sign: Pisces
Moon Phase: 3rd Quarter

Tarot Card: The Star
Herb: Heather
Incense: Cinnamon
Mineral: Emerald
Color: Blue
Name of Power: Aaa-Kheru

13
Friday

Moon Sign: Aries
Moon Phase: 3rd Quarter
Festival: Japanese Bon Festival;
    Feast of Lanterns

Tarot Card: The Moon
Herb: Heart Liverleaf
Incense: Frankincense
Mineral: Garnet
Color: Green
Name of Power: Eloyn

14
Saturday

Moon Sign: Aries
Moon Phase: 3rd Quarter

Tarot Card: The Sun
Herb: Virginia Mouse-ear
Incense: Sandalwood
Mineral: Jade
Color: Black
Name of Power: Pramori

15
Sunday

Moon Sign: Taurus
Moon Phase: 4th Quarter

Tarot Card: Judgment
Herb: Jimson Weed
Incense: Myrrh
Mineral: Lapis Lazuli
Color: Yellow
Name of Power: Rauni

JULY

S	M	T	W	T	F	S
1	2	3	4	5	6	7
8	9	10	11	12	13	14
15	16	17	18	19	20	21
22	23	24	25	26	27	28
29	30	31				

16 *Monday*

Moon Sign: Taurus
Moon Phase: 4th Quarter

Tarot Card: The World
Herb: Leek
Incense: Jasmine
Mineral: Lapis Lingus
Color: White
Name of Power: Gefion

17 *Tuesday*

Moon Sign: Gemini
Moon Phase: 4th Quarter

Tarot Card: The Fool
Herb: Maidenhair
Incense: Benzoin
Mineral: Lapis Lingurius
Color: Red
Name of Power: Ama-terasu-
O-Mi-Kami

18 *Wednesday*

Moon Sign: Gemini
Moon Phase: 4th Quarter

Tarot Card: Ace of Cups
Herb: Mezereon
Incense: Pine
Mineral: Moonstone
Color: Purple
Name of Power: Epona

19 *Thursday*

Moon Sign: Cancer
Moon Phase: 4th Quarter
Festival: Opet

Tarot Card: Two of Cups
Herb: Water Mint
Incense: Cinnamon
Mineral: Opal
Color: Blue
Name of Power: Mut

20   *Friday*

Moon Sign: Cancer
Moon Phase: 4th Quarter

Tarot Card: Three of Cups
Herb: Mullein
Incense: Frankincense
Mineral: Pearl
Color: Green
Name of Power: Damo

21   *Saturday*

Moon Sign: Leo
Moon Phase: New Moon

Tarot Card: Four of Cups
Herb: Violet Bloom
Incense: Sandalwood
Mineral: Ruby
Color: Black
Name of Power: Damo

22   *Sunday*

Moon Sign: Leo
Moon Phase: 1st Quarter
Sun enters Leo

Tarot Card: Five of Cups
Herb: Papaya
Incense: Myrrh
Mineral: Sardonyx
Color: Yellow
Name of Power: Lilyi

			JULY			
S	M	T	W	T	F	S
1	2	3	4	5	6	7
8	9	10	11	12	13	14
15	16	17	18	19	20	21
22	23	24	25	26	27	28
29	30	31				

1990   *July*   1990

23   *Monday*

Moon Sign: Leo
Moon Phase: 1st Quarter
Festival: Rise of Sothis-Sirius

Tarot Card: Six of Cups
Herb: Pimpernel
Incense: Jasmine
Mineral: Topaz
Color: White
Name of Power: Sothis

24   *Tuesday*

Moon Sign: Virgo
Moon Phase: 1st Quarter

Tarot Card: Seven of Cups
Herb: Winter Fern
Incense: Benzoin
Mineral: Turquoise
Color: Red
Name of Power: Iemanja

25   *Wednesday*

Moon Sign: Virgo
Moon Phase: 1st Quarter
Festival: Furrinalia

Tarot Card: Eight of Cups
Herb: Primrose
Incense: Pine
Mineral: Coral Agate
Color: Purple
Name of Power: Furrina

26   *Thursday*

Moon Sign: Libra
Moon Phase: 1st Quarter

Tarot Card: Nine of Cups
Herb: Ragwort
Incense: Cinnamon
Mineral: Greenstone
Color: Blue
Name of Power: Omulu

27
Friday

Moon Sign: Libra
Moon Phase: 1st Quarter

Tarot Card: Ten of Cups
Herb: Rock-Rose
Incense: Frankincense
Mineral: Hawaiite
Color: Green
Name of Power: Hatshepsut

28
Saturday

Moon Sign: Scorpio
Moon Phase: 1st Quarter
Festival: Start of Gathering
       Time in Keltic
       calendar

Tarot Card: Page of Cups
Herb: Sarsaparilla
Incense: Sandalwood
Mineral: Imperial Jade
Color: Black
Name of Power: Mitatron

29
Sunday

Moon Sign: Scorpio
Moon Phase: 2nd Quarter

Tarot Card: Knight of Cups
Herb: Shinleaf
Incense: Myrrh
Mineral: Jet
Color: Yellow
Name of Power: Khesef-Hra-
       Khemiu

JULY

S	M	T	W	T	F	S
1	2	3	4	5	6	7
8	9	10	11	12	13	14
15	16	17	18	19	20	21
22	23	24	25	26	27	28
29	30	31				

30 *Monday*

Moon Sign: Scorpio
Moon Phase: 2nd Quarter

Tarot Card: Queen of Cups
Herb: Star Anise
Incense: Jasmine
Mineral: Tiger Eye
Color: White
Name of Power: Zevao

31 *Tuesday*

Moon Sign: Sagittarius
Moon Phase: 2nd Quarter
Festival: Lughnas Eve

Tarot Card: King of Cups
Herb: Wild Hyssop
Incense: Benzoin
Mineral: Mexican Onyx
Color: Red
Name of Power: Frija

Wednesday

Thursday

Egyptian
Magic and Ritual

Gordon T. G. Hudson

During its long history, Egypt was pre-eminent in the art of magic. The word "magic" as applied here is used in the ritualistic sense of casting spells or conjuring demons to do one's bidding. Magic demands much more sheer knowledge than is possessed by the average man or woman, knowledge of the laws of physical inter-relationship between phenomena as well as of the conditions and laws governing that obscure territory in which physical phenomena are extended into a freer, more unpredictable realm. Magic is concerned with the widening of frontiers between the visible and invisible, reality and illusion, spirit and matter, Deity and man. It is also concerned with the increase and development of every variety of sense perception.

To be a successful magician one must possess an almost encyclopedic knowledge of physical laws, and be able to control the frontiers of all things pertaining thereto. One must investigate all phenomena with the eye of the scientist, scorning no possible hypothesis nor neglecting to take into the fullest consideration the complete structure of our actual and potential being. One must first acquire humility, endless patience, intelligence and much knowledge concerning this Earth and its inhabitants.

In ancient times, by the utterance of a few simple words, magicians were able to change inanimate things to animate, to heal the sick or to bring down the wrath of God upon the un-worthy. The way they did this was by discovering early how to manipulate substance. They knew or realized that Life in its myriad forms was One and everything was part of the Cosmic Plan. It was a small step from that realization to the inescapable

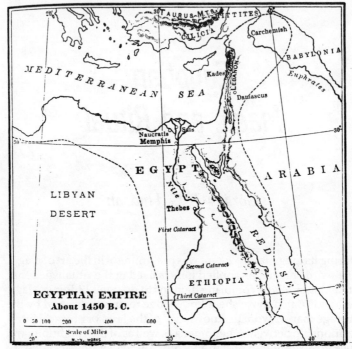

EGYPTIAN EMPIRE
About 1450 B. C.

conclusion the inescapable conclusion that all things are inter-woven into a universal pattern and that *unity* meant sharing a common substance.

What is meant by "substance"? Substance is that which underlies everything in the phenomenal universe—the ether, if you will. Magicians studied the laws of substance and discovered how to manipulate it. They were intimately acquainted with the etheric makeup of matter and, by altering it, were able to make matter do their bidding. Thus the population of ancient Egypt revered all magicians, from the High Priest on down. To give one example, they were able to secure tombs against possible theft. We know that 21 people lost their lives after Tutankhamen's tomb was opened in 1922. We do not, however, know what the death toll was in connection with others which were defiled in the past; the total may well have been in the thousands. What remained of those tombs and their once proud and illustrious occupants is, alas, sad to behold, as in some cases their very persons were violated in the thieves' effort to discover gold and other precious items.

Ritual, the established form for a ceremony, or the order of words prescribed for a special event, was the other side of the coin. It was through ritual, precisely followed, that the Hierarchy ruled the Two Lands. Ritual, correctly performed, was the hand-maiden of magic. Magical prowess and perfect ritual came from the disciplined mind and senses, the virtues of indefatigable industry, the cultivation of a high standard of personal morality and the avoidance of everything which saps insight and spirit. There were risks indeed. The magician imperfectly equipped was liable to be torn to bits mentally, spiritually and physically by the very forces he had summoned and unleashed. One does not beard the lion in his den, still less does one fool around with an angry god!

It was a lonely world because the magician could only hold converse with others of the same ilk. So-called normal folk, with whom he could not commune, were on a totally different wave-length. He was intimately concerned with naked force, elemental as well as cosmic. God was not mocked and neither was the Devil. Let the frivolous and the dilettante beware. So much, then, for background.

The spirit was summoned and dominated in a series of com-manding incantations, through which the magician brought all the resources of his will to bear on the operation. But before he could begin the Ceremony itself, he had to make the necessary preparation.

A magical operation of any difficulty could not be performed in a normal condition of mind and body, and the magician began by consecrating or dedicating himself to the work. This meant he cut himself off from his everyday surroundings and concerns, and excluded all distractions from his mind. The insistence on austerity and the presence of prayers and celebrations of Holy Communion (or its equivalent) in these rituals are surprising at first sight, but they are the result of the principle that magical powers work automatically and regardless of motives. The power of the God in question can be tapped by the use of His name and through forms of prayer to Him (or Her).

There is an apparent dichotomy between the ritual of religion and the seemingly vacuous mouthings of cult priests who tried to put in a good word for their recently deceased Pharaoh or other notable. As an example of the first: "Oh Ra, your son has arrived; gather him to your heart; enfold him in your arms! Oh King, the attainer of purity, take thy place in the boat of the Sun, and range across the sky. Mut will conduct you in your journey of a million years. Travel then, with the imperishable stars!" What the cult priests said I leave to your imagination.

Over a period of time, the Hierarchy had tried numerous

methods of propitiating the gods, and some of these methods were found to be successful. But instead of rejecting the rituals which were found wanting, the priesthood used them for other purposes because they were averse to rejecting anything; they were hoarders in a very real sense. "If it doesn't work for this, then it will work for that," they said. The old was kept, even though it was superceded by superior knowledge.

Not only rituals were retained, but gods were too, which is why there was an enormous number of them. Apep is a case in point. Although he was slain through sympathetic magic with monotonous regularity, he had to be slain repeatedly. The Hierarchy couldn't just get rid of him once and for all; they speared him, cut him with knives, decapitated him, roasted him and finally consumed him by fire, and his evil followers also, *ad nauseum*.

The methods used by the Egyptian priesthood for purification embraced all sorts of processes, including those for making love talismans, or wax images; but they reserved their most impressive ceremonies for the attempt to summon up a "spirit:" a supernatural force or entity of some kind which could be subjugated by the magician and forced to carry out his orders or reveal what it knew. It is this type of operation to which, in the European context, the term "Ritual Magic" particularly refers. The end justified the means in all that the magicians and ritualists did. The goal wasn't oppression of the masses, but conformity to the Will of The Most High in all things. Thus, everything was done in its season, and if procedures were not followed, then disaster overcame the miscreants. This was the atmosphere in which the ancient Egyptian people were surrounded, and perhaps from this we can better understand how priests were able to secure tombs by occult means more efficiently than by other mundane methods.

How then, was the magician able to persuade the gods to do his bidding? It was through words of Power, correctly intoned and following a definite pattern and technique, which furnished him with his weapon against the Gods. If they would not respond to his prayers nor yield to pleading, then he would exert pressure by means of certain words. Sound! That was the secret. He who had mastered sound had mastered all.

In spite of their apparent obsession with death and its trappings, the Egyptians were a happy and contented people. They had a strictly defined moral code to which they adhered. Insofar as *The Book of the Dead* is concerned, it was really a funerary text, usually written on papyrus and only occasionally on leather, placed with the burial of those people sufficiently wealthy to be able to afford a copy. It consisted of detailed instructions on how the deceased was to comport himself or herself in the Underworld, and for that reason it was called the *Book of Coming Forth by Day* (as it was always daylight in the Afterlife). The quality and length of the copy varied in relation to the owner's standing and provision for his or her burial. The *Book of Coming Forth by Day* consists of a number of Chapters or Spells (one source lists 174 Chapters), aimed at the protection of the deceased in the netherworld. The text is found written in hieroglyphs as well as hieratic and demotic scripts, and the best copies are embellished with vignettes at the heads of the chapters and various scenes throughout. The most popular scenes represented are the "Ceremony of the Opening of the Mouth" and the "Weighing of the Heart" in the Hall of Judgment before Osiris. Among the finest extant papyrus copies for private persons are those of Ani and Hunefer (19th dynasty), and the best royal examples are those of Queen Nodjmet and the Princess Nesitanebashru (21st dynasty). Each of these came from the great cache of royal mummies officially discovered in 1881 at Deir El Bahri, where Queen Hatshepsut had her Temple built. All four papyri are in the British Museum in London.

The *Book of Coming Forth by Day* stands at the culmination of a long line of funerary texts. These began with the Pyramid Texts in the 5th and 6th dynasties and graduate through the Coffin Texts of the Middle Kingdon to their fullest form at the beginning of the New Kingdom. The Coffin Texts were inscribed in a conventional sequence on the interior and exterior of the wooden coffins of the First Intermediate Period and Middle Kingdom. The spells were meant to secure access to the next world for the dead person and the preservation of his or her spirit from the manifold dangers which could and would beset it. The rolls of papyrus range from lengths of 120 feet to a miserable scrap on which a spell or two has been inscribed for the benefit of a poor man.

Other books include the *Book of Gates*, the *Book of What is in the Underworld* and *Seeking the Abode of the Most High*. The number of chapters in any one copy varies, as does the content and the selection of the chapters to be included by the individual owners.

Priests owned a large proportion of the land, and manned at their own expense their very own fleet of merchantmen. Temples prospered during the reign of Ramses III, as he made vast donations out of public funds to the priesthood of Amen-Ra. Good and benevolent as he was, Ramses III discovered a plot against his life hatched by one of his secondary wives. The scheme was brought to light and, during the trial, it was revealed that a number of conspirators, resorting to magic, had made statuettes of wax with the names of individuals inscribed whom they wished to bewitch. Magic scrolls were also found. Nearly forty people were involved, each of whom took his or her own life. Ramses III died before the trial ended, perhaps showing how efficacious the power of magic was!

As mentioned earlier, magic figured prominently in safe-guarding the repose of royalty. Their tombs were sealed not only with stones, mortar and locks but with the most potent spells and curses known to man. The forces in the ether seem to become more concentrated and virulent as time passes. One does not mock the gods nor their emissaries, for priests in one form or another are the custodians of the Mysteries and the guardians of tradition. One does not obliterate a civilization or a way of life by killing off the priests who are its guardians, for they transcend mortality and will be with us to the end. Thus occult knowledge and practice live on.

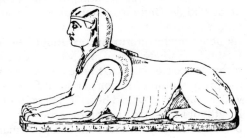

Isis

deTraci Regula

Ancient and beloved, Isis nurtured her native Egypt and then wandered with the Greeks and Romans across the face of the Western world. Her priesthood was admired because of the wisdom and purity of her clergy, yet Isis was also a goddess of erotic and romantic love. She counted among her followers emperors and commoners, freewomen and slaves, merchants and seafarers. All races were admitted to her temple and to the ranks of her priesthood, which accepted both unmarried men and women and married couples. She turned away none, and has been revered since classical times as the one deity above fate, who could rewrite the stars' forebodings. Artists and craftsmen invoked her as the ultimate muse, while at the same period early scientists felt her presence among their alembic and crucibles, and texts on alchemy were written in Isis' name. Along with Serapis, a dynamic aspect of her slain husband Osiris, she presided over the magnificent Library of Alexandria and the school of medicine which set the standard for the education of physicians. At the same time, many of her followers were cured of their ailments merely by spending a night in her temple in the hope of receiving a healing dream or a vision of the goddess.

As the Roman Legions traveled, so did the worship of Isis. She was worshipped in ancient London and at many places in France and Germany. Throughout the Middle East and on the islands of the Aegean Sea her temples were common, and she was often referred to in the same breath as the native goddesses, creating titles such as Isis-Aphrodite.

When the temples of other gods and goddesses were burned and broken, their priests and priestesses fled to the walls of the sanctuaries of Isis and were welcomed to worship their fallen deities within the refuge of her temples. Hers was the last pagan temple to hold worshippers, on the sacred island of Philae in Upper Egypt. But in C.E. 595, centuries after the official banning of the pagan faiths by Constantine in 383, her last sanctuary was closed by force and its priesthood disbanded. Then she became Isis Amenit, the Hidden Goddess, and draped her worship in disguise. Many of her titles were applied to the increasingly popular Virgin Mary, and statues of Isis nursing her son Horus were renamed and placed in churches. A medieval manuscript even preserved the name of Isis, mentioning an "Ysis, Ladye of Herbs," showing that Isis' skill in creating medicines was not forgotten.

In the past century there has been a great resurgence of interest in and worship of Isis, beginning with the expansion of archeological research in the mid-nineteenth century. Known to both Witches and Magicians, Isis is simultaneously a "safe" deity for a beginner to contact yet also a powerful and indomitable Goddess. As one ceremonial magician commented with surprise, "She's no lightweight. You can't just order her to appear!" However, when requested in great need or with genuine devotion, she will make her presence known to her worshippers.

The worship of Isis has always been a revealed, initiatory faith, with great emphasis placed on the would-be initiate's personal contact with the goddess, usually through dreams. In Apuleius' *Metamorphoses*, a second-century "magical novel," the aspirant Lucius is first rescued by the goddess Isis from his imprisonment in the body of an ass, when she appears to him with instructions on what he is to do to restore himself to human form. She then appears that same night in a dream to one of her priests, to assure that Lucius is given the chance to carry out her instructions. Later she appears again to him in dreams, indicating that she wishes Lucius to undergo various initiations. It is clear that the decision to permit an aspirant to experience an initiation was not the decision of either the priesthood or the prospective initiate, but that of Isis alone.

Modern followers of Isis number in the tens of thousands, with about seven thousand members of the Fellowship of Isis based in Enniscorthy, Ireland. Many others are members of neo-Egyptian religious groups or practice their faith alone. Since the personal guidance of the goddess is essential to the practice of the worship of Isis, a good portion of her devotees prefer to rely on dreams and intuition to help them explore their relationship with the goddess. But exclusive devotion to Isis as sole deity has never been necessary; she has always welcomed other god forces into her temples. Several worshippers have noted that her energies blend especially well with Herne, the stag-headed hunting god of Celtic Britain. Among the Egyptian gods, besides Osiris, Isis resonates with Tahuti (Thoth), the jackal- or dog-headed Anubis, who is a guide to both the souls of the dead and the souls of those who are engaged in astral projection; and Min, an ever-erect god of fecundity and sexuality. Among the goddesses, Isis is often paired with her sister Nephthys and frequently takes on the aspects of Hathor, goddess of love, to the point that their images in Egyptian art are often indistinguishable. Isis was also associated with the cat-goddess Bast. Since the Egyptian word for Isis was *Ast* or *Auset*, and a word for soul was *ba*, some Egyptians believed that Bast was a symbol of the soul of Isis.

Throughout her 6,000-year history, Isis has been an evolving, changing goddess, taking on new attributes and skills as the centuries passed. She is a perfect Goddess-figure for us today, when our lives are beset by rapid changes. As a Goddess of Light she can illuminate many areas darkened by confusion and despair, and as a Star-Goddess she can beckon us onward as we become an interplanetary and interstellar species. Think of this when you next look at the night sky and see Sirius, her sacred star, sparkling at the heel of the constellation Orion, the stars sacred to her husband Osiris. Sirius, which is also known as Sothis, should be easy to locate—it's the brightest star in the sky.

Egyptian Magick

The Foundation of Modern Religion and Magick

Gerald and Betty Schueler

Webster's Dictionary defines magic as : "the pretended art of producing effects or controlling events by charms, spells, and rituals supposed to govern certain natural or supernatural forces . . ." Religion is defined as "1. belief in a divine or superhuman power or powers to be obeyed and worshipped as the creator(s) and ruler(s) of the universe. 2. expression of this belief in conduct and ritual." To the casual reader, the definitions of magic and religion seem to be the same. It is the word "pretended" in Webster's definition of magic that sets the two words apart, both in the dictionary and in the minds of Christians. This is unfortunate, because it has divided mankind into two major opposing factions: the "true" believers (Christians) and the heathens (non-Christians). It has only been in the last century that Christians have learned to tolerate and accept other legitimate forms of religion in the world.

With this new toleration has come a renewed interest in the roots from which modern religions have evolved. For unlike the other inhabitants of our planet, the human species deliberately builds upon the foundations laid by its forebears. By understanding the composition of our religious foundations, we are able to use that knowledge to strengthen and improve our current religious convictions.

Although modern archaeological findings constantly change the concepts of our history, at the present historians agree that the Mediterranean area was the cradle of civilization and Egypt the center of that civilization. The religious practices of the ancient Egyptians probably influenced all of our contemporary major religions, at least to some degree. The accompanying chart shows the six major religions of the world and their probable evolution from the ancient Egyptian religion. The arrows on the chart show the likely paths of evolution and interaction that might have occurred between the religions.

ANCIENT EGYPTIAN RELIGION

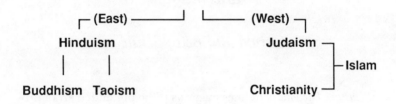

The ancient Egyptians' civilization was an amalgamation of many diverse cultures. The people of Egypt were very tolerant of foreigners and often adopted their customs and deities, modifying them to suit their own needs. As a result, they were probably the most polytheistic people who ever lived. As the early Egyptian civilization matured, its religion became a homogenized blend of theology, superstition, myth, and magick. The religion had something to offer everyone. If it didn't, a person was free to alter the religion to suit himself. Some of the Egyptian theological concepts that have endured through today are those of reincarnation, resurrection, creationism, divine will, monotheism, polytheism, afterdeath judgment, and divine justice (karma), to name just a few.

The theology of the ancient Egyptians was intrinsically bound with colorful strands of myth and superstition. The same could be said of ancient Egyptian Magick, a magick that was used to form the cornerstone of all Western occultism. Most of the teachings and magickal techniques found in modern schools of magick were taught in some form in ancient Egypt.

The Egyptians taught that invisible worlds surrounded our physical Earth, and that these worlds were ruled by powerful and intelligent beings. They taught that man has a series of subtle bodies housed within the physical body, and that consciousness could travel about in these subtle bodies and visit the subtle worlds and their inhabitants. Today we would call these regions planes and subplanes. The magickal ability to visit the various planes is called astral traveling, or out-of-the-body experiences.

Magick can be defined as: the deliberate use of the will to bring about a desired change in one's self or in one's environment. There are two main modes of magick, Low Magick and High Magick. Egyptian Magick contains both of these forms.

Low Magick was practiced to control the physical world. It was a very practical magick, usually selfish in nature. It was used to cast spells, concoct potions, and control other people. Probably the best known Low Magick operation was the creation of protective talismans. The Egyptians used many talismans for protection, but the best known, and most widely used, were the Amulet of Isis, the Tet of Osiris, the Eye of Horus, and the Scarab of Kephera. The Amulet of Isis was used to protect against decay, decomposition, and forgetfulness. The Tet of Osiris gave the bearer stability, and power over all manner of confusion and disorder. The Eye of Horus was probably the most popular of all. It was used for many reasons, from general protection against evil to enhancing the "third eye" of occult vision. The Scarab of Kephera gave protection over births, and was often used to ensure a good beginning in any new venture. Egyptian High Magick was practiced for spiritual development. The ultimate goal was to unite the microcosmic self with the macrocosmic Godhead, the human with the divine. This goal was not only a philosophical concept but it was also religion in the true sense of the word. That is why it is almost impossible to separate Egyptian religion from Egyptian Magick. The Egyptians blended the two together indistinguishably.

Both Low Magick and High Magick make use of specialized rituals. Some have been translated from the walls of ancient tombs and are called the Pyramid Texts. Those written on papyrus, and buried with the dead, are called Coffin Texts. They comprise what we call *The Book of the Dead.*

Signs in common use.	Signs employed more rarely.	Equivalent in English.
	—	A (as in father).
	—	I (sounded as ee in see).
	—	U (sounded as oo in food).
		B
		P
	—	F
		G (deep guttural).
		K
		KH (sounded like the Hebrew ח).
	—	D
		T
		M
		N
		L
		S
	—	SH
		H
		J

Many of the ancient Egyptian texts have been adapted and/or enhanced by the Western magick groups. Dr. W. W. Westcott, one of the founders of the Hermetic Order of the Golden Dawn at the end of the last century, called these texts the *"Per-em-Hru . . . the oldest book in the world as yet discovered."* He went on to say, *"The Ritual of the Dead,* generally speaking, is a collection of hymns and prayers in the form of a series of ceremonial Rituals to enable the man to unite himself with Osiris the Redeemer. After this union he is no longer called the man, but Osiris, with whom he is now symbolically identified." (*The Pillars*).

The Egyptian funerary texts are traditionally called *The Book of the Dead*, but the title of Chapter 1 is translated "The Beginning of the Chapters of Coming into the Light." The phrase "coming into the light" is the Egyptian title for these texts. The *Book of the Dead* should really be called *Pert Em Hru* or simply *Coming into the Light*. The first word, *pert*, means "coming forth" or "appearing." The second word, *em*, can be almost any preposition. The third word, *hru*, usually means "day" but it can also mean "light" and "sun." The phrase *pert em hru* can therefore mean "coming forth like (or with) the sun (or day)" or "appearing with light (or the sun)."

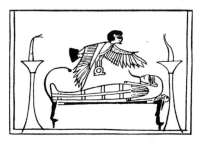

Magick teaches that light is a symbol of consciousness. Therefore, this title refers to a process of coming into conscious awareness, especially when such a process is also highly creative. The process of creative consciousness was represented by the scarab god Khepera, the god of creative manifestation and of dawning consciousness. Khepera was the rising sun and thus he was an aspect of Ra, the chief solar deity of the ancient Egyptians. Technically, Kephera was the sun during sunrise, Ra was the sun at noon, and Tem (sometimes spelled Tmu) was the sun at sunset.

The Egyptians believed that the daily rising and setting of the sun was a solar expression of the same principle by which man lived on earth. As the sun set in the West, and disappeared from the world, so man died at the end of his life. As the same sun rose again in the morning, so man would come into birth again in a new incarnation. This idea of a repeated embodiment in flesh (reincarnation) was represented by the lunar god Osiris. *Asa* or *Ausar* is the personification of the reincarnation principle. The name means "the god who created (caused) a throne." Here the throne refers to the ego, the center or seat of power for every human being. Another spelling of the name Osiris contains the glyph *as*, which is a "chair" exoterically and "embodiment" esoterically. This ideograph for Osiris means "the cause of embodiment." It can also be translated as "the Osirified" in the sense of that which can be embodied in the same way that Osiris was resurrected by the magick of Isis, his sister/wife. In occultism, this "Osirified" is called the Oversoul or Reincarnating Ego. Another meaning of Osirified is "initiated." The title "Osiris" was given to magicians who were successfully initiated into the Egyptian system of magick. In *The Papyrus of Ani*, for example, the scribe Ani is called "Osiris Ani," or "the Osirified Ani" to show that he was an initiate of the Egyptian mysteries and therefore similar to the god Osiris.

As Osiris oversees the reincarnation process, so the ibis-headed Thoth oversees the good and evil that we accumulate during our lifetime. The Egyptians equated *karma*, the universal law of cause and effect, with *maat*. The goddess Maat was the consort of Thoth. She was symbolized by a feather which literally could mean: "truth," "justice," "righteousness" or "law."

The *Pert Em Hru* is a collection of sacred texts in the form of rituals and spells used by the magicians of ancient Egypt. Many address the various states and stages of the invisible worlds. The named used as a general term for the invisible worlds was *Neter-Khert*. It is usually translated as "underworld," but in a magical sense refers to the Magical Universe. This universe was divided into many regions. Probably the largest was called *tuat*, which literally means "astral plane." Many states and stages were known. For example, there were twenty-one Pylons of Osiris, seven Arits (the word *arit* literally means "reception hall"), the fields of the Sekhet-Hetep, and a huge hall of Maati where the nome-deities resided (the country of Egypt was divided into 42 states or *nomes*, and each nome was presided over by a local deity). The Hall of Maati bears striking similarities with the kama-loka of modern theosophy. The Sekhet-Hetep (literally "fields of peace and nourishment") bears striking similarities with the devachan of modern theosophy, and the summerland of the spiritualists. The table below shows the main planes taught by the ancient Egyptians and their correspondences with modern occultism.

TABLE OF THE COSMIC PLANES

Occult	Egyptian
Spiritual	———
Abyss	Abyss
Mental	Sekhet-Hetepet
Astral	Tuat
Etheric	Amentet

The chapters of *The Book of the Dead* provide advice and give guidance to the magician during the ascent into the subtle planes above the physical world of matter as well as during the return back to the physical body. They consist of both rituals and spells and contain the bulk of Egyptian magickal tradition. The ancient Egyptians believed that man consists of much more than a physical body. They divided man's constitution into a graduated series of parts.

Overshadowing, or enveloping, the physical body was a series of subtle bodies, each more ethereal than the last. The first of these, and the most dense, was the shadow or *khaibit*. The next was the *ka*, the body of emotions. This was followed by the heart, *ab* (or *hati-ab,* which can be literally translated "outer heart"). The next was the soul or *ba* which was linked to the ka through the ab. The ba rested in the spirit-body or *sah* (sometimes *sahu*), which was presided over by the spirit or *khu* (quite often the word *khu* was used to denote the subtle body in general, rather than a specific component). These, and other designations for man's components, were all governed by the highest, the *khabs*, the divine component which means a star.

The principle of man's divided constitution was adopted by many groups, including the Vedanta Hindus and Western occultists. The chart below shows the relationship of the parts according to the various ideologies.

TABLE OF MAN'S MAJOR COMPONENTS/BODIES

Vedanta	Occult	Egyptian
atma	divine	khabs
buddhi	spiritual	khu
manas	higher mind	ba
	lower mind	ab
kama	desire	ka
prana	etheric	khaibit
rupa	physical	khat

In order to conduct many of the rituals outlined in *The Book of the Dead*, you must construct a god-form and then speak or act as if you were that deity. This magickal technique is well known to modern magick. For example, it was taught by the Hermetic

Order of the Golden Dawn as well as by Aleister Crowley. To construct a god-form, you must imagine that your aura or Body of Light (the Egyptians often used the *khu* as a general term for the Body of Light) has the appearance of the deity. This is possible because the Body of Light is plastic and can change its shape easily under conscious direction. Enter your Body of Light and then concentrate on the form of the deity and will your own Body of Light to take on this appearance. It may be helpful to place your physical body in a special position, or hold a special device similar to that held by the deity. For example, to assume the god-form of Horus the child (Harpocrates), you might place your index finger against your lower lip, as Horus is often shown doing. If you want your god-form to be authoritative, you might hold a scepter, the symbol for power and authority. A god-form of Ra might hold an ankh, the symbol of life, and so on. If holding a physical object helps you to produce a god-form, then do so. If imagining such an object is just as easy for you, then use your imagination to construct a "thought-form" of the object. To perform these rituals successfully, you must be able to feel like you are the deity, and whatever it takes to do this is what you should use. There are no hard and fast rules.

After three thousand years of greatness, the Egyptian empire fell to foreign invaders. Much of the Egyptian religious heritage degenerated and was lost. Fortunately, the lofty ideas and psycho-physiological insights expressed by the original authors still exist today. They can be found in their pure form in the hieroglyphic texts that have survived the centuries. They can also be found, in an adapted form, in the major religious and occult ideologies of today.

An Egyptian Ritual

Gerald and Betty Schueler

The following ritual is in two parts. The first part is to be conducted at sunrise, just as the sun rises over the Eastern horizon. The second part is to be conducted at sunset, just as the sun descends into the West.

SUNRISE.

Stand facing the rising sun with your arms outstretched toward its first rays of light. You should be wearing gold in some form, either jewelry or perhaps a gold robe. The smell of olibanum should be in the air. Say,

"Honor to you Kephera, the self-manifested Beautiful One. You shine light from the horizon. You shine light on the world. Your radiant light is penetrating. I have come before you. May you be with me throughout the day."

See the sun rising up before you as the beetle-headed god Kephera. Feel the first rays of the sun entering your body and say,

"Honor to you who are in the Boat of Radiant Light. Sunlight, even a single ray of sunlight, can exalt me and protect me for one million years. The god Kephera is in his boat. He has overcome the serpent Apep. Like Kephera, I too will overcome my enemies. I will be truth speaking. I will be protected against evil."

Visualize the rays of Khepera bathing your body in a protective aura of light and feel gratitude for his protection. Assume the god-form of Kephera. Visualize the rising sun as the Atet Boat (Boat of Relationships). Close by saying,

"Before my two eyes appears the shining spirit that is above flesh. My heart expands with the breaths of truth in the Atet Boat. I am eternity and everlastingness."

Bathe in the sunlight and spiritual protective power of the rising sun for a few moments.

SUNSET. Stand facing the setting sun and say,

"Honor to you, O Ra, who shines as the god Tem when you set. Beautiful is your radiant light. You shine upon your own mother. You rise up as the King of the Gods, and cause the Goddess of the Night Sky to show obeisance to your face. Your cyclic pilgrimage across heaven expands your heart."

See the sun setting in the West before you as the human-headed god Tem. Feel the last rays of the sun entering your body and say,

"O Lord of Eternity, whose many transformations are mighty, O Lord of the Secret Chamber, the Guide of the Tuat, you are the governor of those where you set in the night sky. The goddess Isis embraces you when you set, and she drives the demons away from the entrance of your pathways. Your light shines over the world like fine gold."

Visualize the rays of Tem bathing your body in a protective aura of light and feel gratitude for his protection. Assume the god-form of Tem. Visualize the setting sun as the Sektet Boat (Boat of Dreams) and close by saying,

"I pass in strength across heaven, and then I set in the Sektet Boat. May the beauty of the Sektet Boat strengthen my consciousness. May I have the strength of a Master of the Earth. May I rise up and be strengthened like Tem every day without faltering."

The Sistrum

Egyptian Sistrum

At temples throughout the length of Egypt, the ritual silence would be abruptly broken by the call of the magickal rattle called a sistrum. Sacred to both Hathor and Isis, the sound of a sistrum being shaken was considered to be an offering as tangible as food and incense. Traditionally, the sistrum was made of metal and consisted of three or four rods set loosely in a loop of metal and attached to a crossbar which was in turn attached to a handle. Often metal disks were strung on the rods to increase the sound. Ancient sistra varied considerably in tone, ranging from a sweet, musical sound to a harsh clashing as the disks jolted together and against the sides of the loop.

Since the form of the sistrum resembled an ankh, sistra were considered symbols of life. Plutarch wrote in his book *Isis and Osiris* that the shaking of sistra in the temples was a sign of the continual motion necessary to life. Today, the sistrum is still used to accompany religious ceremonies by the Coptic Christian churches.

—deTraci Regula

The Souls of Osiris and Ra meeting to embrace each other in Busiris.

Magickal Names

It was believed by the ancient Egyptians that to know the name of a god, or entity, and to address him by it, would not only force an answer but would force the god to obey the caller in all things. Sir James Frazer (*The Golden Bough*, Macmillan, 1922) gives the Myth of Ra and Isis, which tells how she obtained the most secret name of Ra, and by doing so was able to become a goddess herself. Isis was described as "a woman who possessed words of power," highly skilled in the healing arts. At this time Ra had grown old and "dribbled at the mouth, his spittle falling upon the earth." Isis made a serpent, from a mixture of earth and of Ra's spittle, magick-ally gave it life and laid it in the path where she knew Ra would walk. The serpent then bit Ra and he cried out for help from "the children of the gods." Isis came running "with her craft (of healing), whose mouth is full of the breath of life, whose spells chase pain away, whose word maketh the dead to live." Ra told her how he had been bitten and she said "Tell me thy name, divine Father, for the man shall live who is called by this name." Ra told her many of the names by which he was known, all the time growing weaker. But Isis refused to help, saying "That was not thy name that thou speakest unto me. Oh tell it me, that the poison may depart; for he shall live whose name is named." Finally Ra gave her his true name and she caused the poison to flow away. And she became "the Queen of the Gods, *she who knows Ra and his true name.*"

The name that was the object of a curse brought down evil upon its owner, while the name that was the object of a blessing brought many good things. To the Egyptian the name was as much a part of a man's being as his soul. In the text inscribed on the walls of the pyramid of Pepi I (c. 3200 BCE) it states: "Pepi hath been purified. He hath taken in his hand the *mah* staff, he hath provided himself with his throne, and he hath taken his seat in the boat of the great and little companies of the gods . . . Pepi goeth forward with his flesh, Pepi is happy with his name, and he liveth with his *ka* (double)." Curiously enough only the body and name and double of the king are mentioned, just as if these three constituted his whole economy; and it is noteworthy what importance is attached to the name in this passage.

There is similar mention of names in the pyramid of Pepi II. There we read "If the name of Shu, the lord of the upper shrine in Annu, flourisheth then Pepi shall flourish. If the name of Tefnut, the lady of the lower shrine in Annu, flourisheth the name of Pepi shall be established and this, his pyramid, shall be established to all eternity. If the name of Seb flourisheth at the 'homage of the earth,' then the name of Pepi shall flourish and this, his pyramid, shall flourish . . ." and so on, with mention of many other gods and their names. This prayer was the origin of most of the prayers and texts which had for their object the "making the name to germinate or flourish." They were copied frequently in the Saite, Ptolemaic and Roman periods.

Without a name no man could be identified in the judgment, and as a man only came into being upon this earth when his name was pronounced, so the future life could only be attained after the gods of the world beyond the grave had become acquainted with it and had uttered it. When the deceased comes to the Hall of Judgment, at the very beginning of his speech he says: "Homage to thee, O Great Lord, thou Lord of Maati, I have come to thee, O my Lord, and I have brought myself hither that I may behold thy beauties. I know thee, and I know thy name, and I know the names of the two and forty gods who exist with thee in this Hall of Maati."

After the Judgment he acquires the mystical name of "He who is equipped with the flowers and the dweller in his olive tree," and it is only after he has uttered this name that the gods say "Pass onwards." There then follows a great exchange of names of gods and even of the many different sections of the Hall of Maati. Eventually he passes through seven such halls, each with a gate guarded by a doorkeeper, a watcher, and a herald. Beside the seven halls there are twenty-one hidden pylons of the house of Osiris in the Elysian Fields, each bearing a name.

This example of the use of names possessing magickal powers illustrates the semi-religious views on the subject of names which the Egyptians held.

—*Egyptian Magic*, Sir Wallis Budge, 1899

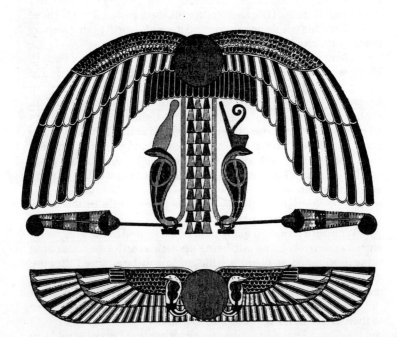

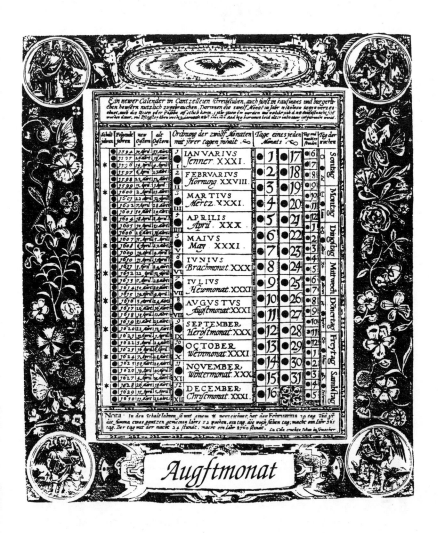

Augstmonat

August

Monday

Tuesday

1   *Wednesday*

Moon Sign: Sagittarius   Tarot Card: Ace of Pentacles
Moon Phase: 2nd Quarter   Herb: Althea
Festival: Lughnasadh;   Incense: Pine
         Fire Festival   Mineral: Montana Ruby
                                 Color: Purple
                                 Name of Power: Lugh

2   *Thursday*

Moon Sign: Capricorn   Tarot Card: Two of Pentacles
Moon Phase: 2nd Quarter   Herb: Barberry
                                 Incense: Cinnamon
                                 Mineral: Ox-eye
                                 Color: Blue
                                 Name of Power: Nas/Boi

3

Friday

Moon Sign: Capricorn
Moon Phase: 2nd Quarter

Tarot Card: Three of Pentacles
Herb: Birthwort
Incense: Frankincense
Mineral: Pigeonblood Agate
Color: Green
Name of Power: Hapiu

4

Saturday

Moon Sign: Capricorn
Moon Phase: 2nd Quarter

Tarot Card: Four of Pentacles
Herb: Blue Flag
Incense: Sandalwood
Mineral: Rainbow Agate
Color: Black
Name of Power: Elchim

5

Sunday

Moon Sign: Aquarius
Moon Phase: 2nd Quarter

Tarot Card: Five of Pentacles
Herb: Buttercup
Incense: Myrrh
Mineral: Topaz
Color: Yellow
Name of Power: Osiris

			AUGUST			
S	M	T	W	T	F	S
				1	2	3	4
5	6	7	8	9	10	11
12	13	14	15	16	17	18
19	20	21	22	23	24	25
26	27	28	29	30	31	

6   *Monday*

Moon Sign: Aquarius
Moon Phase: Full Moon (Wort)

Tarot Card: Six of Pentacles
Herb: Celandine
Incense: Jasmine
Mineral: Star Topaz
Color: White
Name of Power: Baramy

7   *Tuesday*

Moon Sign: Pisces
Moon Phase: 3rd Quarter

Tarot Card: Seven of Pentacles
Herb: Comfrey
Incense: Benzoin
Mineral: Zebra Stone
Color: Red
Name of Power: Yemanjá

8   *Wednesday*

Moon Sign: Pisces
Moon Phase: 3rd Quarter

Tarot Card: Eight of Pentacles
Herb: Desert Tea
Incense: Pine
Mineral: Aquamarine
Color: Purple
Name of Power: Neri

9   *Thursday*

Moon Sign: Aries
Moon Phase: 3rd Quarter

Tarot Card: Nine of Pentacles
Herb: English Ivy
Incense: Cinnamon
Mineral: Beryl
Color: Blue
Name of Power: Tarchimache

10   *Friday*

Moon Sign: Aries
Moon Phase: 3rd Quarter

Tarot Card: Ten of Pentacles
Herb: Feverfew
Incense: Frankincense
Mineral: Chrysoberyl
Color: Green
Name of Power: Yasodhara

11   *Saturday*

Moon Sign: Taurus
Moon Phase: 3rd Quarter

Tarot Card: Page of Pentacles
Herb: Ginger
Incense: Sandalwood
Mineral: Alexandrite
Color: Black
Name of Power: Clare

12   *Sunday*

Moon Sign: Taurus
Moon Phase: 3rd Quarter

Tarot Card: Knight of Pentacles
Herb: Hedge Bindweed
Incense: Myrrh
Mineral: Golden Beryl
Color: Yellow
Name of Power: Felicitas

AUGUST

S	M	T	W	T	F	S
			1	2	3	4
5	6	7	8	9	10	11
12	13	14	15	16	17	18
19	20	21	22	23	24	25
26	27	28	29	30	31	

13

Monday

Moon Sign: Taurus
Moon Phase: 4th Quarter

Tarot Card: Queen of Pentacles
Herb: Herb Robert
Incense: Jasmine
Mineral: Morganite
Color: White
Name of Power: Hecate

14

Tuesday

Moon Sign: Gemini
Moon Phase: 4th Quarter

Tarot Card: King of Pentacles
Herb: Houseleek
Incense: Benzoin
Mineral: Spinel
Color: Red
Name of Power: Ababaloy

15

Wednesday

Moon Sign: Gemini
Moon Phase: 4th Quarter
Festival: Asunción
          Dog Days end

Tarot Card: Ace of Swords
Herb: Juniper
Incense: Pine
Mineral: Topaz
Color: Purple
Name of Power: Diana

16

Thursday

Moon Sign: Cancer
Moon Phase: 4th Quarter

Tarot Card: Two of Swords
Herb: Lemon
Incense: Cinnamon
Mineral: Garnet
Color: Blue
Name of Power: Tana

17
Friday

Moon Sign: Cancer
Moon Phase: 4th Quarter

Tarot Card: Three of Swords
Herb: Mallow
Incense: Frankincense
Mineral: Cape Ruby
Color: Green
Name of Power: Amenartus

18
Saturday

Moon Sign: Leo
Moon Phase: 4th Quarter

Tarot Card: Four of Swords
Herb: Milfoil
Incense: Sandalwood
Mineral: Almandine
Color: Black
Name of Power: Sachiel

19
Sunday

Moon Sign: Leo
Moon Phase: 4th Quarter
Festival: Vinalia

Tarot Card: Five of Swords
Herb: Mistletoe
Incense: Myrrh
Mineral: Spessartite
Color: Yellow
Name of Power: Venus

AUGUST

S	M	T	W	T	F	S
			1	2	3	4
5	6	7	8	9	10	11
12	13	14	15	16	17	18
19	20	21	22	23	24	25
26	27	28	29	30	31	

20   *Monday*

Moon Sign: Virgo
Moon Phase: New Moon

Tarot Card: Six of Swords
Herb: Shepherd's Club
Incense: Jasmine
Mineral: Topazolite
Color: White
Name of Power: Mata

21   *Tuesday*

Moon Sign: Virgo
Moon Phase: 1st Quarter

Tarot Card: Seven of Swords
Herb: Nutmeg
Incense: Benzoin
Mineral: Hyacinth Zircon
Color: Red
Name of Power: Mes-Ptah

22   *Wednesday*

Moon Sign: Libra
Moon Phase: 1st Quarter

Tarot Card: Eight of Swords
Herb: Pawpaw
Incense: Pine
Mineral: Watermelon Tour-
    maline
Color: Purple
Name of Power: Rogdno

23   *Thursday*

Moon Sign: Libra
Moon Phase: 1st Quarter
Sun enters Virgo
Festival: Moira's Day

Tarot Card: Nine of Swords
Herb: Pinkroot
Incense: Cinnamon
Mineral: Quartz Crystal
Color: Blue
Name of Power: Moira

24   *Friday*

Moon Sign: Libra
Moon Phase: 1st Quarter

Tarot Card: Ten of Swords
Herb: Poison Parsley
Incense: Frankincense
Mineral: Violet Tourmaline
Color: Green
Name of Power: Mania

25   *Saturday*

Moon Sign: Scorpio
Moon Phase: 1st Quarter

Tarot Card: Page of Swords
Herb: Privet
Incense: Sandalwood
Mineral: Kunzite
Color: Black
Name of Power: Ops

26   *Sunday*

Moon Sign: Scorpio
Moon Phase: 1st Quarter

Tarot Card: Knight of Swords
Herb: Cocash Weed
Incense: Myrrh
Mineral: Smoky Quartz
Color: Yellow
Name of Power: Lolmischo

AUGUST

S	M	T	W	T	F	S
			1	2	3	4
5	6	7	8	9	10	11
12	13	14	15	16	17	18
19	20	21	22	23	24	25
26	27	28	29	30	31	

27
Monday

Moon Sign: Sagittarius
Moon Phase: 1st Quarter

Tarot Card: Queen of Swords
Herb: Rosemary
Incense: Jasmine
Mineral: Amethyst
Color: White
Name of Power: Nut

28
Tuesday

Moon Sign: Sagittarius
Moon Phase: 2nd Quarter

Tarot Card: King of Swords
Herb: Sassafras
Incense: Benzoin
Mineral: Citrine
Color: Red
Name of Power: Nephthys

29
Wednesday

Moon Sign: Sagittarius
Moon Phase: 2nd Quarter

Tarot Card: Ace of Swords
Herb: Skullcap
Incense: Pine
Mineral: Prasiolite
Color: Purple
Name of Power: Hathor

30
Thursday

Moon Sign: Capricorn
Moon Phase: 2nd Quarter

Tarot Card: Two of Wands
Herb: Sticklewort
Incense: Cinnamon
Mineral: Aventurine
Color: Blue
Name of Power: Charisteria

31   *Friday*

Moon Sign: Capricorn
Moon Phase: 2nd Quarter

Tarot Card: Three of Wands
Herb: Wax Myrtle
Incense: Frankincense
Mineral: Bucklandite
Color: Green
Name of Power: Gana

Saturday

Sunday

AUGUST

S	M	T	W	T	F	S
			1	2	3	4
5	6	7	8	9	10	11
12	13	14	15	16	17	18
19	20	21	22	23	24	25
26	27	28	29	30	31	

A witch working a magickal cure on a man's foot.
(After Ulrich Molitor, De Lamiis, 1489)

The Magick of the Old Religion

Raymond Buckland

In the popular mind the word "Witch" is interchangeable with
"magician" or "caster of spells." For the unthinking person there
is usually no concept of the religious aspects of Wicca. Indeed, the
most common reason for people to be accused of "witchcraft" in
the Middle Ages was because their neighbors said they had
"bewitched" them, or their cattle or crops. Bewitched them meant
put a spell on them.

Of course it is not necessary to be a Witch in order to work
magick, be it putting spells on people or things, or healing the
sick, or manifesting one's desires. Anyone can do these things (or
attempt to do them) and in so doing that person becomes a
"Magician," not a Witch. Magick is a practice, whilst Witchcraft is
a religion. Yet, as with practitioners of virtually all religions,

Witches can, and do, do magick.

What sort of magick do Witches actually do? First and foremost, regardless of the objective, it is a *positive* form of magick. In Wicca there is but one law and that is: *An' it harm none, do what thou wilt* (in other words, do whatever you wish to do but, in doing it, make certain it will harm no one, not even yourself).

One of the magickal beliefs in Wicca is that there is a "power" which emanates from the human body. Exactly what constitutes this power we do not know. It seems sufficient that it is there, has been proven so to our satisfaction, and it can be used to cause things to happen, to work magick. Certainly science has agreed with Wicca on this point. The late Dr. Gerald Gardner pointed out that there had been experiments done at Cornell University which confirmed this belief. In the magazine *Everyday Science and Mechanics*, as long ago as 1932, there appeared an article which stated: "Rays emitted from human blood, fingertips, noses and eyes, kill yeasts and other micro-organisms, according to Professor Otto Rahn, working at Cornell University. Yeast, such as used in making bread, was killed in five minutes merely by the radiation from the fingertips of one person. When a quartz plate, ½-inch thick, was interposed it took fifteen minutes for the yeast to die. In tests of fingers it was found that the right hand was stronger than the left, even in strong-handed persons."

As I point out in my book *Buckland's Complete Book of Witchcraft*, Professor Rahn spoke on the subject at a meeting of the American Association for the Advancement of Science, and Dr. Harold S. Burr, of Yale University, spoke of similar experiments when addressing the Third International Cancer Congress. In my book I go on to give experiments you can do to prove to yourself the existence of this power emission, for everyone possesses it.

But this is not only a power to destroy. Far from it. It is a power that can be directed over immense distances and can be used to do tremendous good.

There are many different traditions, or denominations, of Wicca. Each has its own way of working. Solitary Witches also have their own preferences. All I can do here, therefore, is to give some idea of just a few of the ways used by various individuals and groups I have encountered over the past quarter of a century.

Let's look at ways to draw off this power. The main essential seems to be to get the blood really coursing through the body. Gardner speaks of dancing to generate this energy, and dancing certainly seems to be the most common method. Working within a magick circle (which is consecrated and is there to serve as a

The four witches. Engraving by Albrecht Dürer, 1497.

container for this power), the group starts out slowly, dancing around within the confines of a circle. Almost imperceptibly the speed increases. Gradually the dancers move around faster and faster. What is finally achieved is what is termed *ekstasis*—a form of ecstasy, a "getting out of oneself." Whirling around the circle, the participants lose all sense of where they are and what they are doing. This is found in many societies in all ages. The ecstasy of Voodoo participants, which leads to possession by their gods, is a well-known example.

As with other workings of Magick (Voodoo especially), one of the most important ingredients towards raising the power is music. "Music" can be as simple as one person slapping hands on thighs, or beating a stick against a stone, or it can be as complex as a recording of a full orchestra. Wiccans use both. One of the first pieces of music to which I worked was a fantastic recording of Carl Orff's *Carmina Burana* (which, of course, is a pagan piece anyway). It is ideal in that it starts slowly and then gradually builds up to a crescendo. But equally effective, I have found, has been the beating of a small drum or tambourine, or simply what the Scots call "mouth music." If a coven is working with a live musician, or musicians, however, it is as well for him, her or them not to also try to be part of the power-raising group. They need to concentrate on the music. By studying the participants they can then see when they need to speed up, by how much, and when to stop. The most important part of any such music is the beat. There must be a very definite, very positive, heavy, regular beat.

Recordings of primitive music of all types can be very effective for power-raising dancing. Native American music is especially good. This is a music which is predominantly vocal, frequently at a monophonic or unison stage, and sometimes accompanied by percussion instruments such as drums, bells, gourd rattles and scraping sticks. In the repertoire of any one tribe there may be found songs for the grinding of corn, for success in hunting, fishing, gambling, and warfare, songs for lovemaking and for entertainment. There are also songs for personal power and chants and songs dedicated to the welfare of the tribe. The *Sun Dance* of the Plains tribes, the *Corn Dance* of the Pueblos, the *Snake Dance* of the Hopi, and the *Mountain Chant* of the Navaho are all powerful, energy-raising pieces that can be used profitably by the Wicca. Similarly with the *Petro Dance*, the *Yanvalou of Agwé and Damballah*, and the *Mahi lété* of Voodoo. The African "tamtam" beats and Arab cross-rhythms and poly-rhythms are all effective. *Akiwowo, Oya,* and *Jin-Go-Lo-Ba* from Nigeria are all exciting pieces of drumming that can do much to raise power. There are many such

Dance of the Elves in a 'fairy ring'. From Olaus Magnus, De gentibus septentrionalibus, *Rome, 1555. The elves are assimilated by Olaus to the fauns, lemures, satyrs, larvae, and all the host of Pan in Roman magic.*

recordings available from around the world.

The power which is raised is seen to form in the shape of a cone, having its base on the line of the circle. This is the famous "Cone of Power" of Wicca. In his book *Wicca: A Guide for the Solitary Practitioner*, Scott Cunningham says that "there are three main sources of energy—personal power, Earth power and divine power." He defines Personal Power as the life force that "sustains our earthly existences" and that is released through movement, exercise and sex. He goes on to say: "In magic, personal power is aroused, infused with a specific purpose, released and directed towards its goal."

In some traditions of Wicca there is a High Priestess, or other leader, who acts as a funnel and projector for this raised power. In other traditions the individual Witches send it out themselves. Either way, at some point when it is felt that the power has been generated as highly as is possible, the dancing stops and the participants concentrate on projecting that power to the object of their desire. It might be to heal someone who is sick; it might be to get someone a job; it might be to relocate someone—it could be any one of a number of objectives, though all of them positive and none of them likely to harm another. The exact mechanics of this power raising and projection are explained in my book. It is something which can take a great deal of effort and can leave the coveners exhausted, though this is not always the case.

Witches concocting an ointment to be used for flying to the Sabbath.
By Hans Baldung Grien, Strasburg, 1514.

As an example of what can be done by Wiccans: a young man named Bill was in an automobile accident and, as a result of it, ended up confined to a wheelchair. The medical opinion was that he would never walk again. He was only twenty-two years old and the prospect of spending the rest of his life this way was almost more than he could bear.

Bill's cousin, Frank, came in contact with a coven of Wiccans and told them the story. They promised nothing more than that they would see what they could do, if anything. They subsequently worked on the case for a period of about a month or so. Certainly with magick of this type there is no "flash and bang" with immediate results, as in stage prestidigitation! The group worked at it, drawing off the power at their meetings and directing it towards healing Bill. One morning, several weeks after his first contact with the coven, Frank was working in his front garden when he heard someone walking up the driveway. He turned and was amazed to see his cousin. Bill was walking towards him. He was leaning on a couple of canes ... but he was walking, something the doctors had said he would never do again.

Something like this can easily be shrugged off by the skeptic as "coincidence" (such a handy word!). Certainly Wiccans don't bother to keep any documentation to *prove* what they have done. They believe in it themselves and that is all that matters. And they have had enough of these "coincidences" come to pass that they have no doubt at all that their own raised "power" is responsible.

Other methods of working involve the use of cords. This is an ages-old practice. There are ancient woodcuts showing Witches selling knotted cords to sailors. Winds have been magickally tied up in the knots so that, should the sailor find himself becalmed, he can untie a knot and have a favorable wind! But cord magick can be done for just about any purpose. It is used more by Solitary Wiccans and by Witches working in pairs than it is by full covens, though it certainly can be used by a group.

Sex magick is something which receives unnecessary prominence. Yet it is really only yet another method of raising the power, of getting the blood coursing through the body. Again it is a centuries-old method. It is found in Tantric Yoga in the East, and in many forms around the world. Sex magick can be done in conjunction with cord magick. Poppet magick, candleburning magick, rune-casting; all these, and more, are ways of Wiccan magick.

Witchcraft on the Isle of Man

Gerald Gardner

From time immemorial the people of the Isle of Man have been believers in fairies and Witches. There have been a number of Witch trials in the island, but it appears from the records that the favorite verdict of a Manx jury in cases of alleged Witchcraft was "Not Guilty, but don't do it again"!

The only recorded execution of a Witch in the Isle of Man took place within a short distance of the Old Mill when, in 1617, Margaret Ine Quane and her young son were burned alive at the stake near the Market Cross in Castletown. She had been caught trying to work a fertility rite to get good crops, and as this was the time when the Lordship of Man was temporarily in the hands of the Witch-hunting King James I, she suffered the extreme penalty.

One cannot understand history without some knowledge of our ancestors' beliefs, and what they did because of those beliefs. What manner of people were these magicians and Witches? What went on in their minds?

Ceremonial magick gave its rites a Christian form, whereas Witches were pagans and followed the Old Gods. Hence the Witch cult was fiercely persecuted, while ceremonial magick was sometimes studied and practiced by churchmen. The idea behind ceremonial magick is that of *commanding* spirits, good or evil, in the names of God and His Angels, and thus making the spirits do your will; and the proof that this is how magicians' minds worked is to be found in the old magickal books called *grimoires*. The procedure laid down in them is complicated, and requires a certain amount of education, often involving a knowledge of Latin and Hebrew, to understand it. Also, the rites they specify needed costly equipment, such as swords, wands, magickal robes, pentacles of silver and gold, etc. Hence it was only members of the upper classes, or of the learned professions, who could work such rites.

The Witch cult, on the other hand, was something much closer to the soil. Its practitioners could be, and probably most often were, completely illiterate. It is the remains of the original pre-Christian religion of Western Europe, and its followers possessed traditional knowledge and beliefs which had been handed down by word of mouth for generations. In spite of the great persecutions, the cult has never died. Some remnants of it still exist to this day.

[*The late Gerald Gardner was the driving force behind the resurgence of Wicca, in the 1950s* —Ed.]

Bessie Dunlop and the Fairy Folk

The case of Bessie Dunlop is typical of the Scottish belief in Witchcraft and in fairies. Bessie's trial took place in Lyne, Ayrshire, Scotland, in 1576. At the trial she was charged with practicing Witchcraft because of her seeming ability to predict the future (especially regarding impending illness), and to find lost and stolen property. Bessie claimed that she herself did not have that power. She said that she simply consulted with a certain Thome Reid. He it was who was able to give her accurate answers to anything she asked. The only problem with this explanation lay in the fact that Thome Reid had died at the Battle of Pinkie, thirty years previously!

When the startled judges had pulled themselves together sufficiently to question her further, she told how she had first come to meet this deceased gentleman. It seems that one day she was taking her cows to pasture and was absorbed in her own misfortunes. Both her child and her husband were sick, many of the farm animals were dead or dying, and she felt very ill herself. She wept as she herded the cattle along, so was surprised when she was addressed by a man. Looking up, she saw Thome Reid. He asked her what was wrong and she told him.

"It is all because you have displeased the Lord," he said. "When you return home you will find your child has died, but your husband will recover, as will you. You will lose two sheep but no more." Then, suddenly, he turned and disappeared through a tiny crack in a stone wall! Bessie was astonished.

After another brief encounter with Reid, when he offered her vast wealth if she would renounce Christianity (she refused), she next met him in her own house. There were other people present at the time but they did not see him. Bessie, however, followed him outside, where she found a whole crowd of people waiting for her. They greeted her in friendly fashion but, when she refused to go off with them, they howled with rage and disappeared. All except Thome Reid, who explained to her that they had been fairy folk "who dwelt in the Court of Elfland." If she wished, he said, she could become one of them. She did not wish. Reid also explained that the reason Bessie had been singled out was that, when she was younger, she had done a good service to a stranger, a woman who happened to be the Queen of Fairies. The Queen had therefore instructed Reid to approach Bessie and try to get her to join them.

From then on Bessie received a number of visits from the dead man. He advised her on many problems. If someone had asked Bessie about the health of a friend or relative, or for the location of lost or stolen property, Bessie was able to give them an answer, after first getting it from Reid. Reid also gave her various healing ointments to use on the sick. For these she would charge a fee of a peck of meal and some cheese.

Under questioning from the judges, Bessie reported that she ran many errands for Reid. She had never known him when he was alive though she did know that he had been an officer to the laird of Blair, and that his son was now in that position. She said that she was sometimes instructed to go to the Reid family and give them certain confidential information to prove that she was in touch with Thome. Then she would give further instructions so that the family could correct various wrongs that Thome Reid had committed when alive.

The court was very impressed with Bessie's story. Many questions were asked, which she seemed only too happy to answer. Unfortunately they only served to convince the court that she was, indeed, in league with the Devil. She was sentenced to be burned at the stake.

Goals of a Natural Magician

- To walk in harmony with nature, never taking without giving.
- To understand that magic is an alliance between humans and the Earth for the betterment of all.
- To use magic as an instrument of loving change, not hateful destruction.
- To see the spiritual in the physical and to understand that neither is higher nor more perfect than the other.
- To wisely use natural energies only when in genuine need, not for greed.
- To know that nothing is impossible if we will work beyond personal limitations.
- To work magic for others only with their permission.
- To celebrate magic as a union with the energies that gave us our physical forms.
- To improve ourselves, our friends and our world for the greater good of all.

—Scott Cunningham

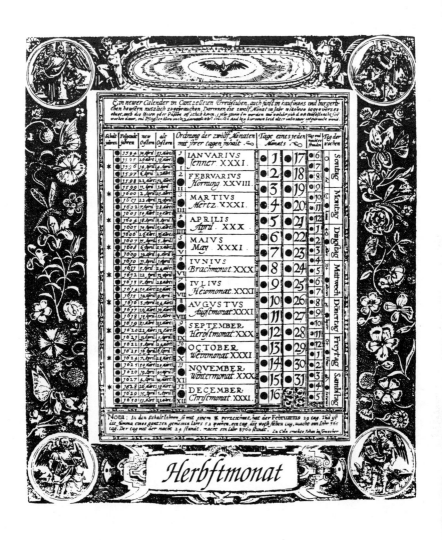

September

Autumn Fires

In the other gardens
And all up the vale,
From the autumn bonfires
See the smoke trail!

Pleasant summer over
And all the summer flowers
The red fire blazes,
The gray smoke towers.

Sing a song of seasons!
Something bright in all!
Flowers in the summer,
Fires in the fall!

—Robert Louis Stevenson

Friday

1 *Saturday*

Moon Sign: Aquarius
Moon Phase: 2nd Quarter

Tarot Card: Four of Wands
Herb: Amaranth
Incense: Sandalwood
Mineral: Sphene
Color: Black
Name of Power: Radha

2 *Sunday*

Moon Sign: Aquarius
Moon Phase: 2nd Quarter

Tarot Card: Five of Wands
Herb: Basil
Incense: Myrrh
Mineral: Amethyst
Color: Yellow
Name of Power: Lief
Tree: Vine

SEPTEMBER						
S	M	T	W	T	F	S
						1
2	3	4	5	6	7	8
9	10	11	12	13	14	15
16	17	18	19	20	21	22
23	24	25	26	27	28	29
30						

3 *Monday*

Moon Sign: Pisces
Moon Phase: 2nd Quarter

Tarot Card: Six of Wands
Herb: Bistort
Incense: Jasmine
Mineral: Peridot
Color: White
Name of Power: Anpu

4 *Tuesday*

Moon Sign: Pisces
Moon Phase: Full Moon
        (Barley)

Tarot Card: Seven of Wands
Herb: Blue Vervain
Incense: Benzoin
Mineral: Obsidian
Color: Red
Name of Power: Kita

5 *Wednesday*

Moon Sign: Pisces
Moon Phase: 3rd Quarter

Tarot Card: Eight of Wands
Herb: Calendula
Incense: Pine
Mineral: Cat's Eye
Color: Purple
Name of Power: Akau

6 *Thursday*

Moon Sign: Aries
Moon Phase: 3rd Quarter

Tarot Card: Nine of Wands
Herb: Celery
Incense: Cinnamon
Mineral: Fluorite
Color: Blue
Name of Power: Baruch

7
Friday

Moon Sign: Aries
Moon Phase: 3rd Quarter

Tarot Card: Ten of Wands
Herb: Coral Root
Incense: Frankincense
Mineral: Fluorspar
Color: Green
Name of Power: Forneus

8
Saturday

Moon Sign: Taurus
Moon Phase: 3rd Quarter
Festival: Navidad de la Virgen

Tarot Card: Page of Wands
Herb: Ma-Huang
Incense: Sandalwood
Mineral: Pearl
Color: Black
Name of Power: Miriam

9
Sunday

Moon Sign: Taurus
Moon Phase: 3rd Quarter

Tarot Card: Knight of Wands
Herb: Ergot
Incense: Myrrh
Mineral: Carnelian
Color: Yellow
Name of Power: Obatalah

SEPTEMBER

S	M	T	W	T	F	S
						1
2	3	4	5	6	7	8
9	10	11	12	13	14	15
16	17	18	19	20	21	22
23	24	25	26	27	28	29
30						

10   *Monday*

Moon Sign: Gemini
Moon Phase: 3rd Quarter

Tarot Card: Queen of Wands
Herb: Feverweed
Incense: Jasmine
Mineral: Opal
Color: White
Name of Power: Tcaridyi

11   *Tuesday*

Moon Sign: Gemini
Moon Phase: 4th Quarter

Tarot Card: King of Wands
Herb: Ginseng
Incense: Benzoin
Mineral: Cerussite
Color: Red
Name of Power: Mestha

12   *Wednesday*

Moon Sign: Cancer
Moon Phase: 4th Quarter

Tarot Card: Ace of Cups
Herb: Hedge Garlic
Incense: Pine
Mineral: Morganite
Color: Purple
Name of Power: Legba

13   *Thursday*

Moon Sign: Cancer
Moon Phase: 4th Quarter
Festival: Lectisternium

Tarot Card: Two of Cups
Herb: Hibiscus
Incense: Cinnamon
Mineral: Gold
Color: Blue
Name of Power: Minerva

14   *Friday*

Moon Sign: Leo   Tarot Card: Three of Cups
Moon Phase: 4th Quarter   Herb: Hyssop
Festival: Egyptian Ceremony of Incense: Frankincense
        Lighting the Fire   Mineral: Ulexite
                               Color: Green
                               Name of Power: Eleguah

15   *Saturday*

Moon Sign: Leo   Tarot Card: Four of Cups
Moon Phase: 4th Quarter   Herb: Khus-khus
Festival: Los Siete Dolores   Incense: Sandalwood
                               Mineral: Tiger's Eye Matrix
                               Color: Black
                               Name of Power: Anael

16   *Sunday*

Moon Sign: Virgo   Tarot Card: Five of Cups
Moon Phase: 4th Quarter   Herb: Lettuce
                               Incense: Myrrh
                               Mineral: Red Tourmaline
                               Color: Yellow
                               Name of Power: Nut

SEPTEMBER

S	M	T	W	T	F	S
						1
2	3	4	5	6	7	8
9	10	11	12	13	14	15
16	17	18	19	20	21	22
23	24	25	26	27	28	29
30						

17 *Monday*

Moon Sign: Virgo
Moon Phase: 4th Quarter

Tarot Card: Six of Cups
Herb: Mandrake
Incense: Jasmine
Mineral: Jade
Color: White
Name of Power: Gamache

18 *Tuesday*

Moon Sign: Virgo
Moon Phase: New Moon

Tarot Card: Seven of Cups
Herb: Milk Thistle
Incense: Benzoin
Mineral: Blue Opal
Color: Red
Name of Power: Agwé

19 *Wednesday*

Moon Sign: Libra
Moon Phase: 1st Quarter

Tarot Card: Eight of Cups
Herb: Golden Bough
Incense: Pine
Mineral: Golden Beryl
Color: Purple
Name of Power: Horus

20 *Thursday*

Moon Sign: Libra
Moon Phase: 1st Quarter

Tarot Card: Nine of Cups
Herb: Velvet Dock
Incense: Cinnamon
Mineral: Silver
Color: Blue
Name of Power: Loco

21
Friday

Moon Sign: Scorpio
Moon Phase: 1st Quarter
Festival: Autumnal Equinox
　　　　Feast of Divine Life

Tarot Card: Ten of Cups
Herb: White Oak
Incense: Frankincense
Mineral: Onyx
Color: Green
Name of Power: Mestha

22
Saturday

Moon Sign: Scorpio
Moon Phase: 1st Quarter

Tarot Card: Page of Cups
Herb: Parsley
Incense: Sandalwood
Mineral: Tufa
Color: Black
Name of Power: Loco-Atissu

23
Sunday

Moon Sign: Sagittarius
Moon Phase: 1st Quarter
Sun enters Libra
Festival: Eleusinian Mysteries
　　　　(1st day)

Tarot Card: Knight of Cups
Herb: Pipsissewa
Incense: Myrrh
Mineral: Obsidian
Color: Yellow
Name of Power: Ceres

SEPTEMBER

S	M	T	W	T	F	S
						1
2	3	4	5	6	7	8
9	10	11	12	13	14	15
16	17	18	19	20	21	22
23	24	25	26	27	28	29
30						

24
Monday

Moon Sign: Sagittarius
Moon Phase: 1st Quarter

Tarot Card: Queen of Cups
Herb: Pokeweed
Incense: Jasmine
Mineral: Tektite
Color: White
Name of Power: Proserpina

25
Tuesday

Moon Sign: Sagittarius
Moon Phase: 1st Quarter

Tarot Card: King of Cups
Herb: Primwort
Incense: Benzoin
Mineral: Alabaster
Color: Red
Name of Power: Tonantzin

26
Wednesday

Moon Sign: Capricorn
Moon Phase: 2nd Quarter

Tarot Card: The Magician
Herb: Life Root
Incense: Pine
Mineral: Meerschaum
Color: Purple
Name of Power: Nibo

27
Thursday

Moon Sign: Capricorn
Moon Phase: 2nd Quarter

Tarot Card: The High Priestess
Herb: Rowan
Incense: Cinnamon
Mineral: Coral
Color: Blue
Name of Power: Mert

28
Friday

Moon Sign: Aquarius
Moon Phase: 2nd Quarter

Tarot Card: The Empress
Herb: Savory
Incense: Frankincense
Mineral: Ivory
Color: Green
Name of Power: Cassiel

29
Saturday

Moon Sign: Aquarius
Moon Phase: 2nd Quarter

Tarot Card: The Emperor
Herb: Skunk Cabbage
Incense: Sandalwood
Mineral: Ruby
Color: Black
Name of Power: Michael

30
Sunday

Moon Sign: Aquarius
Moon Phase: 2nd Quarter

Tarot Card: The Hierophant
Herb: Queen's Root
Incense: Myrrh
Mineral: Opal
Color: Yellow
Name of Power: Meditrina
Tree: Ivy

SEPTEMBER

S	M	T	W	T	F	S
						1
2	3	4	5	6	7	8
9	10	11	12	13	14	15
16	17	18	19	20	21	22
23	24	25	26	27	28	29
30						

The Lords
of the Gates and Levels

Alan Richardson

There is a spark in each of us, buried deep within the layers of our psyches, which holds that we do not really belong here, that we are all strangers. It is that same spark which sees Magick as a means of transport: through it we can create the roads and the vehicles which will take us home.

There are two directions that can be taken in Magick to achieve this. We can go "up," or we can go "down." Both directions will, ultimately, take us out of this dimension entirely. Both directions will take us to the same Place. Whichever way we go we become like Isis in Search, picking up bits and pieces of that which was once most precious, until that moment of completeness when Osiris can rise and step forth.

The Law of the traditional magickal path is "As above, so below—but after another manner." This is the path of intellect and erudition, of robes and rituals and Fire and Air. It takes us "up" toward the Hawks.

The Law of the other path states: "As without, so within—there is no difference." It is the path of simplicity and heart, Water and Earth. It spirals us "down" through the levels toward the Dragon that sleeps below.

Hawk or Dragon—they can both carry us Home . . .

The basis of this came through to me in the early 1980s, when I was busy researching *Priestess*, the first full biography of that enigmatic lady Dion Fortune, who has always seemed to me to be Womanhood's answer to Aleister Crowley.

Briefly, and at risk of gross over-simplification, the dominant Secret Chief within Dion's lodge was an entity known as Thomas Erskine (1749-1823), who was held to be a reincarnation of St. Thomas More. This was the entity they linked with psychically during their inner rituals; this was the entity who gave the lodge its energy. Now both Erskine and More held the position in British politics of Lord Chancellor, of which more later. But at the same time that Dion Fortune and her Adepti were making contacts with "Lord E," as they called him, bringing through power and knowledge of very real importance, others within her lodge were doing similar things with a certain Lord Eldon (1751-1838), who had also been Lord Chancellor.

Was this a case of mistaken identity? Were the Adepti confused? Or was there something magickally special about British Chancellors? . . . a fact that was hard to accept given the sheer ordinariness of the men who have held that position in recent times.

As I later hinted in *Ancient Magick*, it was the actual role of Chancellor which provided the clue, for the *cancellarius* was originally someone who was stationed at doorways to admit and introduce. This later became the King's Chief Secretary, to whom petitions were referred. Since the rank of Chancellor was, technically, higher than that of Prime Minister, the position provided what was essentially a link between the political structures of the Common Man and the time-lost bloodlines of Royalty.

Dion, as she was fully aware, worked her magick for the benefit of her people, and ultimately her race. She could experience the British psyche as a corporate unit, a complete entity, within which she functioned like a particularly active brain cell. Changes in her own consciousness would, in time, influence the collective consciousness of her nation. To her the inner and outer structures of Britain—on *all* levels—were necessarily analogous of each other. The Royal Family would be symbols of Divine

Levels of consciousness; the Common Man would relate to everyday consciousness. Thus the Chancellor, as a link between these two aspects of British society, would necessarily be a parallel of that figure who is greater than human but not quite Divine: in short, Merlin—or whichever figure from mythic realms most resonates within the imagination as a Master Magician. It can be argued, of course, that had Dion and her Adepti pressed beneath the images of those Chancellor figures they would have glimpsed the Arch-mage of Britain. But magicians are, by and large, pragmatic souls. Such interrogative and intellectual pressure upon an inner contact can often destroy the link, just as the first and fragile love between a man and woman can be destroyed by insecurity, doubt, and constant testing. As they were all fully aware, no one can ever *really* know what these otherworld entities are. But we must hold the link as something most precious and beautiful, and work with them, and learn from them. We do not need to have a physicist's knowledge of electricity before we can work under its light. We make the best of it.

Simply, magicians know that when they come to that inner Gate which leads to stellar realms, the entity who meets, directs and guides them is real, separate, potent—and *alive*. To try to reduce it to the realms of psychological compensation or projection is a waste of opportunity. The Chancellor, the Merlin, stands at that gap between Human and Divine consciousness to help us, if only for the briefest of moments. He can transform us if we let him.

It may well be that those historical figures who attained the position of Lord Chancellor *were* exalted beings in their own right. No one can know. Certainly Lord Erskine, a sharp, acid and witty Scot, became the object of intense public adulation to a degree that we might find bewildering today. It was as though he himself became, briefly, so conscious of his particular role, so identified with these great surges of public admiration, that he stepped momentarily into the image of Merlin in his Enchanter aspect. He became larger and wiser; he sparkled. We can compare this with what happened to a particular Chancellor who gained world attention in the 20th century, when the man in question opened Gates within his nation's psyche—though very Dark Gates indeed—and for a few brief and cataclysmic years spoke with a medium's voice, uttering the darkest and most destructive wishes of his people. This began in Germany in the 1920s. It ended in a Berlin bunker in 1945.

In an infinitely more diluted form, and at an infinitely lower level, we have a class of people unique to the present time who

seem to fulfill this Chancellor role as regards the public perception. These people seem, to the excited masses, somewhat greater
than human, though admittedly not quite Divine. They are the
people whom Hollywood has branded—appropriately--as "stars."
Regardless of their true and often dismal natures there is nevertheless something about them which can, for brief moments,
uplift us. In the decades to come will some respectable, highly
trained and efficient Magickal Lodge within America suddenly
find itself making a startling and satisfying contact with a long-
departed soul from the Golden Age of Hollywood? And will they
be stunned to find this near-forgotten star pushing through information of superb originality and wondrous impact? I predict that
this *will* happen.

The Chancellor, then, is that supreme Magician figure who
holds the Stellar Gate, who helps us across the divide between
the Human and the Divine. Yet his very existence points us to the
Other Way, for his staff not only leads the eye upward, but
downward, too. So consider again that image of the Human
Realm with the Spiritual overlaid upon it, separated only by the
narrowest of gaps. Then imagine a third realm, that of Nature,
lying directly *below* the Human Realm. If there is a gap between
the Spiritual and the Human, then there is also a similar one between the Human Realm and the Realm of Nature (and those
who favour the more satisfying complexities of the Kabbalah for
their images of cosmos will find these gaps, or Gates, within the
Places of the Veils upon the Tree of Life).

There is a figure awaiting us here, too. Another Gatekeeper.
This is the Horned God who has been so firmly appropriated by
the pagan cults. He is known by the name *Herne*, or *Gwyn up Nudd*,
or *Cernunnos*—or whatever you will. He is the lower (but by no
means inferior) analogue of Merlin, and the Gate which he holds
open or shut for us is that of the Moon. If Merlin is part man and
part angel, then the Horned One is part man and part beast. If
Merlin can enchant us by stimulating our wonder and curiosity
and intellect, then Herne seduces us by appealing to a more sen-
sual, feeling, and instinctual side. He can seem primitive, savage
and unrelenting, and the intensity of his contact is often too much
for those of an urbane disposition. Nevertheless he and Merlin
are one—but "after another manner."

To a large degree we can study their influences in the way
that Western society is developing today. On the one hand there
are those sections which are, quite literally, attempting to get
beyond this Earth and to the stars, via the most extreme develop-
ments in technology. On the other hand there are those who are

becoming most passionately concerned with the state of the Earth on which all this is happening, and would seek to preserve its wildlife, its rain forests and oceans. Slowly, surely, they are starting to work together. They have to. Interestingly, we can catch a tiny glimpse of this in the career of Lord Erskine. From being a meteor in British politics and society, toasted and lauded by all, he ended up as just another politician, a virtual non-entity in comparison. The only thing he did of note in his last years was to start what might be called an "animal rights" campaign. It was as though he knew that he had, somehow, failed to maintain himself on the stellar path and so chose to try again "downward," picking up something of the old glories via the Moongate of the Natural Realm.

Herne's great revelation is concerned with involving man in a direct and living relationship with the Earth, in particular with the specific geographies in which he conducts his life. Herne teaches us about the Spirit of Place while Merlin takes us to the Place of Spirit. Herne shows us places that are as wondrously alive and conscious as any human associate. He shows us that we can take our places within the Dance of Nature as performed by the animal, vegetable and mineral kingdoms. He makes us understand the Law: "As without, so within—there is no difference."

This is the Shaman Path, the path of the Ancestors and the Land. It is a path of intelligence but not intellect, a path of dreams and moons and dragons; it also is a path of sheer survival, because living with Nature has nothing to do with states of unalloyed bliss, or pretty rites below a Harvest Moon. Nature has its dark side. Nature involves struggle and sheer hard *work*. Herne contains within himself both the wolf and the deer, and so as humans we need not feel compelled to go vegetarian. However we choose to run, or forage, there are problems involved.

Herne can come at times of extreme duress, during those moments when the personality is destroyed, the reasoning mind obliterated, and only the basic and primitive senses are left. He cares little for the rites and mores of society. His concern is to take us into the Wildwood—those staggeringly lush, fertile, verdant and unexplored territories within our hearts. Once there, and managing to survive, he will lead us to our Places of Power, and the caves beneath where the Dragons lie waiting for us.

If the Merlin/Chancellor figure helps us find a world where the structures of society are parallels of spirtual realms, then Herne teaches us that the actual physical realm is itself an actual model of that which can be found on inner levels. The shaman could, for example, climb a steep hill and find that while doing so his consciousness was expanding apace and set fair to burst out in splendor when he glimpsed the sunrise over the brow. Or if he chose to explore certain dark but fecund areas within his (and his tribe's) past, he might do so by entering a narrow valley from which a stream poured forth at one end. All aspects of the shaman's psyche would be paralleled—consciously or no—by aspects of the landscape in which he lives. He *is* the land, and the land is he. There is no difference.

Herne has two qualities which are capable of causing grave upsets if they are not reckoned with. First, although he is often happy to give a person what he asks for, he will *always* take something away at the same time. It is partly to do with that Law of Nature which can be crudely expressed as "Nothing in life is free," and partly because Herne is not that far removed from those Trickster qualities which represent the less refined aspects of Hermes. Second, Herne has a talent for inverting (and sometimes *apparently* rejecting) all the traditional philosophies that a magician may have.

One example. Herne has no regard for the concept of a Higher Self which might be regarded as being tucked away among the stars. His concern is with what might be termed the Rootself, which is buried in the good Earth and which links a man through the Ages, through endless natural cycles, and which holds the wisdom of his Ancestors. He overturns the traditional ideas about reincarnation because of this. Imagine, then, a rosebush. Every year, springing from the root, comes the branch, the bud and flower. We are those flowers. Every year we die, and our branch is cut back so that the bush might flourish again. Sometimes, by a trick of circumstance, light and angle, and by a process of drawing nutrients direct from the root, we can briefly relive the experiences of a bloom long gone. These memories do not necessarily relate to the individual soul in a previous existence, now come back to fulfill some unresolved karma. It is often a case of the Rootself being drawn upon, the Rootself which contains all things, the Rootself which parallels the consciousness at the heart of the Shaman's tribe. The personality flowers; it never reflowers in a later life. The personality dissolves into the Land. It is the Rootself which endures. This means that it is quite possible to get a group of sane, balanced, and wise people in the same room who each have far memories of having been, say, Rameses II in a previous life. They are just separate blooms, tracking back to a common vision as stored in the same root. They should not argue their uniqueness, but act as brothers in vision. They are part of each other.

So we can go Up or we can go Down, via the Path of the Enchanter or the Seducer—the Merlin or the Horned One. Ultimately we will still end up at the same Place, where all paradoxes are resolved, where opposing concepts can yet be simultaneously true. This is when we become whole, and when we return to our true Home, which is to be found both at the far side of Space, amid the stars, and also in the very heart of innermost Earth.

There is no difference.

Opening the Moongates

Alan Richardson

You must learn to make a link with those inner figures who can best teach the Mysteries of Earth. Along with Herne, the Horned God, there is also the feminine aspect. You can visualize this as the Lady with the Moon on her Brow. In striving toward Herne or his Lady, you will be making equal inroads toward yourself. But first you must learn to switch off the internal monologue, that aspect of the reasoning mind which comments on everything.

To do this you must choose a Name. But this will not be quite the same as those Magickal Names used on the Hermetic Path. This one is a simple affair, without meaning, but which is able to be split into two parts, a name which expresses both male and female. Imagine something like Ab/Abba. The sonic "Ab" would relate to the left side of the brain, to the reasoning, interrogative qualities. "Abba," in contrast, would be used to awaken the brain's right side, and bring into use its dark and intuitive aspects. All sorts of Names can be chosen along these lines: Ab/Abba, El/Ella, Am/Aima . . . the list is endless. Find your own.

As you go through daily life, practice sounding *El-la, El-la, El-la* while looking at the world like a camera: without comment, judgment, or interpretation. Just watch and experience. When you have sustained this for as long as possible, take up the outer sonic *El, El, El* . . . then deliberately allow the conscious, reasoning mind to take over again. This method of intonation can be done quite easily in public by keeping the lips tightly closed. Any passers-by would think you were merely humming.

Once some degree of facility has been achieved, the magician can then begin to use an actual God-name in the same way: *Herna, Herna, Herna.* The "h" should be aspirated like the "ch" in the Scottish word *loch*—a sharp, rasping sound. At the same time the magician should, in his imagination, see himself as assuming the form of the Horned God deliberately. You should deliberately feel your own mundane personality changing into something greater and more splendid. On other occasions, preferably on the edge of sleep, you should begin to create a Place within your consciousness where you can come to meet this God. Herne being what he is, this should take the form of a Glade. The magician should visualize a gate, of any kind, beyond which is a wide green field which slopes gently upward toward a cluster of broad-leaved trees. Because you are working by yourself, the magician should then actually *begin* an internal monologue to help maintain concentration: "I am stepping through the gate, which is shaped like . . . I am striding through the long grass and feel . . . The trees ahead are . . ." Visualize a path between the trees which leads into a glade. In the glade are two tall and ancient Standing Stones. This is where you pause. This is where you deliberately invoke the Horned God.

In the early days of practice these will be pictures in the head, no more, often very mushy and invariably sliding away into sleep, or boredom. There will, however, come a time when the picture will vivify itself. It will sparkle. And the deliberately created phantom of the Horned God will suddenly burst into a very real sort of life. And even if, for whatever reason, this never seems likely to happen, the magician is still sending out a signal to Herne which will be answered—at some time and in some way. Always.

The next thing is to link all this with actual places in the physical world. Every magician must find High Places: a Lake, Valley and Stream. You must learn to sit down at these places, talk to them and ask them to teach you. You must will your consciousness down through the soil, down toward the heart of the Earth. You must pay your respects to all those who have gone before, and make peace with your own Ancestors. This can only be done alone. In the magick circle of the Hermetic Lodge the priest must always have his priestess; the power flows between them. But in this solitary type of magick the Land itself becomes your priestess or your priest. You begin to enter into an erotic, feeling, and intuitive relationship. Absurd but true. But it will not happen quickly. There are cycles to be considered, the slow turning of the Natural World. Yet gradually but infallibly the magician will find that the Land will begin to speak. Symbols and omens will appear, new insights.

So find your God or your Goddess, be it Herne, Pan, Cheiron or Whoever. And find your Holy Places. Be humble, be simple, be quiet, be brave—and above all *listen*. The Moongates will open, and the Earth beneath will show you wonders.

Magick in the New Age

Magick is not just something from out of the past; it is not something with no place in the present. Magick has as great a place in the here and now as does, for instance, television or a turbocharged sports car. Magick is making things happen when we want them to happen. Well, certainly we still have things we want to happen, most of us, so there definitely is a place for magick. In fact, magick could bring us a television or that turbocharged sports car! But magick does demand a large amount of effort and a certain amount of faith, faith in the fact that it will work.

There was a young man I once knew, who had read many books on the subject, and who one day decided to give magick a try. He decided he would like a nice, red Porsche sports car sitting in his garage. He prepared his tools for a ritual and, on the night of the full moon, went through that ritual. The following morning he went out to the garage and opened the door. No Porsche! He shrugged his shoulders. "I didn't think it would work," he said.

Of course it didn't work, because he had that doubt in the back of his mind the whole time he was working on the ritual. If he had felt positive, if he had gone through that rite firmly convinced that at the end of it the car would be there, then I believe it would have been. The most important ingredient for the working of magick is not the magick wand, or the incense, or the words of the rite; it is the intensity of feeling on the part of the practitioner. He, or she, must feel so strongly that what is being done is going to succeed that the energy/power/*mana* will surge out and *make* it successful.

If you do a magickal ritual for no other reason than to show that it can be done—if you are trying to prove the existence of magick to someone else, perhaps—then it almost certainly will not work. In the same way if you do magick to bring (for example) money to you, or to someone else, and it's just for the sake of having the money, then it almost certainly won't work. The reason for both these failures is that there would be a lack of intensity. There would be no real *need* for these rituals to work.

There are certain laws concerning magick. As we have seen, one is that you must have faith and another is that there must be a need. And really the one ties in with the other. A young woman I knew had a daughter who had accidentally overdosed on drugs. The daughter was in a coma, and had been for nearly a week when I first learned of it. The mother desperately wanted the daughter to recover, to come out of the coma. I knew them both quite well and agreed to work with the mother to do some magick for the daughter. We both put a tremendous amount of effort into it. We both wanted, so badly, for the girl to recover, and we both believed with all our hearts that the magick would do it. And it did. Within twenty-four hours of our finishing the ritual, the daughter came out of her coma. Today she is fully recovered and, in fact, is now a fine, healthy mother herself. Now if either one of us had not felt as strongly as we did, if we had gone into it just "hoping that something would happen," then we would have been disappointed.

I have personally used magick over the years to bring me things I have needed. I have brought a job promotion to myself, and food and shelter when needed; bought property when I needed to relocate; obtained transportation—I have done many things magickally. Yet I have had my failures as well. In retrospect I can see that those failures were not due to any fault in my technique, in my tools, or timing. They were entirely attributable to the amount of power/feeling I was able to put into the rituals, which in turn was related to the degree of real need I had for what I was striving for.

From the point of view that we really have far more real needs, in modern civilization, than people had in earlier times, we can say that magick actually has *more* of a place in today's society than it has ever had in the past. It is truly a tool for the New Age.

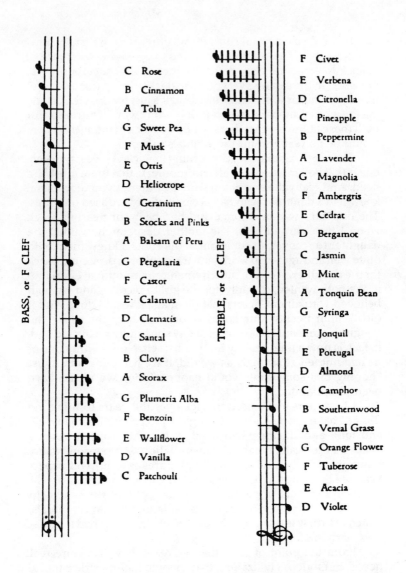

Piesse's Gamut of Scents

Esoteric Aromatics

Raymond Buckland

It is difficult, if not impossible, to describe a smell. Certainly it is virtually impossible to describe it with any accuracy, so that it might be distinguished from a similar aroma. Odor has failed to be harnessed to any mathematical formula that would give it a relationship to the other properties of a chemical.

It was a perfumer named Septimus Piesse who first, in the mid-nineteenth century, established a classification for smells. He did so by equating them with sound, with the notes on a piano. Starting with the lower C of the bass clef (patchouli), he went up through six and a half octaves to F above top C (civet). The complete "odophone scale" is illustrated on the opposite page.

Piesse went on to say that not only was there a correspondence between odors and musical notes, but that there was also the same principle of harmony—certain odors could be "out of tune" with others.

Perfumes have been burned, for their sweet aroma, in magickal and religious ceremonies for thousands of years. Myrrh, cinnamon, and various resinous gums are the oldest ingredients. The odor was thought to be most pleasing to the gods. The oldest perfume containers in existence are probably those that were discovered in the tomb of Tutankhamen. When opened it was found that the perfumes had long since evaporated, but the aromas remained! The ancient Egyptians perfumed everything: mummies of birds and animals as well as those of humans. This was because they associated perfumes with immortality and reincarnation. Happily some of the formulas for these perfumes have survived. They include many natural resins, gums, and scented woods, together with myrrh and frankincense.

The Greeks included perfumes in their religious rites. Greek mythology gives a few clues as to the esoteric meanings of some of the perfumes. The rose, for example, according to a Greek myth mentioned by Virgil, was born from a drop of blood and a kiss by Venus.

In the Old Testament there is also mention of the esoteric power of perfume. Apparently it was on account of the sweet smell of Noah's offering that Jehovah decided "not again to curse the ground any more." And after the Ten Commandments had been delivered to Moses, the offering of the Children of Israel contained anointing oils and sweet resins. In Exodus III, 23-25 is found a formula for a fine perfume: "Five hundred shekels of pure myrrh together with two hundred and fifty shekels of sweet oil of cinnamon, two hundred shekels of sweet oil of calamus, five hundred shekels of cassia, and one hin of olive oil." The list of fragrances mentioned in the Old Testament is long and impressive. In the Song of Songs and the Apocryphal story of Judith there are obvious references to the sexually stimulating properties of perfume.

When reading of the lives of various saints there is often mention of "the odor of sanctity." This has both a symbolic and a pragmatic meaning. In the account of the death of St. Theresa, for example, it is mentioned that the atmosphere was permeated with a sweet flowery odor. When the body of Blessed Marie Pelletier was exhumed thirty-five years after her burial, the surgeon reported that the corpse resembled that of a person no more than three days dead and that it discharged "an inoffensive somewhat aromatic fluid recalling balsam."

Certainly scientists do acknowledge the fact that certain diseases have an "olfactory environment." For example, pulmonary tuberculosis has a strong sweet odor, diphtheria a light sweetish odor, and scarlet fever a smell "not unlike freshly baked bread," according to one physician.

In much medieval magick aromatic herbs are used prominently, especially during the casting of the magick circle. In addition to being thrown onto the brazier, they are frequently spread around the circle itself. Sometimes a small brazier is set on one side especially for the use of burning herbs—pleasant herbs to attract good spirits, herbs such as hemlock and coriander to summon less communicative entities.

Present-day perfumes are sold not so much to cover up natural body odors, but more to create an atmosphere, usually a sexual one. They are created and sold to make a person more attractive to the opposite sex. Their essential purpose, therefore, is to *charm*, to cast a spell over another. Indeed, the very names used frequently indicate their magickal intent! One of the most popular scents for men, incidentally, is musk—the essence obtained from small Asiatic deer—and for women, ambergris from the sperm whale (interestingly enough, the smell of ambergris is not generally appreciated by women but can send men wild!). More than seventeen thousand separate odors have now been identified, some pleasant, others not so pleasant.

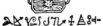

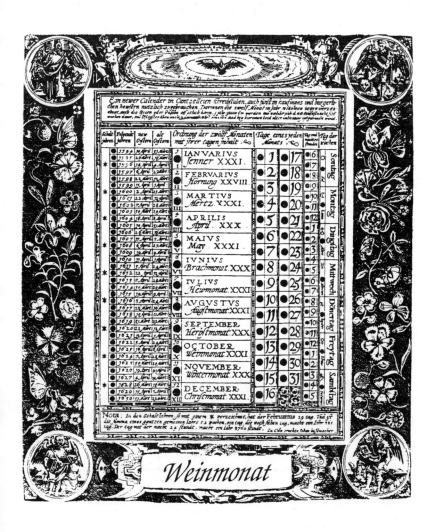

Weinmonat

October

1
Monday

Moon Sign: Pisces
Moon Phase: 2nd Quarter
Festival: Greater Eleusinian
    Mysteries (last day)

Tarot Card: The Lovers
Herb: Centaury
Incense: Jasmine
Mineral: Agate
Color: White
Name of Power: Fides

2
Tuesday

Moon Sign: Pisces
Moon Phase: 2nd Quarter
Festival: Angeles Guardianes

Tarot Card: The Chariot
Herb: Bearberry
Incense: Benzoin
Mineral: Amber
Color: Red
Name of Power: Arawhon

3
Wednesday

Moon Sign: Aries
Moon Phase: 2nd Quarter

Tarot Card: Justice
Herb: Black Alder
Incense: Pine
Mineral: Amethyst
Color: Purple
Name of Power: Meditrina

4
Thursday

Moon Sign: Aries
Moon Phase: Full Moon (Blood)

Tarot Card: The Hermit
Herb: Boneset
Incense: Cinnamon
Mineral: Beryl
Color: Blue
Name of Power: Clare

5

Friday

Moon Sign: Taurus
Moon Phase: 3rd Quarter

Tarot Card: Wheel of Fortune
Herb: Camomile
Incense: Frankincense
Mineral: Bloodstone
Color: Green
Name of Power: Fa

6

Saturday

Moon Sign: Taurus
Moon Phase: 3rd Quarter

Tarot Card: Strength
Herb: Chervil
Incense: Sandalwood
Mineral: Carnelian
Color: Black
Name of Power: Tem

7

Sunday

Moon Sign: Gemini
Moon Phase: 3rd Quarter

Tarot Card: The Hanged Man
Herb: Coriander
Incense: Myrrh
Mineral: Chrysolite
Color: Yellow
Name of Power: Ogoun

OCTOBER

S	M	T	W	T	F	S
	1	2	3	4	5	6
7	8	9	10	11	12	13
14	15	16	17	18	19	20
21	22	23	24	25	26	27
28	29	30	31			

8
Monday

Moon Sign: Gemini
Moon Phase: 3rd Quarter
Festival: Start of Fading Time
       in Celtic calendar

Tarot Card: Death
Herb: Dill
Incense: Jasmine
Mineral: Peridot
Color: White
Name of Power: Durga

9
Tuesday

Moon Sign: Cancer
Moon Phase: 3rd Quarter

Tarot Card: Temperance
Herb: Eucalyptus
Incense: Benzoin
Mineral: Coral
Color: Red
Name of Power: Felicitas

10
Wednesday

Moon Sign: Cancer
Moon Phase: 4th Quarter

Tarot Card: The Devil
Herb: Figwort
Incense: Pine
Mineral: Quartz Crystal
Color: Purple
Name of Power: Simba

11
Thursday

Moon Sign: Leo
Moon Phase: 4th Quarter

Tarot Card: The Tower
Herb: Goat's Rue
Incense: Cinnamon
Mineral: Diamond
Color: Blue
Name of Power: Quetzalcoatl

12   *Friday*

Moon Sign: Leo
Moon Phase: 4th Quarter

Tarot Card: The Star
Herb: Hedge Hyssop
Incense: Frankincense
Mineral: Emerald
Color: Green
Name of Power: Fortuna
                    Redux

13   *Saturday*

Moon Sign: Leo
Moon Phase: 4th Quarter

Tarot Card: The Moon
Herb: Musk Mallow
Incense: Sandalwood
Mineral: Garnet
Color: Black
Name of Power: Apep

14   *Sunday*

Moon Sign: Virgo
Moon Phase: 4th Quarter

Tarot Card: The Sun
Herb: Iceland Moss
Incense: Myrrh
Mineral: Jade
Color: Yellow
Name of Power: Zaka

OCTOBER

S	M	T	W	T	F	S
	1	2	3	4	5	6
7	8	9	10	11	12	13
14	15	16	17	18	19	20
21	22	23	24	25	26	27
28	29	30	31			

15 — *Monday*

Moon Sign: Virgo
Moon Phase: 4th Quarter

Tarot Card: Judgment
Herb: Kidney Vetch
Incense: Jasmine
Mineral: Lapis Lazuli
Color: White
Name of Power: Yemaya

16 — *Tuesday*

Moon Sign: Libra
Moon Phase: 4th Quarter
Festival: Cera

Tarot Card: The World
Herb: Licorice
Incense: Benzoin
Mineral: Lapis Lingus
Color: Red
Name of Power: Cera

17 — *Wednesday*

Moon Sign: Libra
Moon Phase: 4th Quarter
Festival: Tibetan Festival of
          Departed Worthies

Tarot Card: The Fool
Herb: Marjoram
Incense: Pine
Mineral: Lapis Lingurius
Color: Purple
Name of Power: Shinto

18 — *Thursday*

Moon Sign: Scorpio
Moon Phase: New Moon

Tarot Card: Ace of Pentacles
Herb: Milkweed
Incense: Cinnamon
Mineral: Moonstone
Color: Blue
Name of Power: Pandrosus

19
Friday

Moon Sign: Scorpio
Moon Phase: 1st Quarter

Tarot Card: Two of Pentacles
Herb: All-heal
Incense: Frankincense
Mineral: Opal
Color: Green
Name of Power: Minceskro

20
Saturday

Moon Sign: Scorpio
Moon Phase: 1st Quarter

Tarot Card: Three of Pentacles
Herb: Candlewick
Incense: Sandalwood
Mineral: Pearl
Color: Black
Name of Power: Anael

21
Sunday

Moon Sign: Sagittarius
Moon Phase: 1st Quarter

Tarot Card: Four of Pentacles
Herb: Red Oak
Incense: Myrrh
Mineral: Ruby
Color: Yellow
Name of Power: Tutu

OCTOBER

S	M	T	W	T	F	S
		1	2	3	4	5	6
7	8	9	10	11	12	13
14	15	16	17	18	19	20
21	22	23	24	25	26	27
28	29	30	31			

22 *Monday*

Moon Sign: Sagittarius
Moon Phase: 1st Quarter

Tarot Card: Five of Pentacles
Herb: Pasque Flower
Incense: Jasmine
Mineral: Sardonyx
Color: White
Name of Power: Sogbo

23 *Tuesday*

Moon Sign: Capricorn
Moon Phase: 1st Quarter
Sun enters Scorpio

Tarot Card: Six of Pentacles
Herb: Wintergreen
Incense: Benzoin
Mineral: Topaz
Color: Red
Name of Power: Arioch

24 *Wednesday*

Moon Sign: Capricorn
Moon Phase: 1st Quarter

Tarot Card: Seven of Pentacles
Herb: Pomegranate
Incense: Pine
Mineral: Turquoise
Color: Purple
Name of Power: Veleketé

25 *Thursday*

Moon Sign: Capricorn
Moon Phase: 1st Quarter

Tarot Card: Eight of Pentacles
Herb: Quassia
Incense: Cinnamon
Mineral: Peridot
Color: Blue
Name of Power: Oshun

26   *Friday*

Moon Sign: Aquarius
Moon Phase: 2nd Quarter

Tarot Card: Nine of Pentacles
Herb: Raspberry
Incense: Frankincense
Mineral: Obsidian
Color: Green
Name of Power: Hau-Hra

27   *Saturday*

Moon Sign: Aquarius
Moon Phase: 2nd Quarter

Tarot Card: Ten of Pentacles
Herb: Mountain Ash
Incense: Sandalwood
Mineral: Amethyst
Color: Black
Name of Power: Ayida-Wédo

28   *Sunday*

Moon Sign: Pisces
Moon Phase: 2nd Quarter

Tarot Card: Page of Pentacles
Herb: Saw Palmetto
Incense: Myrrh
Mineral: Sapphire
Color: Yellow
Name of Power: Hathor
Tree: Dwarf Elder or Reed

OCTOBER

S	M	T	W	T	F	S
	1	2	3	4	5	6
7	8	9	10	11	12	13
14	15	16	17	18	19	20
21	22	23	24	25	26	27
28	29	30	31			

29

Monday

Moon Sign: Pisces
Moon Phase: 2nd Quarter

Tarot Card: Knight of Pentacles
Herb: Soapwort
Incense: Jasmine
Mineral: Yellow Sapphire
Color: White
Name of Power: Pele

30

Tuesday

Moon Sign: Aries
Moon Phase: 2nd Quarter

Tarot Card: Queen of Pentacles
Herb: Hardhack
Incense: Benzoin
Mineral: Dioptase
Color: Red
Name of Power: Kian

31

Wednesday

Moon Sign: Aries
Moon Phase: 2nd Quarter
Festival: Samhain Eve—
      1st of 3 days of
      Samhain

Tarot Card: King of Pentacles
Herb: Bitter Ash
Incense: Pine
Mineral: Blue Quartz
Color: Purple
Name of Power: Echtge

OCTOBER

S	M	T	W	T	F	S
		1	2	3	4	5	6
7	8	9	10	11	12	13
14	15	16	17	18	19	20
21	22	23	24	25	26	27
28	29	30	31			

LUCIFUGÉ ,
prem. Ministr.

SATANACHIA ,
grand général.

AGALIARPT. ,
aussi général.

FLEURETY ,
lieutenantgén.

LUCIFER,
Empereur.

BELZÉBUT ,
Prince.

ASTAROT ,
Grand-duc.

SARGATANAS ,
brigadier.

NEBIROS ,
mar. de camp.

Magic in Hawaii

Scott Cunningham

An ancient temple lies twelve bumpy miles from Highway 11 on the Big Island of Hawaii. Here, on this isolated spit of land known as Ka Lae, is Kalalela Heiau. The fishermen who still work these waters leave offerings to the Hawaiian deities on the lava stone structure.

Several years ago, the Kapiolani Rose Garden, near Diamond Head on the island of Oahu, was experiencing a rash of thefts. Tourists were stripping off the blooms and whole rose bushes were being spirited away. Charles Kenn, a renowned *kahuna*, was called to protect them. The thefts stopped.

Many students of *hula* make pilgrimages to a temple set on the rocky Na Pali coast of Kauai. There they offer flower *lei* to Laka, the goddess of the hula.

On the edge of Halemaumau, the steaming, sulfurous domain of the demi-goddess Pele at Kilauea on Hawaii, numerous offerings are left by Her worshippers. Leaf-wrapped volcanic rocks, scarlet berries of the *ohelo* (a close relative of the cranberry), incense and other offerings are placed there or thrown into the crater. During recent eruptions, such as those that consumed part of the Royal Gardens subdivision on Hawaii, homeowners who had invoked Pele reported that their houses had been spared the wrath of Her molten rock.

There are those who say that the Hawaiians have forgotten their old ways of worship and magic, that they no longer pray to Kane for rain, that they no longer see Hina in the full moon or Pele in the dancing fountains of fire. There are those who say the magic of Hawaii is long dead, buried under 150 years of Western dominance, religious conversion and tons of concrete. First-time visitors arriving at Honolulu International Airport are apt to believe such statements. The long ride from the airport to Waikiki passes junkyards, heavy industrial areas and shabby warehouses. The beach itself glitters with carefully groomed, imported sand, all but swallowed up by multi-million dollar hotels.

But above Honolulu, in the Tantalus Heights, lies Keaiwe Heiau. Now a state park, this ancient healing temple is still visited by the sick who leave offerings among its stones. An inscription on a plaque there reads:

"A temple with lifegiving powers believed to be a center where the Hawaiian Kahuna Lapa'au or herb doctor practiced the art of healing. Herbs grown in nearby gardens were compounded and prescribed with prayer.
Commission of Historical Sites."

Twenty or thirty minutes away at Wahiawa, in the center of the island, are *pohaku* (stones) with healing powers.

Most Hawaiians today are of "conventional" religious backgrounds. The missionaries, who first arrived in 1820, found the peoples ripe for the new religion. The Mormons made tremendous inroads. Their Polynesian Cultural Center, located in Laie on the island of Oahu, is the single most-visited attraction in the state.

Still, the earlier ways of existence on these islands— reverence for the earth, the sea, the sky, the water and the plants— lives on. In 1984, a botanist told me that she prays to Ku for protection while hiking in the mountains. Time-honored deities are thanked prior to collecting flowers and foliage to create *lei*.

Fishermen still attach *ki* leaves to their boats before setting out.

Many persons of Hawaiian ancestry still grow *dracena* and *ki* plants outside their homes for money and protection, respectively. When ground is broken for new construction, a *kahuna* is often called to bless the area with salt, water and a *ki* leaf. The importance of this last ritual is affirmed by numerous stories of the accidents and strange occurrences at building sites at which it *wasn't* performed. Workmen are killed, the earth itself sinks, heavy pieces of earth-moving equipment are found turned on their sides in the morning.

The *kahuna* is probably the least-understood aspect of ancient Hawaii. Numerous books have been written about them. Most are contradictory and bear little resemblance to the truth. One recently published book seems to combine the reminiscences of a Pleasant Hawaiian Holidays tour, faulty research and some psychic detective work.

The *kahuna* were and are the keepers of the secret. These men (and women) were experts in various fields. In today's world, a person with a PhD in psychology is a type of *kahuna*, as is a master sculptor, a skilled weather forecaster, a miraculously successful healer, an engineer and a well-trained psychic.

There were *kahuna* who specialized in love magic, in navigation, in divination, in the construction of canoes and housing, in prayer. Far from the evil, scary creatures that the missionaries depicted them as, the *kahuna* were respected masters.

One of the best-known contemporary *kahuna* describes his field as philosophical, scientific and magical practice. *Kahuna* aren't merely magicians. Several recent books have described *huna* as a purely psychological system. These are based on the works of Max Freedom Long, a researcher who, through investigating the Hawaiian language, sought to crack what he considered to be the "huna code." Unfortunately Long never spoke to a *kahuna*, though they were around. His books—and those based on them—are sadly incomplete.

What is the heart of old Hawaii? It must lie in her people's views of deity. All their rites of worship, their temples, their magical practices stem from this people's relationship with the forces of nature.

Their deities, the personifications of the wind, the earth, volcanic activity, the fish, birds and all the other features of their string of islands, were conceived of as being *real*, as real as those of any other religion and perhaps more so, since the earthly forms of their deities were all around them. No aspect of life was without religious impact. Fishermen prayed to Ku'ula for good catches; medicinal plants were gathered with prayers to Hina and Ku; all planting, harvesting and eating were accompanied by prayers. Births and deaths, house building, sports of all kinds, even combat—all were overseen and nourished by the deities.

No one deity was revered above all others by all people at all times. Just as in ancient Egypt, certain gods and goddesses rose and fell in favor. Small geographic areas worshipped deities unknown to outsiders. The Hawaiians themselves describe, in the prayers that have been preserved, the 4,000, the 40,000, the 400,000 gods.

Pele is perhaps the most famous of them to outsiders, and yet She wasn't quite a goddess. The woman of flame, who lives in Kiluaea on the island of Hawaii, is the *kupua*, or demi-goddess, who created the islands themselves through volcanic activity. Searching for a home for Herself, Her brothers and sisters, Pele dug pits for her fire that were free of ground water. In turn, she created the islands from Ni'ihau to the Big Island of Hawaii, where she continues to live. On Kauai two caves near Haena can still be seen. They represent earlier attempts of Pele's search to find a home.

Pele has not been forgotten by the Hawaiian people. As mentioned above, She is still given many offerings, and stories of her appearing in fire, steam and mist during eruptions are commonplace. She is also said to show Herself as a beautiful young girl or an old, wrinkled woman. Many drivers have reported picking up a female who stood by the side of the road. Within moments she disappears from the car seat. That is Pele.

Though Pele is the spirit of the volcanoes, She isn't a wrathful being. Many see Her as a true mother goddess, who continues to create new land when lava reaches the sea, stretching the size of the island of Hawaii. And unlike volcanic eruptions in most other parts of the world, those in Hawaii threaten little danger to human life.

There are many other Hawaiian deities:

KANE is seen in sunlight, fresh water, living creatures, forests. Some myths credit Him with creating the universe. Earthly forms of Kane include *ko* (sugar cane) as well as the beautiful *ohia lehua*, a tree bearing feathery red flowers.

LONO is the god of agriculture, fertility, the winds, gushing springs and rain. He presides over many sports. At his *heiau* people prayed for rain and rich crops, and offered plants and pigs to him. All Hawaiians ate from His food gourd. He is seen in the *kukui* tree, whose nuts were once made into lamps and now are

fashioned into durable *lei*. Lono's other early forms include the *'ualu* (sweet potato) and the leaves of the *kalo*. From the root of the *kalo* (Tahitian: *taro*) poi is made.

Ku is the famous war-god of the ancient Hawaiians, the male generative power. It was at his temples that human sacrifices were made. *Kuka'ilimoku*, one of the many forms of Ku, was made famous by Kamehameha I. A huge wooden statue of Kuka'ilimoku can be seen in the Bishop Museum in Honolulu. Other aspects of Ku (all the deities had many) include *Ku'ula*, the fisherman's god. Earthly forms of Ku include the hawk.

Human sacrifice has to be mentioned in any account of the ancient Hawaiians. It is certainly savage to our eyes, but it played an important ceremonial role at certain times. There has been speculation that the practice was introduced to Hawaii from outside its islands. (Before shaking our heads in horror, let's remember our own form of human sacrifice, one carried out on prisoners who are given death sentences. How different are we from the ancient Hawaiians?)

Hina is seen in the setting sun as well as in the moon. She rules over corals, spiny sea creatures, seaweeds and cool forests. Women who beat tree bark into the cloth known as *kapa* (*tapa* elsewhere in the Pacific) prayed to Hina.

It may be surprising that *Poliahu* was revered by early Hawaiians, for She is a goddess of snow. However, Mauna Kea, one of the great volcanoes that make up the Big Island of Hawaii, is often shrouded with snow. It is the home of Poliahu, the beautiful goddess.

Laka oversaw the hula, which was originally both a sacred dance performed for the deities and the *ali'i* (chiefs) as well as a secular activity for the common people. Laka is represented on the hula altars by a block of wood wrapped with kapa cloth. Several plants, especially ferns, are sacred to her.

There are many other deities and demi-gods, such as *Maui*,

the Hawaiian trickster who, among other exploits, fished up the islands from the bottom of the sea with His fishhook. Maui's magical hook can still be seen hanging in the skies over Hawaii, made up of stars. *Kamapua'a*, a demigod who appeared in various forms including that of a pig, had a tempestuous love affair with Pele. The mythology (sacred literature) of Hawaii is filled with passion, adventure, love and magic. It is required reading for anyone wishing to pierce into ancient Hawaiian consciousness.

As we've seen, the ways of the past still live in Hawaii. It was recently proposed to tap a stream from Kilauea Crater in order to produce geothermal energy. Modern-day priestesses of Pele immediately protested, stating that She still lives in all parts of the crater and that the plan would be nothing more than selling part of Her body. To their great dissatisfaction, the priestesses lost and the plans proceeded. Money overcame the old ways, as it often has.

Is there still magic to be found in Hawaii? Yes. It's there in the ground. In the air. In the cries of birds. In the rustling of plants. In the splash of water tumbling down a volcanic cliff. In the sunrise from Haleakala. In the green, white and black sand beaches. In the thundering waves.

Mana—the Hawaiian concept of the natural energy that resides in all things—permeates the very rock upon which these islands formed. The life-force is so vibrant here that the sensitive can feel it on the breeze when stepping off a 747 at the airport.

Yes, the magic of Hawaii still lives, but it can't be found in books that promise to reveal the "secrets" of ancient Hawaiian huna. If you visit there, go to a luau, take in a show and rent a surfboard if you must. But seek out the quiet places, those wild spots where the mana of old Hawaii rises from the trees and the water and the Earth. Listen to the voices of the past whispering from the hibiscus, rustling the wild ginger.

Visit Pele at Her home on the Big Island. Weave a lei of flowers (or buy one) and place it on the ocean. Visit such sites as Keaiwa Heaiu (Oahu), Ka Lae (Hawaii), the Na Pali coastline (Kauai), Pu'uhonua O Honaunau (Hawaii), Haleakala (Maui), Kilauea Crater (Hawaii) and the magnificent petroglyph sites on Maui and Hawaii. Any good guidebook will direct you to such wonders.

The magic of Hawaii lives in its people and the land itself. It is there, waiting, ready to reveal its secrets to anyone who goes with an open heart and an open mind.

And it is alive!

Recommended Reading

Reading is the next best thing to being there! These are some recommended books. If you can't find them at your local bookstore, write to the following address for a catalog. At the time of this writing, all of these books are in print and available from:

Pacific Trade Group
94-527 Puahi Street
Waipahu, HA 06797

Beckwith, Martha. *Hawaiian Mythology.* Honolulu: University Press of Hawaii, 1979.

Cox, J. Halley and Edward Stasack. *Hawaiian Petroglyphs.* Honolulu: Bishop Museum Press, 1970.

Malo, David. *Hawaiian Antiquities.* Honolulu: Bishop Museum Press, 1971.

McDonald, Marie. *Ka Lei: The Leis of Hawaii.* Honolulu: Topgallant/Press Pacifica, 1985.

Mitchell, Donald D. Kilolani, *Resource Units in Hawaiian Culture.* Honolulu: The Kamehameha Schools Press/Bernice P. Bishop Estate, 1982.

Stone, Margaret, *Supernatural Hawaii.* Honolulu: Aloha Graphics and Sales, 1979.

Huna Magick

The word *Huna* comes from a Polynesian word meaning "secret." In Hawaii Huna has grown into a psychoreligious system. Many legends have come down through oral tradition but details of the system's true origins have been lost. A man who did a tremendous amount of research into Huna and the *Kahunas* (practitioners of Huna) was Max Freedom Long.* He spent a great many years investigating the system's origins and has probably come as close as anyone is likely to come in discovering those origins.

The Huna belief is that each person is divided into three "selves": the low, middle, and high. These parts correspond, roughly, to our subconscious, conscious, and supraconscious minds. By embodying the power of *mana*, spiritual awareness of the three selves can be brought about. (The high self actually exists a few feet above, and outside, the body. It is connected to the body by a thin cord of what is known as *aka* substance.)

According to the Polynesians, the whole of creation—mortals, gods, and the whole of nature—is pervaded by mana. Religion was concerned with controlling and directing mana, with increasing it where it was needed, with shielding man from its dangers. Mana power comes down through the divine ancestors and enters into all beings descended from them. A Polynesian chief was regarded as being directly descended from the gods and, therefore, was especially charged with great mana.

It is also a power in itself; it can be protective of taboo objects, for instance. The "power" generated by Wiccans in their magickal rituals can be described as mana, as can that

---

*See *Recovering the Ancient Magic* (1936) and *Growing Into Light* (1955).

awesome power which Australian Aboriginals believe emanates from the *Kadaicha*, or medicine-man.

The Kahunas felt that the Huna power was too powerful, too awesome, to be passed on willy-nilly, and so its use and manipulation was generally handed down from parent to child only. Because of this the great Kahuna clans of Polynesia grew into being. They were later severely diminished by the encroaching Christian missionaries, yet they were never completely destroyed.

The Kahunas exhibited great powers of healing and generally did much good for their communities. Yet since the mana power could be used equally well for bad as for good, it was jealously guarded.

—R.B.

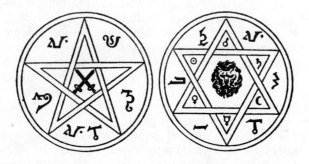

Maori Magick

The "spirits of the dead" play an important part in the lives of the Maoris of New Zealand. The priests, or *Tohungas*, are very like Spiritualist mediums in many ways, acting as a bridge between this world and the world of the dead. The Tohungas are usually trained from early childhood, being presented for this training by their parents. Through years of prayer, fasting, chanting, and meditation, they acquire a "power" for prophecy and spirit communication.

In the early days of the British Empire, when Great Britain was trying hard to tame this wild country, officials frequently wrote home that they were being frustrated by the work of the Tohungas. "They will never be wholly conquered," said one correspondent. "They obtain information of the parties sent out to

attack them. The number of the enemy, the direction from which they will come, the very color of their boats, the hour at which they will arrive—all this and more is known to the Maori through the agencies of the Tohungas. All particulars essential to their safety are invariably communicated to the tribes beforehand by these prophets."

The best natural "prophets" among the Maori were the women. Although the Christian missionaries tried to explain away their powers by attributing them to ventriloquism, or similar, the female Tohungas communicated most effectively with the spirits of their dead. In his book *Old New Zealand*, General Cummings cites an interesting case of Tohungaism.

A young chief had been appointed Registrar of Births and Deaths. He carried out his duties faithfully until, one day, he was killed in an accident. General Cummings then searched for the all-important book of registrations but could not find it. The place was turned upside down but no one could locate the book. The relatives then decided to call in a Tohunga and communicate with the dead chief's spirit. General Cummings was present at this séance: "The appointed time came. Fires were lit. The Tohunga repaired to the darkest corner of the room. All was silent, save the sobbing of the sisters of the deceased warrior-chief. There were thirty of us, sitting on the rush-strewn floor, the door shut and the fire now burning down to embers. Suddenly there came a voice out from the partial darkness. 'Salutation! Salutation, to my family, to my tribe, to you, pakeha, my friend!' Our feelings were taken by storm. The oldest sister screamed and rushed with extended arms in the direction from whence the voice came. Her brother, seizing her, restrained her . . . The spirit spoke again. 'Speak to me, my family.' At last the brother spoke. 'How is it with you? Is it well with you in that country?' The answer came—not in the voice of the Tohunga-medium, but in tones recognized by the family—'It is well with me.' A woman from another part of the room now anxiously cried out: 'Have you seen my sister?' 'Yes, I have seen her. She is happy in our beautiful country.' 'Tell her my love so great for her will never cease.' 'Yes. I will bear the message.'

"I said, 'We cannot find the book with the registered names; where have you concealed it?' The answer came instantly: 'I concealed it between the tahuhu of my house and the thatch, straight over you as you go in at the door.' The brother rushed out to see. All was silence. In five minutes he came hurriedly back, with the book in his hand! It astonished me."

—*RB*

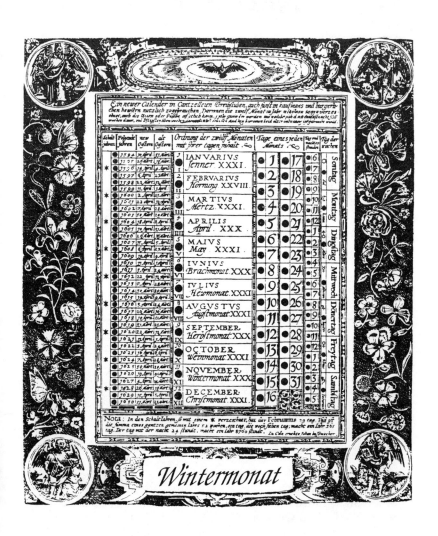

Wintermonat

November

Monday

Tuesday

Wednesday

1

Thursday

Moon Sign: Taurus
Moon Phase: 2nd Quarter
Festival: Assembly of Tara
      2nd day of Samhain
      Fire Festival

Tarot Card: Ace of Swords
Herb: Hellebore
Incense: Cinnamon
Mineral: Amber
Color: Blue
Name of Power: Samhuin

2

Friday

Moon Sign: Taurus
Moon Phase: Full Moon (Snow)
Festival: All Souls' Day
         Last Day of Samhain

Tarot Card: Two of Swords
Herb: Bearded Darnel
Incense: Frankincense
Mineral: Kyanite
Color: Green
Name of Power: Neb-Er-Tcher

3

Saturday

Moon Sign: Gemini
Moon Phase: 3rd Quarter
Festival: Gaelic New Year

Tarot Card: Three of Swords
Herb: Red Alder
Incense: Sandalwood
Mineral: Obsidian
Color: Black
Name of Power: Khepera

4

Sunday

Moon Sign: Gemini
Moon Phase: 3rd Quarter

Tarot Card: Four of Swords
Herb: Borage
Incense: Myrrh
Mineral: Tektite
Color: Yellow
Name of Power: Bibi

NOVEMBER

S	M	T	W	T	F	S
				1	2	3
4	5	6	7	8	9	10
11	12	13	14	15	16	17
18	19	20	21	22	23	24
25	26	27	28	29	30	

5 *Monday*

Moon Sign: Cancer
Moon Phase: 3rd Quarter

Tarot Card: Five of Swords
Herb: Cannabis
Incense: Jasmine
Mineral: Scenic Agate
Color: White
Name of Power: Zaka

6 *Tuesday*

Moon Sign: Cancer
Moon Phase: 3rd Quarter

Tarot Card: Six of Swords
Herb: Chickweed
Incense: Benzoin
Mineral: Amethyst
Color: Red
Name of Power: Hemhemti

7 *Wednesday*

Moon Sign: Cancer
Moon Phase: 3rd Quarter

Tarot Card: Seven of Swords
Herb: Cornflower
Incense: Pine
Mineral: Cape Ruby
Color: Purple
Name of Power: Peklo

8 *Thursday*

Moon Sign: Leo
Moon Phase: 3rd Quarter

Tarot Card: Eight of Swords
Herb: Dogbane
Incense: Cinnamon
Mineral: Yellow Jasper
Color: Blue
Name of Power: Ceres

9 *Friday*

Moon Sign: Leo
Moon Phase: 4th Quarter

Tarot Card: Nine of Swords
Herb: European Centaury
Incense: Frankincense
Mineral: Yellow Diamond
Color: Green
Name of Power: Helena

10 *Saturday*

Moon Sign: Virgo
Moon Phase: 4th Quarter

Tarot Card: Ten of Swords
Herb: Flax
Incense: Sandalwood
Mineral: Green Zircon
Color: Black
Name of Power: Nichevin

11 *Sunday*

Moon Sign: Virgo
Moon Phase: 4th Quarter
Festival: Celtic November Day

Tarot Card: Page of Swords
Herb: Goldenrod
Incense: Myrrh
Mineral: Jet
Color: Yellow
Name of Power: Qrunlah

NOVEMBER

S	M	T	W	T	F	S
				1	2	3
4	5	6	7	8	9	10
11	12	13	14	15	16	17
18	19	20	21	22	23	24
25	26	27	28	29	30	

12 *Monday*

Moon Sign: Libra
Moon Phase: 4th Quarter

Tarot Card: Knight of Swords
Herb: Hedge Mustard
Incense: Jasmine
Mineral: Peridot
Color: White
Name of Power: Shango

13 *Tuesday*

Moon Sign: Libra
Moon Phase: 4th Quarter

Tarot Card: Queen of Swords
Herb: Holly
Incense: Benzoin
Mineral: Spinel
Color: Red
Name of Power: Feronia

14 *Wednesday*

Moon Sign: Libra
Moon Phase: 4th Quarter

Tarot Card: King of Swords
Herb: Imperial Masterwort
Incense: Pine
Mineral: Turquoise
Color: Purple
Name of Power: Herne

15 *Thursday*

Moon Sign: Scorpio
Moon Phase: 4th Quarter

Tarot Card: Ace of Wands
Herb: Knotweed
Incense: Cinnamon
Mineral: Jade
Color: Blue
Name of Power: Oxossi

16 *Friday*

Moon Sign: Scorpio
Moon Phase: New Moon

Tarot Card: Two of Wands
Herb: Linden
Incense: Frankincense
Mineral: Cape Ruby
Color: Green
Name of Power: Hecate

17 *Saturday*

Moon Sign: Sagittarius
Moon Phase: 1st Quarter

Tarot Card: Three of Wands
Herb: Marsh Tea
Incense: Sandalwood
Mineral: Leucite
Color: Black
Name of Power: Patachel

18 *Sunday*

Moon Sign: Sagittarius
Moon Phase: 1st Quarter

Tarot Card: Four of Wands
Herb: Milkwort
Incense: Myrrh
Mineral: Blue Opal
Color: Yellow
Name of Power: Forcas

NOVEMBER						
S	M	T	W	T	F	S
					1	2	3
4	5	6	7	8	9	10
11	12	13	14	15	16	17
18	19	20	21	22	23	24
25	26	27	28	29	30	

19 *Monday*

Moon Sign: Sagittarius
Moon Phase: 1st Quarter

Tarot Card: Five of Wands
Herb: Monarda
Incense: Jasmine
Mineral: Violet Tourmaline
Color: White
Name of Power: Qeth

20 *Tuesday*

Moon Sign: Capricorn
Moon Phase: 1st Quarter

Tarot Card: Six of Wands
Herb: Feltwort
Incense: Benzoin
Mineral: African Jade
Color: Red
Name of Power: Cerberus

21 *Wednesday*

Moon Sign: Capricorn
Moon Phase: 1st Quarter

Tarot Card: Seven of Wands
Herb: Black Oak
Incense: Pine
Mineral: Aquamarine
Color: Purple
Name of Power: Zau

22 *Thursday*

Moon Sign: Aquarius
Moon Phase: 1st Quarter
Sun enters Sagittarius

Tarot Card: Eight of Wands
Herb: Passion Flower
Incense: Cinnamon
Mineral: Zebra Stone
Color: Blue
Name of Power: Siva

23   *Friday*

Moon Sign: Aquarius
Moon Phase: 1st Quarter
Festival: Shinjosai

Tarot Card: Nine of Wands
Herb: Pitcher Plant
Incense: Frankincense
Mineral: Topazolite
Color: Green
Name of Power: Konohana-
                        Hime

24   *Saturday*

Moon Sign: Aquarius
Moon Phase: 1st Quarter

Tarot Card: Ten of Wands
Herb: Quaking Aspen
Incense: Sandalwood
Mineral: Coral Agate
Color: Black
Name of Power: Alcheghek

25   *Sunday*

Moon Sign: Pisces
Moon Phase: 2nd Quarter
Festival: Feast of Santa
         Catalina de Alejandría

Tarot Card: Page of Wands
Herb: Bitter Ash
Incense: Myrrh
Mineral: Olivine
Color: Yellow
Name of Power: Nago-Bolisha

NOVEMBER

S	M	T	W	T	F	S
				1	2	3
4	5	6	7	8	9	10
11	12	13	14	15	16	17
18	19	20	21	22	23	24
25	26	27	28	29	30	

26
Monday

Moon Sign: Pisces
Moon Phase: 2nd Quarter

Tarot Card: Knight of Wands
Herb: Rattlesnake Plantain
Incense: Jasmine
Mineral: Black Tourmaline
Color: White
Name of Power: Amam

27
Tuesday

Moon Sign: Aries
Moon Phase: 2nd Quarter

Tarot Card: Queen of Wands
Herb: Rue
Incense: Benzoin
Mineral: Pyrite
Color: Red
Name of Power: Dantallan

28
Wednesday

Moon Sign: Aries
Moon Phase: 2nd Quarter

Tarot Card: King of Wands
Herb: Scotch Broom
Incense: Pine
Mineral: Yellow Sapphire
Color: Purple
Name of Power: Chanda

29
Thursday

Moon Sign: Taurus
Moon Phase: 2nd Quarter

Tarot Card: Ace of Cups
Herb: Solomon's Seal
Incense: Cinnamon
Mineral: Black Amber
Color: Blue
Name of Power: Malalu

30

Friday

Moon Sign: Taurus
Moon Phase: 2nd Quarter

Tarot Card: Two of Cups
Herb: Woundwort
Incense: Frankincense
Mineral: Fire Opal
Color: Green
Name of Power: Chango

Saturday

Sunday

NOVEMBER						
S	M	T	W	T	F	S
				1	2	3
4	5	6	7	8	9	10
11	12	13	14	15	16	17
18	19	20	21	22	23	24
25	26	27	28	29	30	

Shamanism

Raymond Buckland

The word *shaman* comes from the Siberian tribal language of Tungus (of the Ural-Altaic peoples of the arctic and central Asian regions), though the practice of shamanism is by no means limited to that area.

A shaman is something of a medicine man/priest/healer. Yet he is more than that. While a medicine man will tend to the sick, working with herbs, roots, barks and the like, the shaman works more on the psychological level. He will go on "a journey" for the benefit of the one who is ill; he will direct sacrifices, he will seek out new knowledge, and he will accompany the spirits of the dead on their journey to the afterlife. Yet he is not a medium in the sense of a Spiritualist medium. He does not simply act as a bridge by being possessed by departed spirits and allowing them to speak through him. Rather, he goes out to the spirits and into their realm of existence. How is he able to do this? By what might be termed an out-of-the-body experience.

There are three regions of existence. There is the middle region where we live our everyday lives, then there are the regions of the "lower world" and the "upper world." It is these last two which the shaman is able to visit at will. Typically, when visiting the lower world the shaman enters by way of a (visualized) tunnel into the earth, a cave, an animal's burrow, or down through a hollow tree. To reach the upper world, he will go up from the topmost branches of a tree, or rise with the smoke of a fire, or ride up on a cloud, or on the back of a bird. These are ecstatic journeys, brought about through methods we shall examine. The purpose of the journey is usually to bring back information relating to the diagnosing and curing of a patient, to find the location of necessary resources, or to assist the recently deceased.

Some Siberian tribes have both "white" shamans, who dress all in white, and "black" shamans, who actually dress in blue. The former deal with the gods and the latter with spirits, including evil spirits.

There are several possible ways to become a shaman. Frequently it is a hereditary thing, the trainee being the offspring, or close relative, of the teacher. But occasionally someone shows signs of shamanship—perhaps by their general behavior; by having dreams, by a detachment, a desire for solitude, perhaps even by going into spontaneous trances—and the tribe as a whole elects him to be trained. Another way, closely akin to this, is for the person to be "called," to receive a vision or in some way be specifically directed to the position, presumably by the gods or spirits. Yet another way is when the individual undergoes some traumatic experience. This could be anything from falling out of a tree to being struck by lightning.

However it comes about, there will be a long period of training with the master shaman. In this training the initiate will learn the mythology of the tribe, the traditions, the secret language of the shamans, the actual techniques for leaving the body. He will also almost certainly learn much by actual experience, through dreams and visions, meditations and trances. In this way, then, he is taught both by the master shaman and by the spirits themselves.

With some peoples there is a period when the shaman-to-be will detach himself completely from the rest of the clan and go and live wild in the forest or on the mountain. He may stay away for weeks, or months, living off what he can hunt and gather.

When he eventually returns he may be in a disheveled state, often speaking and behaving like a madman. But eventually he will return to normal. It is believed that during this period of disorder his soul is away being taught by the spirits.

Whatever the form of initiation—and as with all initiations, universally—there is a death and rebirth experience. The shaman may find himself torn to pieces by wild animals or monsters, devoured by demons, dismembered by the spirits. He is subsequently reborn—or pieced back together—as an initiated being. It seems common that the shaman is reduced to a mere skeleton, at some point, then "rebuilt" from those bare bones.

The shaman refers to the "other world" that he visits as a "world of spirits." Psychologists, especially of the Jungian school, would no doubt describe it as the collective unconscious or the realm of archetypes. But to the shaman it is very real. It contains much potential power and wisdom and has its own natural laws.

To reach it the shaman passes into a trance-like state. This may be induced in a variety of ways: dancing, chanting, fasting, drugs, music. Wiccans are familiar with some of these methods of arousing power from within, and use them for the working of Wiccan magick. But the shaman goes a step further. He allows himself to enter into the altered state. This state seems to be of the theta wavelength that is associated with dreams and visionary states.

Drumming is one of the most common methods used for passing into the state. It also happens to be far superior to the use of drugs in that it is more predictable and more controllable. Oftimes the drumming is accompanied by dancing on the part of the shaman. The drumming itself is a repetitive, driving beat, usually in the range of five or six beats per second. This coincides with the frequency of theta waves in the brain. It has been suggested that this may lead to the blocking of the sequential processing function of the left lobe of the brain, allowing the right hemisphere to become dominant.

The shaman sees himself—or, more correctly, actually seems to experience—passing down into the ground (if visiting the lower world). He generally follows down the winding tunnel as it twists and turns, going ever deeper. Eventually he comes out at the far end and finds himself in open country. However, there are

occasions when he will speed down the tunnel so fast that he is hardly aware of its existence, suddenly finding himself out at the far end. From there he might experience any number of things: encounters with monstrous animals, talks with wise men who pass on advice, conversations with the spirits of the mountains or rivers.

There is a movement towards shamanism in many parts of today's society. What might be termed "neo-shamans" are subjecting themselves to sweat lodges, flotation tanks, strobe lights, and many other forms of modern technology designed to bring about the altered state of consciousness experienced by the true shaman. Much of it is very effective, both as a spiritual path and as a path towards self-realization through shamanic counseling. Several psychotherapists have taken an interest in the process and some have even developed additional, modern tools and techniques.

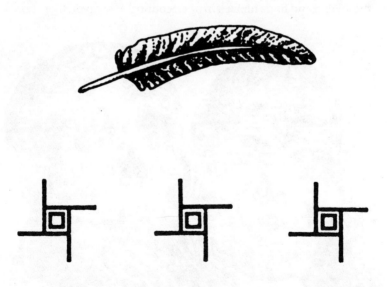

Cat Magic

Kathleen Wilder

When exploring the realm of natural magic, there is no better
guide and companion than the enigmatic cat. Many of us acquire
cats magickally—Poof! One day there's a cat on your doorstep,
the next minute it's in your kitchen and, very quickly, you find the
new arrival is in your heart. Before long it will also be an un-
rehearsed part of your ritual, since most cats seem to have a
natural affinity for magical ceremony, perhaps an inherited mem-
ory of the fine days their ancestors spent in the temples of
Bast in Egypt.

    Several things occur when a cat finds that you have been
using *her* temple space for *your* rituals. Unnecessary clutter on the
altar top is taken care of with a sweep of the well-aimed tail; it is
impossible to curl up comfortably with so many crystals and can-

dles and so on. Besides, these objects are put to much better use as playthings for the High Priests and Priestesses of the Goddess Bast. Lit candles can never be left unattended for fear of singeing the sacred fur, and incense sticks, while admired for their curling smoke and interesting smell, also make excellent toy daggers to be carried crosswise in the teeth when the temple cat feels like playing pirate.

With time and maturity some of these temple antics cease or at least become somewhat less frequent. Some felines have an instinctive sense of appropriate behavior and will dance across the altar with breathtaking grace, disturbing nothing but the air. Others will leave an offering of a whisker.

Magically, cats are an excellent way to avoid allowing your magical and spiritual work to become too etheric. They are grounding influences on you and your environment and are naturally attracted to some varieties of negative energy, which they apparently possess the ability to neutralize without harm to themselves.

If you want to protect your cat from harm, why not inscribe protective runes on the inside of its collar? Other protective symbols can also be used. And if there's anything that cats find truly magical in this world, it is catnip. Catnip mice are easy to make and serve as a very appropriate offering to your sacred cats. Simply take a piece of felt cut into an oval, fill it with a couple tablespoons of dried or fresh catnip, and stitch it up. Use regular sewing thread if possible, since thicker threads and yarn could come undone and present a choking hazard to your pet. If you have a statue of Bast, set the catnip mouse before her and wait. Your cat will make her daily temple rounds and discover it. This is similar to a practice once found in Egyptian temples, where the offerings to the gods were left in front of their statues for a period of time (usually no more than a day) and then consumed by the priests or distributed by them. My statue of Bast is about two feet tall and made of plaster. Similar statues are available at plaster figurine stores and can be either painted or left plain. Around her neck I have placed a string of peridot beads, since green is one of her sacred colors (red is the other). And in front of her I place a bowl of dry cat food and another one of fresh water. Somehow, although their other temple duties are varied and pressing, my cats faithfully consume the offerings every day and remind me if *my* attention to *their* temple is lacking.

May Bast bless and protect you and make certain that your temple never lacks for a full staff of furred priests and priestesses!

The Wild Time

Scott Cunningham

It is important for us, as those who tread the ways of ancient magic, to set aside a few minutes a day, or an hour a week, to be with the wild.

A trip to the countryside may fulfill this obligation. The tall trees swaying above us, the wildflowers and shrubs at our feet and the concrete-free ground stretching out for miles is refreshing to the eyes. Clear air and green energy recharge our magical batteries. These wild times renew our links with nature, the ultimate source of power.

Enter a cave or visit a beach. Climb a small hill and ramble down a leaf-shrouded valley. Sit amidst a plain full of grasses and flowers and drink in pure energy.

The deserts, too, offer stark, unbridled powers. Stand with the cacti and listen to their fiery messages. Feel the stored solar forces beating in the sand beneath your feet.

Gardens, especially those in which seeds are scattered and the plants are allowed to grow unhindered by human hands, are also pools of nourishing Earth powers. Stop awhile in such a place and relax. In winter, celebrate rain and ice and snow.

Those who are fortunate to live on the edge of a wilderness, far from cities, should also venture into it from time to time for no other purpose but to rediscover the wonders at their doorsteps.

The untrodden corners of the Earth are waiting for us. Indulge yourself with a few magical moments of wild time.

Majestic Longevity

Raymond Buckland

Is it possible for any living thing to be alive for three thousand years or more? Very definitely yes. There are ancient Sequoia trees (redwoods) which are that age, and still going strong. The General Sherman Tree, in Sequoia National Park, is 272 feet tall, has an average basal diameter of 30.7 feet, and is estimated to be *3,800 years old!* Trees that live for many hundreds of years are almost commonplace.

Trees are awesome, magickal things, when you pause to study them. They start out as tiny seeds, struggle up out of the earth, battle the elements, and become majestic creatures exuding great power. It was an ancient belief that spirits inhabited trees. Even today, in certain primitive areas, a native will not chop down a tree without first asking permission of the spirit within. In addition, he will knock on the trunk of the tree to give the spirit fair warning and time to get out. In fact it is from this custom that we get the expression "Knock on wood!" for good luck.

From trees we gather fruits of great variety; also syrup. Leaves and barks of various trees have great medicinal qualities. Timber, of course, is invaluable. From it we get such products as rubber and paper. Trees purify the air we breathe and influence the atmosphere. But from the standing, growing tree we can receive tremendous psychic energy. To quote from *Buckland's Complete Book of Witchcraft* (Llewellyn): "If ever you feel completely drained, if ever you are angry or tense, go out and sit against a tree. Choose a good, solid tree (oak or pine are good) and sit down on the ground with your back straight, pressed up against the trunk. Close your eyes and relax. You will feel a gradual change come over you. Your tension, your anger, your tiredness will disappear. It will seem to drain out of you. Then, in its place, you will feel a growing warmth, a feeling of love, and comfort. It comes from the tree. Accept it and be glad. Sit there until you feel completely whole again. Then, before leaving, stand with your arms about the tree and thank it."

It was an ancient custom for women to lie beneath a tree in childbirth. By embracing the tree in the final stages of labor, a woman would transmit her pain to the tree. But the interesting part of this is that the tree accepted the pain, and replaced it with soothing love. Trees work *with* us, and seem aware of our times of need. Another ancient custom was for a mother to bury a new-born child's placenta and umbilical cord at the base of a tree (probably the same tree she clung to in the birthing process) to protect the child as it matured.

From earliest times humans have venerated trees, looking upon them either as deities or as representing deity. Ancient Assyrian and Chaldean engraved cylinders show sacred trees, the tree being a symbol of the Chaldean religion—in particular the cypress or pomegranate. The banyan tree was sacred in India; the cypress in Persia. Sycamores were favored in Egypt, with belief in certain deities dwelling in the trees. The idea of a god or gods dwelling inside a tree is found universally.

Sacred groves were common throughout the ancient world. These were places not only in which to worship the gods but also in which to worship, and pay due reverence to, the trees themselves. Many times the trees were thought to be oracles, their roots reaching down into the underworld and therefore to the wisdom and knowledge available to the dead. There are several such trees mentioned in the Old Testament, most especially the tree "of the revealer" mentioned in Genesis (12:6), and the tree "of the diviners," mentioned in Judges (9:37).

The Tree of Life of the Cabala is well known, representing the universe. In Scandinavian mythology the tree—Yggdrasil—is the universe; similarly in India, where it is the fig tree Asvattha.

Francoise Strachan gives the following list of special tree powers, in her book *Natural Magic* (New York, 1974):

ALMOND—This tree symbolizes virginity. In phallicism it is identified with the yoni. It also symbolizes fruitfulness and self-protection.

ASH—Considered the father of trees. A special guardian spirit resides in it, being especially good for absorbing sickness.

APPLE—Helps fertility.

BANANA—From the shape of the fruit, is regarded as very much a masculine tree.

BANYAN—Imbibes eternal life, productivity, knowledge and happiness. Also it possesses great powers of fertility.

COCONUT—A very feminine and fertile tree. The shell of its fruit represents the womb. Also regarded as a charm against the evil eye.

FIG—A bisexual tree; the fruit being feminine and the leaves masculine.

IVY—Sacred to Bacchus, god of wine and revelry.

MISTLETOE—A healer. Symbolizes love and purity.

OAK—Sacred to the Druids. Associated with Zeus, Thor, and Jupiter.

PALM—Self-renewing. Aids in rejuvenation; symbolizes the matrix of life itself.

PEACH—Abundance. The emblem of marriage.

PINE—Eternal symbol of life and immortality. Especially soothing to be near. To many ancients, symbolic of fire.

WILLOW—Associated with death and sorrow.

YEW—Like the Willow, frequently associated with death and also with black magick rituals.

In his master work, *The Golden Bough*, Sir James Frazer speaks a great deal about trees. He speaks of *Rex Nemorensis*, the "King of the Wood," who served the goddess Diana in her sacred grove. Frazer suggests that this "King" represented the oak-god Jupiter and that union of the god and the goddess was intended to "make the earth gay with the blossoms of spring and the fruits of the autumn, and to gladden the hearts of men and women with healthful offspring." This union was—and still is—celebrated in the festival of May Day, with the Maypole and the May Queen.

Trees are wonderful, awesome, living beings. They deserve respect, grateful thanks and, yes, perhaps even worship.

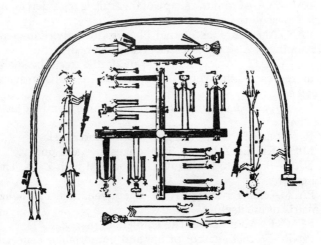

The Hopi Shaman

The patient lay sick on his bed, watching the medicine man carefully. The patient's wife was following tradition and feeding the
visitor a good meal before he started his inspection of the patient.
When he had finished eating, the medicine man wiped his hands
on his clothing and approached the bed.

He loosened the patient's clothing, then started to massage
the sick man's stomach. Every once in a while the old man would
stop and, bringing his right hand up to his mouth, blow into it. He
did this four times, four being a sacred number to the Hopi. On
the fourth blow he opened his hand to show that he had blown
out a small piece of bone. The sick man looked at it and nodded
his head as though he had been expecting something like that.

The medicine man went back to his massaging and hand-blowing. Again, on the fourth blow he displayed a piece of black obsidian. He showed that to the patient, then laid it alongside the bone, on the floor beside the bed. The third time he produced some grains of a blue mineral from which the Hopi make a paint for painting sacred objects.

The old man picked up all three items and cast them into the fire. Sternly he told the patient that they had been "shot" into his stomach by an evil sorcerer, in an attempt to kill him. The patient and his wife nodded their heads. They could believe it. It happened all the time in the Hopi village. With the foreign objects removed from his stomach—and with the benefit of some herbal brew the medicine man also gave him—the patient recovered quickly.

The ability to perform black magick is known as *duhisa*, and that ability is believed to be derived from a familiar animal. The amount of *duhisa* obtained varies with the nature of the sorcerer's associated animal. Coyotes, bull snakes, crows, owls, cats and dogs; all can provide this evil power. The worst provider of all, giving most *duhisa*, is the black ant. Along with this idea of obtaining power from the animals goes the belief that, when a person does so, he or she also comes into possession of a second heart—an animal heart.

No Hopi knows who might or might not be a sorcerer. It could be anyone. It could especially be someone of power, which is why Hopis do not like to accept any high office in their pueblo. If they do have to accept such a post they remain forever extremely sober and restrained, showing a great deal of humility, so that they may not be suspected of being "two-hearted."

Sorcerers maintain their numbers either by accepting voluntary recruits, or by teaching their craft to children too young to really know what is happening. It is said that sorcerers steal away sleeping children to initiate them into their rites. The initiate is taught how to change into his or her beast of association. This transformation is done by somersaulting through a hoop. The change back to human form takes place when the person tumbles backwards through the same hoop. Once having gone through the entire ceremony, the initiate is regarded as now possessing two hearts and being capable of performing sorcery. To prolong his or her own existence, the sorcerer must then cause the death of at least one relative each year. "Shooting" foreign objects into the person's body is the favorite way of bringing this about. The Hopi believe that if the sorcerer grows repentant and fails to do what is expected, he or she will die an early death.

—RB

Chriftmonat

December

Yule Lore

One traditional Yuletide practice is the creation of a Yule tree. This can be a living, potted tree which can later be planted in the ground, or a cut one. The choice is yours.

Appropriate Wiccan decorations are fun to make, from strings of dried rosebuds and cinnamon sticks (or popcorn and cranberries) for garlands, to bags of fragrant spices which are hung from boughs. Quartz crystals can be wrapped with shiny wire and suspended from sturdy branches to resemble icicles. Apples, oranges and lemons hanging from boughs are strikingly beautiful, natural decorations, and were customary in ancient times.

Many enjoy the custom of lighting the Yule log. This is a graphic representation of the rebirth of the God within the sacred fire of the Mother Goddess. If you choose to burn one, select a proper log (traditionally of oak or pine). Carve or chalk a figure of the Sun (such as a rayed disc) or the God (a horned circle or a figure of a man) upon it, with the white-handled knife, and set it alight in the fireplace at dusk on Yule. As the log burns, visualize the Sun shining within it and think of the coming warmer days.

As to food, nuts, fruits such as apples and pears, cakes of carraways soaked in cider, and (for non-vegetarians) pork are traditional fare. Wassil, lambswool, hibiscus or ginger tea are fine drinks for the Simple Feast or Yule meals.

Reprinted from *Wicca: A Guide for the Solitary Practitioner* by Scott Cunningham.

Friday

1

Saturday

Moon Sign: Gemini
Moon Phase: 2nd Quarter

Tarot Card: Three of Cups
Herb: Ivy
Incense: Sandalwood
Mineral: Black Coral
Color: Black
Name of Power: Bruma

2

Sunday

Moon Sign: Gemini
Moon Phase: Full Moon (Oak)

Tarot Card: Four of Cups
Herb: Bear's Garlic
Incense: Myrrh
Mineral: Pigeonblood Agate
Color: Yellow
Name of Power: Pingala

DECEMBER

S	M	T	W	T	F	S
						1
2	3	4	5	6	7	8
9	10	11	12	13	14	15
16	17	18	19	20	21	22
23	24	25	26	27	28	29
30	31					

3 *Monday*

Moon Sign: Cancer
Moon Phase: 3rd Quarter

Tarot Card: Five of Cups
Herb: Smooth Alder
Incense: Jasmine
Mineral: Soapstone
Color: White
Name of Power: Rhea

4 *Tuesday*

Moon Sign: Cancer
Moon Phase: 3rd Quarter

Tarot Card: Six of Cups
Herb: Boxwood
Incense: Benzoin
Mineral: Green Feldspar
Color: Red
Name of Power: Pallas Athena

5 *Wednesday*

Moon Sign: Leo
Moon Phase: 3rd Quarter

Tarot Card: Seven of Cups
Herb: Caraway
Incense: Pine
Mineral: Smithsonite
Color: Purple
Name of Power: Baracata

6 *Thursday*

Moon Sign: Leo
Moon Phase: 3rd Quarter

Tarot Card: Eight of Cups
Herb: Chicory
Incense: Cinnamon
Mineral: Green Zircon
Color: Blue
Name of Power: Saatet-Ta

7
Friday

Moon Sign: Virgo
Moon Phase: 3rd Quarter

Tarot Card: Nine of Cups
Herb: Corydalis
Incense: Frankincense
Mineral: Violet Sapphire
Color: Green
Name of Power: Elohim

8
Saturday

Moon Sign: Virgo
Moon Phase: 4th Quarter
Festival: Feast of Nuestra
      Senora Guadalupe

Tarot Card: Ten of Cups
Herb: Dog Poison
Incense: Sandalwood
Mineral: Blue Opal
Color: Black
Name of Power: Schilalyi

9
Sunday

Moon Sign: Libra
Moon Phase: 4th Quarter
Festival: Feast of Nuestra
      Senora Guadalupe

Tarot Card: Page of Cups
Herb: European Vervain
Incense: Myrrh
Mineral: Beryl
Color: Yellow
Name of Power: Tonantzin

DECEMBER						
S	M	T	W	T	F	S
						1
2	3	4	5	6	7	8
9	10	11	12	13	14	15
16	17	18	19	20	21	22
23	24	25	26	27	28	29
30	31					

10 *Monday*

Moon Sign: Libra
Moon Phase: 4th Quarter

Tarot Card: Knight of Cups
Herb: Foxglove
Incense: Jasmine
Mineral: Carnelian
Color: White
Name of Power: Lux Mundi

11 *Tuesday*

Moon Sign: Libra
Moon Phase: 4th Quarter

Tarot Card: Queen of Cups
Herb: Goldenseal
Incense: Benzoin
Mineral: White Opal
Color: Red
Name of Power: Kore

12 *Wednesday*

Moon Sign: Scorpio
Moon Phase: 4th Quarter

Tarot Card: King of Cups
Herb: Hellebore
Incense: Pine
Mineral: Orange Spinel
Color: Purple
Name of Power: Loco-Atissu

13 *Thursday*

Moon Sign: Scorpio
Moon Phase: 4th Quarter

Tarot Card: Ace of Pentacles
Herb: Hollyhock
Incense: Cinnamon
Mineral: Black Amber
Color: Blue
Name of Power: Koto-Hajime

14 *Friday*

Moon Sign: Sagittarius
Moon Phase: 4th Quarter

Tarot Card: Two of Pentacles
Herb: Indian Corn
Incense: Frankincense
Mineral: Red Spinel
Color: Green
Name of Power: Phra

15 *Saturday*

Moon Sign: Sagittarius
Moon Phase: 4th Quarter
Festival: 1st of Halcyon Days

Tarot Card: Three of Pentacles
Herb: Kola
Incense: Sandalwood
Mineral: Nephite
Color: Black
Name of Power: Alcyone

16 *Sunday*

Moon Sign: Sagittarius
Moon Phase: New Moon

Tarot Card: Four of Pentacles
Herb: Lion's Foot
Incense: Myrrh
Mineral: Sodalite
Color: Yellow
Name of Power: Herachio

			DECEMBER			
S	M	T	W	T	F	S
						1
2	3	4	5	6	7	8
9	10	11	12	13	14	15
16	17	18	19	20	21	22
23	24	25	26	27	28	29
30	31					

17 *Monday*

Moon Sign: Capricorn
Moon Phase: 1st Quarter
Festival: Saturnalia (1st day)

Tarot Card: Five of Pentacles
Herb: Masterwort
Incense: Jasmine
Mineral: Star Sapphire
Color: White
Name of Power: Ops

18 *Tuesday*

Moon Sign: Capricorn
Moon Phase: 1st Quarter

Tarot Card: Six of Pentacles
Herb: Mint
Incense: Benzoin
Mineral: Zoisite
Color: Red
Name of Power: Chevob

19 *Wednesday*

Moon Sign: Aquarius
Moon Phase: 1st Quarter
Festival: Start of Sorrowing
　　　　　Time in Celtic
　　　　　Calendar

Tarot Card: Seven of Pentacles
Herb: Mountain Balm
Incense: Pine
Mineral: Tanzanite
Color: Purple
Name of Power: Khermuti

20 *Thursday*

Moon Sign: Aquarius
Moon Phase: 1st Quarter

Tarot Card: Eight of Pentacles
Herb: Mustard
Incense: Cinnamon
Mineral: Jasper
Color: Blue
Name of Power: Kar

21
Friday

Moon Sign: Aquarius
Moon Phase: 1st Quarter
Sun enters Capricorn
Festival: Winter Solstice;
        Yule Festival (1st day)

Tarot Card: Nine of Pentacles
Herb: Oat
Incense: Frankincense
Mineral: African Jade
Color: Green
Name of Power: Gu

22
Saturday

Moon Sign: Pisces
Moon Phase: 1st Quarter

Tarot Card: Ten of Pentacles
Herb: Pennyroyal
Incense: Sandalwood
Mineral: Beccarite
Color: Black
Name of Power: Rhiannon

23
Sunday

Moon Sign: Pisces
Moon Phase: 1st Quarter
Festival: Laurentalia

Tarot Card: Page of Pentacles
Herb: Plantain
Incense: Myrrh
Mineral: Fire Opal
Color: Yellow
Name of Power: Larunda

		DECEMBER				
S	M	T	W	T	F	S
						1
2	3	4	5	6	7	8
9	10	11	12	13	14	15
16	17	18	19	20	21	22
23	24	25	26	27	28	29
30	31					

24 *Monday*

Moon Sign: Aries
Moon Phase: 2nd Quarter
Festival: Juvenalia

Tarot Card: Knight of Pentacles
Herb: Tacamahac
Incense: Jasmine
Mineral: Cape Ruby
Color: White
Name of Power: Oip-Teaa-
                    Pdoke

25 *Tuesday*

Moon Sign: Aries
Moon Phase: 2nd Quarter
Festival: Christmas

Tarot Card: Queen of Pentacles
Herb: Bitter Wood
Incense: Benzoin
Mineral: Peridot
Color: Red
Name of Power: Hiems

26 *Wednesday*

Moon Sign: Taurus
Moon Phase: 2nd Quarter

Tarot Card: King of Pentacles
Herb: Adder's Violet
Incense: Pine
Mineral: Greenstone
Color: Purple
Name of Power: Ortagu

27 *Thursday*

Moon Sign: Taurus
Moon Phase: 2nd Quarter

Tarot Card: The Magician
Herb: Safflower
Incense: Cinnamon
Mineral: Labradorite
Color: Blue
Name of Power: Arawhon

28
Friday

Moon Sign: Gemini
Moon Phase: 2nd Quarter
Festival: End of Halcyon Days

Tarot Card: The High Priestess
Herb: Scurvy Grass
Incense: Frankincense
Mineral: Spectrolite
Color: Green
Name of Power: Malalu

29
Saturday

Moon Sign: Gemini
Moon Phase: 2nd Quarter

Tarot Card: The Empress
Herb: Sorrel
Incense: Sandalwood
Mineral: Jet
Color: Black
Name of Power: Kharebutu

30
Sunday

Moon Sign: Cancer
Moon Phase: 2nd Quarter

Tarot Card: The Emperor
Herb: Wormwood
Incense: Myrrh
Mineral: Red Zircon
Color: Yellow
Name of Power: Nago-Iki

DECEMBER

S	M	T	W	T	F	S
						1
2	3	4	5	6	7	8
9	10	11	12	13	14	15
16	17	18	19	20	21	22
23	24	25	26	27	28	29
30	31					

JANUARY 1991

S	M	T	W	T	F	S
		1	2	3	4	5
6	7	8	9	10	11	12
13	14	15	16	17	18	19
20	21	22	23	24	25	26
27	28	29	30	31		

31

Monday

Moon Sign: Cancer
Moon Phase: Full Moon
　　　　　(Wolf)
Festival: Hogmanay

Tarot Card: The Hierophant
Herb: Sweet Flag
Incense: Jasmine
Mineral: Mexican Onyx
Color: White
Name of Power: Sekhmet

Tuesday

Wednesday

Thursday

Magickal Power in the Spoken Word

Raymond Buckland

In themselves words can be a means of emotional control over persons and events. The words of a chant, a spell, can imbue a person with feelings of power and, by so doing, can help generate that power into reality. The foundation of successful spell casting lies in the power and mystery of "the word." In medieval times it was believed that some words were so powerful in themselves that they could not, or should not, ever be pronounced. Others were powerful enough that great care had to be exercised as to when and where they were spoken.

To quote from *Tyrall of Witch-craft* (London, 1616): "Galen writeth, that a certain Sorcerer, by uttering and muttering but one word, immediately killed, or caused to die, a serpent or scorpion; Benivenius in his *De Abd. morb. Caus.*, affirmeth, that some kind of people have been observed to do hurt, and to surprise others, by using certain sacred and holy words."

Eliphas Levi said: "In magick to have said is to have done; to affirm and will what ought to be, is to create." These are the two necessary ingredients of magick. They are the strong belief/ desire, willing that it be so, and the right words. Finding those right words is usually either a question of trial and error, or of discovering previously effective (in other words, time-tested) words.

According to the Book of Genesis, "God said, 'Let there be light,' and there was light . . . And God said, 'Let there be a firmament in the midst of the waters . . .' And God said, 'Let the waters under the heaven be gathered together unto one place, and let the dry land appear . . .' And God said, 'Let the earth bring forth grass . . .' " And all these things came to pass, because God *said* them. According to the Old Testament, God created the world with *words*. This is a good example of the constructive power of words, of the power of The Word. And in magick we are doing exactly the same thing: using powerful words (and *appropriate* words) together with a concentration of power. It doesn't matter that we are not as powerful as God, incidentally, since we are not trying to create a whole world!

The words themselves must be spoken in a particular way. They must be spoken with authority. They must be spoken with *familiarity* (which is one of the reasons why modern-day magicians have little success using ancient Latin, Greek and other mystical texts they do not understand). And they must be spoken rhythmically. Chants and spells should either rhyme or, at the very least, have a repetitive, heavy, sonorous beat to them. This can, and should, contribute to a gradually rising state of excitement within the magician, adding immeasurably to the amount of power produced. In *The Power of Magic Chants* (Reward Books, 1980) I bring up a point that I find interesting and relevant to this. It is the fact that so many of today's rock songs feature constant (almost to the point of aggravation!) repetition of a word or phrase. The same word, or the same line of a song, is repeated over and over and over again. And these are the recordings that are at the top of the charts. Could it be that the very fact of that repetition is helping put them there, I wonder?

The power of the spoken word is implicitly believed in, especially if emanating from a known expert of the magickal art, and even more so if in foreign or uncommon language. The Egyptian texts say that the priest-magicians of ancient Egypt used foreign words for their magickal workings. Herodotus, the earliest Greek historian whose words have come down to us, tells that magickal chanting by the Egyptian magicians was what enabled them to lift the great blocks with which they built the pyramids. The magicians of the Middle Ages also used foreign languages, as did the medicine men of the Amerindians. The Houngan and Mambo of Voodoo speak in *langage*, a magical language taught them by the Loa (gods). It is even of note that the Ecumenical Council of 1963 only voted to allow the Catholic Mass to be said in languages other than Latin if the Latin was retained for "the precise verbal formula which is essential to the sacrament" (in other words, the words which are spoken by the priest to transform the bread and wine into the Body and Blood).

But, as I said above, it is essential that the person using the words know what they mean. It is no good repeating something parrot-fashion, or phonetically, in the hopes that these "great words of power" will be as effective for you as they were for the magicians who used them in the past. If you don't know what they mean, you *cannot* put the true, and necessary, feeling into them. And if you cannot put the necessary feeling into them, the magick will not work.

Circles

A Roman ambassador in a foreign country would draw a circle around himself with his staff to show he was safe from attack; the Babylonians drew a circle of flour on the floor round the bed of a sick man to keep demons away; German Jews, in the Middle Ages, would draw a circle round the bed of a woman in labor to protect her from evil spirits. The use of a circle to mark the boundary of a sacred area is very ancient (for example, Stonehenge). But the circle not only keeps the unwanted power out, it also keeps the wanted—the raised power, the magickal energy—in.

When magick is to be done, the Circle *must* be constructed with more care than might otherwise be the case. (It) must be very carefully cast and consecrated at the *Erecting the Temple*. Make sure the point of the sword, or athame, follows the line of the Cir-

cle exactly. The person casting the Circle should direct as much
personal energy down through the instrument and into the Circle as possible. Give a good, thorough sprinkling and censing.
Magick is done at the Esbat Circle, of course, so the *Esbat* and/or
Full/New Moon ceremony will be conducted, followed by the
Cakes and Ale. At this latter the coven will discuss fully what work
(magick) is to be done and *exactly how* it is to be done. Then—just
before actually starting the work—let the Priest/ess once more go
around the Circle with sword or athame, to reinforce it (second
sprinkling and censing not necessary, however). A few moments
should then be spent meditating on the whole picture of what is
to be done. In the actual working of magick you will be concentrating on the end result but for now, right at the start, meditate on
all that is to be accomplished.

—Buckland's Complete Book of Witchcraft
Llewellyn, 1988

Myth and Magick Survival in Dance and Rhyme

Folk rhymes and many nursery rhymes frequently contain elements of myth and magickal workings. Similarly, many dances—both children's and adult—contain ancient ritual steps and gestures. Obvious examples of the latter are the English Morris dances and, especially, the well-known Horn Dance from Abbots Bromley. A good example of the former is the children's rhyme:

"Ride a cockhorse to Banbury Cross
To see a fine lady upon a white horse;
With rings on her fingers and bells on her toes,
She shall have music wherever she goes."

A "cockhorse" was a hobbyhorse, which is featured in many Morris dances. Indeed, there is even a hobbyhorse as part of the Abbots Bromley Horn Dance ceremony. A hobbyhorse is made of a wooden framework, which hangs from the "rider's" shoulders, with a horse's head at the front (usually with snapping wooden jaws) and a tail at the rear. A skirt is attached around the frame to hide the performer's legs and there are often bells hanging from "martingales." Beryl de Zoete (in *Dance and Drama in Bali*) tells of a similar performer in a Balinese dance who, through ritual dance and rhythmic movement, throws himself into an ecstatic trance.

The white horse is a very ancient figure in British folklore. There are many huge figures of horses carved into the white chalk of hillsides, in the south of England. Lady Godiva rode a white horse through the streets of Coventry, and it seems probable that the lady riding to Banbury Cross was a similar personage.

The Goddess Epona was especially associated with horses. She, or her earthly representative, would have been greeted

Raising the Maypole
(from "The Book of Days" 1735)

with bells and general rejoicing. She would certainly have had "music wherever she goes." However, St. George, the patron saint of England, was originally the old god of sheep, cattle, horses, and vegetation. In his honor bells were often rung to drive evil spirits from the animals and the plants. So the bells on the toes of the riding lady might also connect with such an exorcism. Additionally, it was traditional on St. George's Day to parade a white horse, bedecked with bells, through the streets of London (specifically the Strand), and of Leicester and other towns and cities . . . possibly including Banbury?

There is a possibility, then, that the traditions associated with Epona and with George became confused, or perhaps were brought together for some unknown reason. George was not adopted as the patron saint of England until 1348. Prior to that he was a Spring culture hero and, according to Lewis Spence, "slew a dragon and thus let loose the magickal tank of life-giving moisture which the monster guarded." Spence further suggests: "His legend may have been superimposed upon that of an ancient British goddess of fructification, whose female worshippers passed to their secret rites in a state of nature [naked—*Ed.*]."

A final point is that the rhyme refers to the lady going to Banbury *Cross*. This would indicate a *crossroads* at Banbury. The crossroads was always a magickal place. It was, incidentally, frequently a place where three roads came together rather than the four we automatically seem to think of today.

Two of the most common forms of surviving ritual dances in England are the Morris dances and the Sword dances. The Morris dances are many and varied, the variations being as numerous as there are villages in England. Originally they were only danced by the men of the village but today there are quite a few excellent women's teams.

The origins of the dances are lost in time but many certainly originated as pagan fertility rituals, for both crops and humans. They were then performed by priests or others chosen especially for the parts. The "dibbling" of the sticks into the ground tied in with the planting of the seeds. In some dances the dancers leap high in the air, in the same way that the Witches of old did as part of their sympathetic magick to show the crops how high to grow.

The clashing of sticks, in some of the stick dances, or the furious weaving of white handkerchiefs, was intended to disperse evil spirits who otherwise might inhibit the fertility.

Dancing around the Maypole, on May Day, is a truly ancient custom. The Maypole itself has been traced back to pre-history. There is a fine representation of dancers around the Maypole in the stained glass windows at Batley, in Staffordshire, England, dating from the reign of Henry VIII. The figures dancing include the hobbyhorse, a jester, and the May Queen. Stubbes, the Elizabethan chronicler, described the Maypole as the "cheefest jewell" of the populous, saying "their Maie poole, which they bring home with great veneration: they have twentie or fourtie yoke of oxen, every oxe having a sweet nosegay of flowers tyed to the tippe of his hornes, and these oxen drawe home this Maie poole which is covered all over with flowers and herbes, bounde rounde about with strynges, from the top to the bottome, and sometyme painted with variable colours, with twoo or three hundred men, women and children following it. And thus beyond reared up, with handkerchiefs and flagges streamyng on the toppe, they strewe the grounde aboute, binde greene boughes about it, sett up Bowers and Arbours hard by it. And then fall they to banquet and feast, to leap and daunce aboute it."

The dance footed around the Maypole seems to have been of the nature of an ordinary round dance in which the performers sometimes took hands, at other times capered singly. Occasionally it took the form of "plaiting" the Maypole. There is a recorded instance of this being done in the Tudor period, to the tune of "Sellenger's Round."

—RB

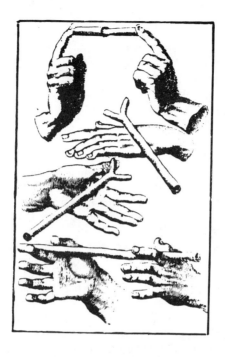

Ancient Celtic Invisibility Spells

One of the most potent spells used by the ancient Celts was known as the *Fith-fath* (pronounced "fee-fah") spell. This was used to cause invisibility or to change something from one form into another. In Gaelic *faeth*, or *fàth*, was an incantation or form of poem. In Scotland it was associated with women who were supposed to be able to change themselves into the shape of deer.

Fith-fath is sometimes found as *fath-fith* but the two are interchangeable. One of the extant rhymes for the spell goes:

"A magick cloud I put on thee,
From dog, from cat,
From cow, from horse,
From man, from woman,
From young man, from maiden,
And from little child,
Till I again return."

This is as much as to say, "Let none of these animals and people be able to see the enchanted." This was a favorite charm for hunters and, especially, for smugglers and poachers. Supposedly the charm was originally given to the Tuatha De Danann by the god Manannan. The Irish god Angus made much use of it, living invisible to mortals in his Brugh of the Boyne.

Invisibility was also thought to be conferred through use of the fern seed. Sir Walter Scott says that the seed becomes visible only on St. John's Eve, "and at the very moment that the Saint was born"! It is probably through confusion between Herodius (who danced before her father, Herod, and asked for John's head on a plate) and Herodias, the Fairy Queen of the Middle Ages, that the seed came to be associated with St. John's Eve. But it was believed that there was a great deal of danger attached to harvesting the seed. You could be attacked by evil spirits, according to Jackson (*The Originall of Unbelief*), for it was in the keeping of the King of Fairies. In *Henry IV* (ii. 1), Shakespeare has one of the characters say: "We have the receipt of fern-seed, we walk invisible."

—RB

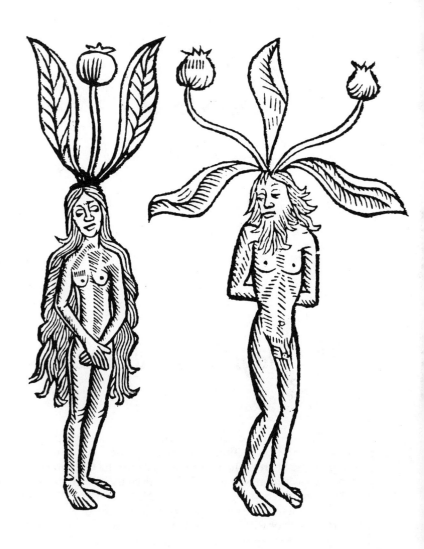

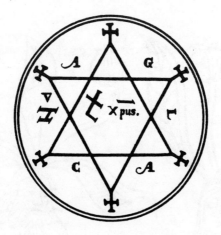

The Magick of Talismans

Raymond Buckland

A talisman is a man-made object endowed with magickal powers, usually either for protection or for bringing luck, in one form or another, to the bearer. The Hermetic Order of the Golden Dawn stated that a talisman is "a magickal figure charged with the force which it is intended to represent." Donald Michael Kraig (*Modern Magick,* Llewellyn, 1988) defines a talisman as "any object, sacred or profane, with or without appropriate symbols, which has been charged or consecrated by appropriate means and made to serve a specific end."

Talismans may be used for any aspect of health, wealth, love, or luck. Similarly, they may be made of virtually any material, though there are traditional materials preferred by serious magicians. These are as listed below, together with the days of the week they are associated with and the properties associated with them:

GOLD—*Sun*—Sunday—Fortune; Hope; Money
SILVER—*Moon*—Monday—Merchandise; Dreams; Theft
IRON—*Mars*—Tuesday—Matrimony; War; Enemies; Prison
MERCURY—*Mercury*—Wednesday—Debt; Fear; Loss
TIN—*Jupiter*—Thursday—Honor; Riches; Desires; Clothing
COPPER—*Venus*—Friday—Love; Friendship; Strangers
LEAD—*Saturn*—Saturday—Protection; Life; Building

It can be seen from this, then, that a talisman for Love would be best made of copper and made on a Friday in the hour of Venus. Certainly this would give that particular talisman its greatest impact. However, if it is not possible to get copper, the talisman could be made on parchment without subtracting too much of its potency. Similarly, what should be a gold talisman could be made of copper; a lead one could be of tin; or any one of them could be done on parchment. But for greatest potency and best chance of success, the listed metals, days, and hours should be adhered to. Mercury, of course, is a liquid metal and not a good choice for engraving! These days aluminum is frequently substituted.

The shape of the talisman is not generally important; most are done on coin-size discs and worn suspended on chains about the neck. They can, of course, also be made as rings.

What is engraved, or drawn, on the talisman depends entirely on the objective. It should certainly be first personalized by putting the name of the person on one face. A talisman is best made by the person who is going to use it. You certainly can make one for someone else but it will never be as effective as the one he or she makes. The reason is the same as for any other form of magick; the person most directly concerned is the one who will put the most power (*mana*) into the ritual, and thereby into the talisman.

Also on the talisman place a symbol for that which you desire. If you're working for money, dollar signs will do; if for matrimony, wedding bells; if for health, a picture of someone running or leaping about. There are more traditional symbols and "sigils" that can be used. These are found in many of the old *grimoires*, or books of magick. I also show them in detail in my book *Practical Color Magick* (Llewellyn, 1983).

Use of one or other of the so-called Secret Magickal Alphabets is encouraged. This way you will be working with figures which are not familiar to you and, therefore, will be concentrating more and thereby putting power into what you are working on.

When the talisman has been completed it should be consecrated by dipping it into sacred (salted) water and then holding it in the smoke of incense. This should be done while boldly stating its purpose. The talisman should be made in the appropriate phase of the Moon (see Almanac) and then worn next to the skin for at least seven days.

The Planetary Hours

The selection of an auspicious time for starting any affair is an important matter. The ancients paid special attention to determining a favorable time for the erection of important edifices, and many of these structures are still standing today as a constant source of wonder and admiration.

When a thing is once commenced its existence tends to be of a nature corresponding to the conditions under which it was begun. Not only should you select the appropriate date, but when possible you should also start the affair under an appropriate *Planetary Hour.*

Each hour of the day is ruled by a planet, and so the nature of any time during the day corresponds to the nature of the planet ruling it. Not only can you start important matters according to the appropriate planetary hour, but you can judge the nature of a matter (say a letter you receive) from the planetary hour in which you first are aware of it, or when it is first brought into contact with you.

The nature of the planetary hours is the same as the description of each of the planets, except that you will not need to refer to the descriptions for Uranus, Neptune and Pluto as they are considered here as higher octaves of Mercury, Venus and Mars respectively. If something is ruled by Uranus, you can use the hour of Mercury.

The only other factor you need to know to use the Planetary Hours is the time of your local Sunrise and Sunset for any given day. This is given in the chart following.

Having determined the times of Sunrise and Sunset, you merely divide the daylight hours, and then the night-time hours, into 12 equal parts. They will only once in a awhile turn out to be periods of 60 minutes in length, for during our summer time there is more daylight than night, and during the winter more night than day. Having charted the times when each of these 12 night periods and 12 day periods occurs, you now refer to the table and ascribe to each such period the planetary rulership in the order listed.

Hour	Sun	Mon	Tue	Wed	Thu	Fri	Sat
			Sunrise				
1	☉	☽	♂	☿	♃	♀	♄
2	♀	♄	☉	☽	♂	☿	♃
3	☿	♃	♀	♄	☉	☽	♂
4	☽	♂	☿	♃	♀	♄	☉
5	♄	☉	☽	♂	☿	♃	♀
6	♃	♀	♄	☉	☽	♂	☿
7	♂	☿	♃	♀	♄	☉	☽
8	☉	☽	♂	☿	♃	♀	♄
9	♀	♄	☉	☽	♂	☿	♃
10	☿	♃	♀	♄	☉	☽	♂
11	☽	♂	☿	♃	♀	♄	☉
12	♄	☉	☽	♂	☿	♃	♀
			Sunset				
1	♃	♀	♄	☉	☽	♂	☿
2	♂	☿	♃	♀	♄	☉	☽
3	☉	☽	♂	☿	♃	♀	♄
4	♀	♄	☉	☽	♂	☿	♃
5	☿	♃	♀	♄	☉	☽	♂
6	☽	♂	☿	♃	♀	♄	☉
7	♄	☉	☽	♂	☿	♃	♀
8	♃	♀	♄	☉	☽	♂	☿
9	♂	☿	♃	♀	♄	☉	☽
10	☉	☽	♂	☿	♃	♀	♄
11	♀	♄	☉	☽	♂	☿	♃
12	☿	♃	♀	♄	☉	☽	♂

☉ Sun; ☿ Mercury; ♄ Saturn; ♂ Mars;
♀ Venus; ☽ Moon; ♃ Jupiter.

SUNRISE

UNIVERSAL TIME FOR MERIDIAN OF GREENWICH

LAT		+10°	+20°	+30°	+40°	+42°	+46°	+50°
		h m	h m	h m	h m	h m	h m	h m
JAN	2	6 16	6 34	6 55	7 21	7 28	7 42	7 58
	14	6 21	6 38	6 57	7 21	7 26	7 39	7 54
	26	6 23	6 37	6 54	7 14	7 19	7 30	7 42
FEB	7	6 22	6 34	6 47	7 03	7 07	7 15	7 25
	19	6 19	6 27	6 37	6 49	6 51	6 57	7 04
	27	6 16	6 22	6 29	6 37	6 39	6 44	6 49
MAR	7	6 12	6 16	6 20	6 25	6 26	6 29	6 32
	19	6 05	6 06	6 06	6 06	6 06	6 06	6 06
	27	6 01	5 59	5 56	5 53	5 52	5 51	5 49
APR	12	5 52	5 45	5 37	5 28	5 26	5 21	5 15
	20	5 48	5 39	5 29	5 16	5 13	5 06	4 58
	28	5 44	5 33	5 21	5 05	5 01	4 53	4 43
MAY	6	5 41	5 28	5 13	4 55	4 50	4 41	4 29
	18	5 38	5 23	5 05	4 43	4 37	4 25	4 11
	26	5 38	5 21	5 01	4 37	4 31	4 17	4 02
JUN	3	5 38	5 20	4 59	4 33	4 26	4 12	3 55
	15	5 39	5 20	4 58	4 30	4 24	4 09	3 50
	23	5 41	5 22	5 00	4 32	4 25	4 09	3 51
JUL	1	5 43	5 24	5 02	4 34	4 28	4 13	3 55
	9	5 45	5 27	5 06	4 39	4 33	4 18	4 01
	17	5 47	5 30	5 10	4 45	4 39	4 25	4 09
	25	5 48	5 33	5 14	4 51	4 46	4 34	4 19
AUG	2	5 50	5 36	5 19	4 59	4 54	4 43	4 30
	10	5 51	5 38	5 24	5 06	5 02	4 52	4 41
	18	5 51	5 41	5 29	5 14	5 10	5 02	4 53
	26	5 51	5 43	5 33	5 21	5 19	5 12	5 05
SEP	3	5 51	5 45	5 38	5 29	5 27	5 22	5 17
	11	5 50	5 46	5 42	5 36	5 35	5 32	5 29
	19	5 49	5 48	5 46	5 44	5 43	5 42	5 41
	27	5 49	5 50	5 51	5 52	5 52	5 52	5 53
OCT	13	5 48	5 54	6 00	6 08	6 09	6 13	6 18
	21	5 49	5 57	6 05	6 16	6 19	6 24	6 31
	29	5 50	6 00	6 11	6 25	6 28	6 35	6 44
NOV	6	5 52	6 04	6 17	6 34	6 38	6 47	6 57
	14	5 54	6 08	6 24	6 43	6 48	6 58	7 10
	22	5 57	6 13	6 30	6 52	6 58	7 09	7 23
	30	6 01	6 18	6 37	7 01	7 07	7 19	7 35
DEC	8	6 05	6 23	6 43	7 09	7 15	7 28	7 45
	16	6 09	6 27	6 49	7 15	7 21	7 35	7 52
	24	6 13	6 32	6 53	7 19	7 26	7 40	7 57
	30	6 17	6 35	6 56	7 22	7 28	7 42	7 59

SUNSET

UNIVERSAL TIME FOR MERIDIAN OF GREENWICH

LAT		+10°	+20°	+30°	+40°	+42°	+46°	+50°
		h m	h m	h m	h m	h m	h m	h m
JAN	2	17 48	17 30	17 09	16 43	16 36	16 22	16 06
	14	17 57	17 40	17 21	16 57	16 52	16 39	16 24
	26	18 02	17 48	17 32	17 11	17 06	16 56	16 43
FEB	7	18 07	17 55	17 42	17 26	17 22	17 13	17 04
	19	18 09	18 01	17 51	17 40	17 37	17 31	17 24
	27	18 10	18 04	17 57	17 49	17 47	17 43	17 38
MAR	7	18 11	18 07	18 03	17 58	17 57	17 54	17 51
	19	18 11	18 11	18 10	18 10	18 10	18 10	18 10
	27	18 11	18 13	18 15	18 19	18 19	18 21	18 23
APR	12	18 10	18 17	18 25	18 35	18 37	18 42	18 48
	20	18 11	18 20	18 30	18 43	18 46	18 53	19 01
	28	18 11	18 22	18 35	18 51	18 55	19 03	19 13
MAY	6	18 12	18 25	18 40	18 59	19 04	19 14	19 25
	18	18 14	18 30	18 48	19 11	19 16	19 28	19 43
	26	18 16	18 33	18 53	19 18	19 24	19 37	19 53
JUN	3	18 18	18 36	18 57	19 24	19 30	19 45	20 02
	15	18 22	18 40	19 02	19 30	19 37	19 52	20 11
	23	18 23	18 42	19 04	19 33	19 39	19 55	20 13
JUL	1	18 25	18 43	19 05	19 33	19 39	19 55	20 13
	9	18 25	18 43	19 04	19 31	19 37	19 52	20 09
	17	18 25	18 42	19 02	19 27	19 33	19 46	20 02
	25	18 25	18 40	18 58	19 21	19 27	19 39	19 53
AUG	2	18 23	18 37	18 53	19 13	19 18	19 29	19 42
	10	18 20	18 32	18 46	19 04	19 08	19 18	19 29
	18	18 17	18 27	18 39	18 53	18 57	19 05	19 14
	26	18 13	18 21	18 30	18 42	18 45	18 51	18 58
SEP	3	18 08	18 14	18 21	18 29	18 31	18 36	18 41
	11	18 03	18 07	18 11	18 16	18 18	18 20	18 24
	19	17 58	18 00	18 01	18 03	18 04	18 05	18 06
	27	17 53	17 52	17 51	17 50	17 50	17 49	17 49
OCT	13	17 44	17 39	17 32	17 24	17 23	17 19	17 14
	21	17 40	17 33	17 24	17 13	17 10	17 05	16 58
	29	17 38	17 27	17 16	17 02	16 59	16 52	16 43
NOV	6	17 36	17 23	17 10	16 53	16 49	16 40	16 30
	14	17 35	17 21	17 05	16 45	16 40	16 30	16 18
	22	17 35	17 19	17 01	16 39	16 34	16 22	16 09
	30	17 36	17 19	17 00	16 36	16 30	16 17	16 02
DEC	8	17 39	17 21	17 00	16 35	16 28	16 15	15 59
	16	17 42	17 23	17 02	16 36	16 29	16 15	15 58
	24	17 46	17 27	17 06	16 39	16 33	16 19	16 02
	30	17 50	17 32	17 11	16 45	16 39	16 25	16 08

MOONRISE

UNIVERSAL TIME FOR MERIDIAN OF GREENWICH

LAT		+10°	+20°	+30°	+40°	+42°	+46°	+50°
		h m	h m	h m	h m	h m	h m	h m
JAN	2	10 20	10 22	10 25	10 29	10 30	10 31	10 33
	14	21 02	20 57	20 52	20 45	20 43	20 40	20 36
	26	6 03	6 21	6 41	7 07	7 13	7 27	7 43
FEB	7	16 10	15 51	15 28	14 58	14 51	14 35	14 16
	19	1 15	1 38	2 05	2 39	2 48	3 07	3 30
	27	7 40	7 35	7 31	7 25	7 24	7 21	7 18
MAR	7	15 01	14 43	14 23	13 58	13 52	13 38	13 22
	19	.. ..	0 21	0 48	1 23	1 31	1 50	2 14
	27	6 15	6 09	6 01	5 52	5 49	5 45	5 39
APR	12	20 08	20 28	20 50	21 18	21 25	21 40	21 59
	20	1 52	2 03	2 15	2 30	2 34	242	2 51
	28	8 43	8 20	7 53	7 19	7 11	6 52	6 29
MAY	6	15 44	15 50	15 58	16 07	16 10	16 15	16 20
	18	0 29	0 37	0 46	0 57	1 00	1 06	1 12
	26	7 29	7 06	6 39	6 06	5 58	5 39	5 16
JUN	3	14 27	14 36	14 47	15 01	15 04	15 12	15 20
	15	23 49	23 49	23 49	23 49	23 49	23 49	23 49
	23	6 12	5 51	5 25	4 53	4 45	4 27	4 06
JUL	1	13 09	13 21	13 35	13 53	13 57	14 07	14 18
	9	19 44	19 59	20 16	20 37	20 42	20 52	21 05
	17	0 50	0 33	0 13	.. ..	.. ..	.. ..	23 48
	25	8 41	8 39	8 35	8 32	8 31	8 29	8 26
AUG	2	15 12	15 35	16 02	16 36	16 44	17 03	17 26
	10	21 13	21 06	20 58	20 49	20 46	20 41	20 36
	18	3 46	3 27	3 05	2 38	2 32	2 17	1 59
	26	10 31	10 48	11 07	11 32	11 37	11 51	12 06
SEP	3	17 02	17 11	17 22	17 35	17 38	17 45	17 53
	11	23 35	23 12	22 45	22 12	22 03	21 45	21 22
	19	6 00	6 02	6 05	6 09	6 09	6 11	6 13
	27	12 35	12 56	13 21	13 52	14 00	14 17	14 37
OCT	13	1 27	1 14	0 59	0 41	0 36	0 27	0 15
	21	7 56	8 16	8 40	9 09	9 16	9 33	9 52
	29	14 09	14 13	14 18	14 25	14 26	14 29	14 33
NOV	6	21 22	21 01	20 37	20 06	19 58	19 41	19 21
	14	3 26	3 35	3 44	3 56	3 59	4 05	4 13
	22	9 58	10 15	10 36	11 01	11 07	11 21	11 37
	30	15 50	15 33	15 13	14 49	14 44	14 31	14 16
DEC	8	23 50	23 48	23 46	23 44	23 43	23 42	23 41
	16	5 29	5 51	6 17	6 49	6 57	7 15	7 37
	24	11 20	11 19	11 18	11 16	11 16	11 15	11 14
	30	16 36	16 14	15 48	15 15	15 07	14 49	14 27

(.. ..) INDICATES PHENOMENON WILL OCCUR NEXT DAY.

MOONSET

UNIVERSAL TIME FOR MERIDIAN OF GREENWICH

LAT		+10°	+20°	+30°	+40°	+42°	+46°	+50°
		h m	h m	h m	h m	h m	h m	h m
JAN	2	22 39	22 39	22 39	22 39	22 39	22 39	22 39
	14	8 50	8 57	9 05	9 14	9 16	9 21	9 27
	26	17 56	17 39	17 21	16 57	16 51	16 39	16 23
FEB	7	4 19	4 40	5 04	5 35	5 43	5 59	6 19
	19	12 57	12 33	12 06	11 31	11 23	11 03	10 40
	27	20 14	20 20	20 28	20 38	20 40	20 46	20 51
MAR	7	3 07	3 26	3 48	4 15	4 21	4 36	4 53
	19	11 39	11 16	10 49	10 14	10 06	9 47	9 23
	27	18 56	19 06	19 17	19 31	19 34	19 41	19 50
APR	12	7 10	6 53	6 33	6 08	6 02	5 49	5 33
	20	13 56	13 47	13 37	13 24	13 21	13 15	13 07
	28	21 57	22 20	22 46	23 19	23 27	23 46	.. ..
MAY	8	3 12	3 08	3 03	2 57	2 56	2 53	2 49
	18	12 38	12 32	12 26	12 18	12 16	12 11	12 06
	26	20 41	21 02	21 27	21 59	22 07	22 24	22 45
JUN	3	1 50	1 42	1 34	1 24	1 21	1 16	1 10
	15	11 23	11 21	11 18	11 15	11 14	11 12	11 10
	23	19 22	19 42	20 05	20 35	20 42	2058	21 17
JUL	1	0 26	0 16	0 04	.. ..	.. ..	.. ..	23 48
	9	6 50	6 33	6 13	5 49	5 43	5 29	5 14
	17	13 53	14 12	14 35	15 04	15 11	15 26	15 45
	25	21 05	21 06	21 06	21 07	21 07	21 07	21 07
AUG	2	2 03	1 40	1 14	0 40	0 32	0 13	.. ..
	10	8 59	9 03	9 08	9 15	9 16	9 19	9 23
	18	16 45	17 01	17 20	17 43	17 48	18 01	18 15
	28	22 21	22 02	21 42	21 15	21 09	20 55	20 39
SEP	3	4 17	4 05	3 51	3 34	3 29	3 20	3 09
	11	11 45	12 07	12 33	13 07	13 15	13 33	13 56
	19	18 14	18 09	18 04	17 57	17 56	17 52	17 48
	27	.. ..	.. ..	23 36	23 06	22 59	22 42	22 22
OCT	13	14 12	14 22	14 34	14 48	14 52	14 59	15 08
	21	19 42	1921	18 57	18 26	18 19	18 02	17 42
	29	1 34	1 27	1 19	1 09	1 07	1 02	0 56
NOV	6	9 29	9 51	10 16	10 48	9 54	10 12	10 35
	14	15 29	15 19	15 07	14 53	14 50	14 42	14 33
	22	21 48	21 32	21 13	20 49	20 44	20 31	20 16
	30	3 49	4 04	4 22	4 44	4 49	5 01	5 15
DEC	8	11 32	11 36	11 40	11 46	11 47	11 50	11 53
	16	17 12	16 50	16 24	15 52	15 44	15 25	15 04
	24	23 47	23 50	23 54	.. ..	.. ..	.. ..	.. ..
	30	4 43	5 05	5 31	6 04	6 12	6 30	6 52

(.. ..) INDICATES PHENOMENON WILL OCCUR NEXT DAY

FULLY UPDATED!
1990 ASTROLOGICAL CALENDAR

For years the *Llewellyn Astrological Calendar* has been the calendar of choice among astrologers. Now it has a new look, more accurate data and new features. The late Gary Duncan, a well-known computer scientist and astrologer, created the best astrological program to date just before his death. This new program gives our calendar the edge on all others.

Included are Moon phases and signs, voids, eclipses, aspects, planetary motion, monthly ephemerides, and much more. Fascinating articles on using astrology, understanding the planets and signs, planting and fishing by the Moon, relationships, vacation planning, financial planning and the history of astrology are included!

Our exclusive fold-down time conversion table makes using the calendar in any time zone a breeze. The times given are set for Central Standard Time. This full-sized (10" by 13"), two-color wall calendar, lavishly illustrated, offers you a daily guide to the heavens and the latest in astrological expertise.
0-87542-452-X, 52 pgs., $7.95

Please use order form on back page.

A SELL-OUT EVERY YEAR!
THE BEST ASTROLOGICAL DATEBOOK

***Llewellyn's 1990 Daily Planetary Guide* is fast becoming the only engagement calendar people will ever need.** We have included all of the astrological information necessary to plan your day. Just open a page in the Guide and you will find all of the lunar data, all of the aspects for the day with their exact times, voids, retrogrades, planetary motion, holidays, and more. The times are set in *both* Eastern and Pacific times so that even bi-coastal folks can use it with ease!

We have included a business section, planetary hour chart, address blanks, introductory material on the planets, signs and more, monthly ephemeris pages, and plenty of room to write in appointments. The book is spiral bound so that it will lie flat and is a convenient 5 x 8 size. The information is from an all-new computer program and is the most accurate to date of any available.

0-87542-453-8, 176 pgs, mass market, $6.95

Please use order form on back page.

HOROSCOPES FOR ALL 12 SIGNS
ALL IN ONE EXCITING BOOK!

Llewellyn's 1990 Sun Sign Book is America's most popular all-in-one yearly guide. If you are the least bit curious about what is in store for you in 1990, this book is a must! This handy book gives the whole year's horoscopes for all 12 signs so that you can chekc out the trends for aoo your friends, too! That's not all. With the *Sun Sign Book* you also receive special activity tables giving you the best dates for each month for a variety of activities. Know the best time to sign a contract or throw a party.

The forecasts were written this year by best-selling author Gloria Star, a professional astrologer, lecturer, counselor and radio and TV personality. Her book *Optimum Child* has been a popular guide for parents interested in using astrology to help their kids develop to their fullest.

Also included are feature articles by famous astrologers from around the country. Read about interpreted signs, finding love, Archetrynes, oppositions and much more.

0-87542-454-6, 368 pgs, mass market, $3.95
Please use order form on back page.

SAVE BIG ON
LLEWELLYN DATEBOOKS AND ALMANACS

Llewellyn offers several ways to save money on our great line of almanacs and calendars. With the four-year subscription you receive your books automatically when they are published. With the subscription the price remains the same for four years even if there is a price increase! Llewellyn pays postage and handling as well. *Buy any 2 subscriptions and take $2.00 off! Buy 3 and take $3.00 off! Buy four and take an additional $5.00 off the cost!*

Subscriptions (4 years, 1991–1994)

☐	Astrological Calendar	$27.80
☐	Sun Sign Book	$15.80
☐	Moon Sign Book	$15.80
☐	Daily Planetary Guide	$31.80

Order by the dozen and save 40%! You may sell them or give them as much-appreciated gifts. We pay all postage and handling on quantity orders.

Quantity Orders: 40% OFF!

1990 1991

☐	☐	Astrological Calendar	$57.24
☐	☐	Moon Sign Book	$28.44
☐	☐	Sun Sign Book	$28.44
☐	☐	Daily Planetary Guide	$50.04

When you order more than one copy, you save money because we pay the postage and handling! Of course, you may order just one copy and pay $2.00 P&H (for orders under $10.00).

Single Copies of all Llewellyn's Almanacs and Calendars

1990 1991

☐	☐	Astrological Calendar	$7.95
☐	☐	Daily Planetary Guide	$6.95
☐	☐	Sun Sign Book	$3.95
☐	☐	Moon Sign Book	$3.95
☐		Goddess Book of Days	$12.95
☐		Zodiac Art Calendar	$8.95

Please use order form on last page

by Scott Cunningham

A BOOK OF MAGICAL RECIPES

Llewellyn presents a revised and updated edition of Scott Cunningham's *The Complete Book of Incense, Oils and Brews.* These recipes come primarily from European sources and are *not* the ones you will find in other sources on magical workings. Some are original, some come from very old manuscripts, some were passed down from teachers and some are indeed ancient.
0-87542-128-8, $12.95

Please use order form on last page.

FOR THE SOLITARY PRACTITIONER

Wicca: A Guide for the Solitary Practitioner is a positive, practical introduction to the religion of Wicca. This is a book of life and how to live magically, spiritually and wholly attuned with Nature. Exercises designed to develop magical proficiency, a self-dedication ritual, herb, crystal and rune magic, and recipes for Sabbat feasts are included in this excellent guide.
0-87542-118-0, $9.95

Please use order form on last page.

MAGICAL HERBALISM

Cunningham's Encyclopedia of Magical Herbs brings to light the occult properties of plants. Over 400 herbs are discussed, with exact magical procedures for using them. Extensive tables, a cross-reference of folk names, a listing of herb suppliers, glossary, annotated bibliography and hundreds of illustrations make this an infinitely practical book.
0-87542-122-9, $12.95

Please use order form on last page.

CRYSTALS/GEMSTONES/METALS

Crystals, gemstones and metals have their own inherent powers and abilities just waiting to be used! The secrets of these powers have been hidden in rare and unusual books. In the pages of *Cunningham's Encyclopedia of Crystal, Gem & Metal Magic* you will find ways to make positive changes in your life—with a complete course in natural magic.
0-87542-126-1, $12.95

Please use order form on last page.

by Gerald and Betty Schueler

A NEW AGE TAROT

The Enochian Tarot explains in detail the meaningful correspondences behind the structure of the Enochian Deck. A powerful path to spiritual enlightenment, Enochian Magick was revealed to John Dee, court astrologer to Queen Elizabeth I of England, and his partner Edward Kelly. This book contains detailed information, including gematria correspondences and magical formulas for those who are interested; but it is written so that anyone can use the deck immediately if so desired.

0-87542-708-1, 86 cards/booklet/box, $12.95
0-87542-709-X, book, $9.95

Please use order form on last page.

THE EGYPTIAN MAGICKAL UNIVERSE

Coming Into Light is the name that the ancient Egyptians gave to a series of magickal texts known to us today as *The Book of the Dead.* In this updated rendition of the text entitled *Coming Into the Light,* the Schuelers introduce the major deities of the Egyptian pantheon in the ancient rituals and in 24 beautifully drawn color plates. *Coming Into the Light* demonstrates that these fascinating rituals were originally used by living magicians as effective practices of a complex form of Magick.

0-87542-713-8, $14.95

Please use order form on last page.

HERMETIC MAGIC FOR EVERYONE

Enochian Magick is a complete and easy-to-read textbook that can be used by the magical novice. This manual contains the complete theory behind the system, with explanations and tabulated data, together with step-by-step instructions and detailed examples. Any student willing to spend time and effort will have a corresponding degree of success.

0-87542-710-3, $12.95

Please use order form on last page.

YOU DON'T HAVE TO BE A PHYSICIST

to understand the ideas presented in *Enochian Physics.* With straightforward prose and over 50 illustrations, Gerald Schueler introduces Enochian Magick to the concepts of modern physics, providing a much-needed rationale for seemingly irrational experiences, and structured knowledge for the control and direction of psychic abilities.

0-87542-712-X, $12.95

Please use order form on last page.

SIMPLIFIED MAGIC
by Ted Andrews

This is the first book of the New Age Qabala. It is an introduction to the the Qabala as the basis of magic—the highly ethical, moral and spiritual system that is also the metaphysical basis for Judaism and Christianity. This is an easy-to-understand, easy-to-use book that has the key to a better, more positive future.
0-87542-015-X, $3.95

Please use order form on last page.

GODWIN'S CABALISTIC ENCYCLOPEDIA
by David Godwin

The ancient tradition of gematria is a method of revealing the archetypal significance of numbers. Here is a valuable source book for students of the cabala which *you* can use to bring to consciousness the significance of numbers and archetypal images occurring in whatever endeavor in which you are engaged. This is a complete guide to cabalistic magick which brings gematria into practical understanding and usage.
0-87542-292-6, $15.95

Please use order form on last page.

STROKING THE PYTHON
by Diane Stein

The Python is women's psychic power and Goddess image. To stroke the python is to invite, choose and accept psychic knowledge, power and responsibility. In this book are fascinating accounts of women's psychic experiences. Learn how to develop your own, natural psychic abilities through the extensive advice given in *Stroking the Python.*
0-87542-757-X, $12.95

Please use order form on last page.

THE GODDESS BOOK OF DAYS
by Diane Stein

This is a perpetual calendar of Goddess dates, holidays and festivals and holy days, a reference book of great interest to anyone involved with women's spirituality, Goddess cultures, magick, the Wiccan religion, and women's herstory. As a planner this is an important tool in a busy world, and it uniquely connects daily life and appointments to the rebirth and growth of the Goddess in the modern world.
0-87542-758-8, $12.95

Please use order form on last page.

ANCIENT MAGICKS FOR A NEW AGE
by Alan Richardson and Geoff Hughes
This is a book about a "Magickal Current." It details the work of magicians from two different eras. These magicks of Christine Hartley and Geoff Hughes are like the poles of some hidden battery which lies hidden beneath the Earth, and beneath the years. The energy is there for you to tap. If you simply want to learn how real magicians work their rituals, and to discover the results and experiences they have, this book is a must!
0-87542-671-9, $12.95

Please use order form on last page.

THE AZTEC CIRCLE OF DESTINY
Understand the *Tonalpouhalli*, the ancient Mesoamerican calendar and divination system. Bruce Scofield and Angela Cordova's kit provides the means to do complete divinatory readings while learning the Aztec astrological system. The 260-day sequence along with interpretations for each day sign and number are given. The kit consists of a 256-page book, 20 cards, 13 wooden number chips, a cloth bag and a colorful box.
0-87542-715-4, $24.95

Please use order form on last page.

THE WISDOM OF SOLOMON THE KING
This new kit created by Priscilla Scwei allows you to understand and use the knowledge of a king. A 208-page book gives interpretations of the 72 cards of the *Spirits of Solomon* complete with a zodiacal sign and degree range, a general planetary ruler, the sign's decanate and its ruler, and an elemental association. The cards are also correlated with a day of the week and its corresponding planetary hour and zodiacal ruler.
0-87542-701-4, $12.95

Please use order form on last page.

THE A-Z HOROSCOPE MAKER
This is one of the most popular beginning books on astrology ever. Written by one of the first major astrologers, Llewellyn George, this book is a virtual encyclopedia and textbook on all aspects of astrology. It includes how to set up charts, a dictionary of terms, and everything you need to begin your study of astrology.
0-87542-264-0, $12.95

Please use order form on last page.

LLEWELLYN ORDER FORM
LLEWELLYN PUBLICATIONS
P.O. Box 64383-455, St. Paul, MN 55164-0383

You may use this form to order any of the Llewellyn books or services listed in this publication.

Give Title, Author, Order Number and Price

_____

_____

_____

_____

_____

_____

Postage and handling: include $2.00 for orders under $10.00 or $3.50 for orders over $10.00. We ship UPS so please use street address. MN residents add 6% sales tax. Outside USA, add $5.00 per book. You may charge on your ☐ Visa, ☐ MC or ☐ Am. Express.

Account No._____

Exp. Date_____Phone_____

Signature_____

Name_____

Address_____

City, State, Zip_____

CHARGE CARD ORDERS (minimum $15.00) may call 1-800-THE-MOON (in Canada, 1-800-FOR-SELF) during regular business hours, Monday-Friday, 8:00 a.m. to 9:00 p.m., CST. Other questions please call 612-291-1970.

☐**Please send me your FREE CATALOG!**